To Kitty K.
   a fine biographer
This is my best work.
           Warmly
           Fred Gmils

D0872368

STAN

Also by Fred Lawrence Guiles

NORMA JEAN: THE LIFE OF MARILYN MONROE
MARION DAVIES
HANGING ON IN PARADISE
TYRONE POWER: THE LAST IDOL

STAN

FRED LAWRENCE GUILES

MICHAEL JOSEPH · LONDON

First published in Great Britain by
Michael Joseph Ltd.,
44 Bedford Square, London WC1
1980

© Fred Lawrence Guiles 1980

All Rights Reserved. No part of this
publication may be reproduced, stored in a
retrieval system, or transmitted in any form
or by any means, electronic, mechanical,
photocopying, recording or otherwise,
without the prior permission of the copyright
owner.

ISBN 0 7181 1908 8

Phototypeset by Western Printing Services Ltd, Bristol
and printed and bound by Billing and Sons
London, Guildford and Worcester

For Charles Lederer (1910–1976) and for
Carlos MacMaster, whose idea this was

Contents

Illustrations

Between pages 192 and 193

Introduction

It has taken far too long for even film scholars to realize that Stan Laurel ranks with Chaplin and Keaton in the pantheon of great film clowns. The scholars did not elevate him to that level; the public did.

Oliver Hardy's rotund shadow has made it hard to see the true dimensions of Stan's genius in detail, and, as a performer, Hardy belongs next to Stan. But Stan was more than a comic, more than an actor. He was a film-maker in every sense, and this aspect of his career has only recently begun to find its way into film history.

Stan chose "small" comedies as his *métier*, although he could have moved into meaningful comedy as easily as Chaplin; he knew the Karno brand of pathos as well as he did. Like the great Charlie, he was a vaudeville and music-hall clown who had brought his gags and routines to the screen. There they were perfected so that in very short order he was one of the finest music-hall comedians ever, bringing laughter to many millions who didn't know what a music-hall was.

Once launched with producer Hal Roach, he quickly acquired the technical knowledge necessary to put a film together. He understood direction, camera work and editing as well as story- and gag-construction. For a very long time, Stan Laurel was one of the few performers in Hollywood who told the director what he wanted, as well as the cameraman and the cutter, without getting a credit line on the screen for those contributions.

Possessing none of Chaplin's hard-headedness in business matters and little of the commanding authority which was characteristic of Keaton throughout the twenties, Stan Laurel and Oliver Hardy lived and worked in ignorance of the pervasiveness of the team's popularity from their first short comedies of 1927 until their first European tour in 1932. Stan knew only that producer Roach was doing exceptionally well booking their comedies and that there seemed to be an insatiable demand for them. He did not know for five years that Laurel and Hardy had become as universally identified with the movies as Chaplin himself and, from 1928 onwards, Mickey Mouse.

But Stan did know that he, as well as Hardy, was a star. Self-effacing on the screen, Stan was conscious of the prerogatives of stardom on the set. For a professional skinny man, he threw a great deal of weight around on the Roach lot and was not loved by all of his co-workers. A great deal of eulogistic nonsense has been written about Stan's "lovableness", yet with few exceptions, the great comics have not been lovable men off camera. Stage and screen comedy relied heavily upon the humiliations of life, more perhaps than any other medium including the pitiless creations of advertising. Since comedy stars had to be targets for custard pies and kicks in the pants, many of them, including Stan, felt that society owed them considerable apology, and they were quick to draw upon this debt.

Stan relied upon fellow troupers from his vaudeville days and Roach writers and directors for companionship, but he was never a snob and there were a number of grips and other crew members who knew him well. There was an unconscious reverse snobbery in Stan. He prided himself on having no pretensions.

Stan distrusted women, although he was forever pursuing them, marrying them or keeping them as diversions from the pressures of his craft. The liberated woman would have appalled him. It is something of a wonder that the scandal surrounding Stan's affairs with the ladies did not seriously cripple his screen career. It *did* affect his income. The growing ledger of sexual indiscretions by Stan, assiduously maintained by Roach and his executives, kept Stan from the huge earnings that independence would have brought him, as it had done Chaplin and Lloyd. His private life simply seemed too irresponsible for bankers ever to be seriously interested in backing him and Hardy as independent film-makers. There were ironic moments when he was besieged by ex-wives and mistresses seeking alimony and settlements, the penalty demanded of Stan for always being in love, and his economic and personal disasters were headlined everywhere, making it more and more difficult to keep his professional reputation and fortunes on the level that he deserved.

His off-screen life was chaotic at best and lurid at worst. Yet he succeeded in his fundamental goal, making people laugh. For this he felt he was born and in this he had no peer. It is no exaggeration to say that, universally, Laurel and Hardy have provoked more decibels of laughter than anyone else in films. This is because they were superior comics. Stan would have been the first to say that Chaplin stood alone. Nor is it because their material was better: more often than not it was predictable and obvious, with comic invention being passed over in favour of Stan's comic memory. Stan was not turning out his gags and routines for posterity or for the scholars to mull over, but for the millions of suffering people around the world who needed a few laughs. The quality of what he was doing was only rarely a consideration, and that was late in his career when he believed that everything they did was second-rate. He knew even at the time when he was making those great comedies with Leo McCarey that Keaton's work was purer cinematic art and less reliant upon gags. And he knew, too, that Chaplin's was more significant (and how he carried on about that!), touching as it did such plagues as poverty, industrialization, dictatorships and the isolation of modern man.

Almost in spite of Stan's intentions, there was something timeless in their comedy. Stan and Ollie were the archetypal fall guys. Society demanded that they shape up or drop out. They were usually outside, trying this way and that to get a foot in the door but getting pinched toes for their efforts. Why they even bothered when those on the inside are made to seem so unattractive is a question never answered.

We *care* about Laurel and Hardy. It is the edge they have over

Abott and Costello and other, lesser teams. There is a fundamental innocence about them, a primal innocence. They evoke a concern not unlike that we feel as we glance through a maternity ward window at a new-born baby. When Ollie gallantly tips his bowler to a passing lady he truly means the gesture, and when he is repaid with a cold stare, he is devastated. Stan's smile seems to suggest that he possesses no memory of pain or previous miscalculations. The whimpering cry is nearly always provoked by bewilderment.

During the great depression, when many normally successful men were jobless and when Stan and Ollie were actually filming *Sons of the Desert*, *Them Thar Hills*, and *Way Out West* (to name but three of forty-seven comedies they made during the thirties), most everyone suffered, class and achievement barriers were destroyed, and the team's travails had a sense of pertinence and cock-eyed reality for millions. Their appeal seemed strongest with those at the very bottom, the have-nots, and with those at the top. Perhaps the tycoons and presidents and dictators enjoyed them so hugely because everything the boys did turned out so disastrously. Failure, of course, makes the bourgeoisie uncomfortable and the women squirm; a taste for Laurel and Hardy must be developed among them, like the taste for yogurt.

What is even more interesting and regrettable is the fact that as times improved with the outbreak of war in Europe and the Far East (war production sparking the economy to sudden life), Stan and Ollie were among the first victims of the new prosperity. Doubtless even Hitler regretted that. Certainly Mussolini did, since he collected prints of all their comedies and screened them frequently. Hollywood studios were too beholden to their stockholders to take any risks on improvised whimsey such as Stan's. "Winging it", with only an idea, a rough script and some gags, was no longer even thinkable. And for reasons that must be traced carefully back to their beginnings in the late twenties, low or pratfall comedy was considered outdated by the powerbrokers in American films – Darryl F. Zanuck, Louis B. Mayer, Sam Goldwyn, Jack Warner, Harry Cohn and David O. Selznick. This was a mortal blow to Mack Sennett and would have been to Hal Roach, the boys' producer, but Roach always had a finger up to the wind and he switched to the more sophisticated gags of *Topper*, which had the distinction of being based on a novel by Thorne Smith. By that time and mostly through Stan's knack for doing the right thing at the wrong time, he and Ollie were adrift in Hollywood. For the rest of their declining careers, they were hirelings of studios that looked upon them as performers whose films could be handled by the assembly-line chief (i.e., Sol Wurtzel at Twentieth Century-Fox) wherever they worked. Their movies, once considered prestige bookings by cinemas like the New York Astor or Capitol, became programmers, the lower half of double bills. Stan was no longer asked to collaborate on the scripts; he was barred from the cutting room; he was not allowed to apply the clown white for which he was so well known, but was made up in darker tones devised by the Fox make-up department. They were packaged almost into oblivion.

Stan lived to see a turn-about. Before his death in 1965, nearly all of their films played somewhere, the good and the indifferent, in theatres, on television, in the private collections of film buffs and an astonishing number of world leaders, and even in banks to amuse those waiting in line. Stan thought they were popular because people could see "how much love we put into them". Perhaps he was right. It is man's custom to prize most what is rarest, and in our time, the consumption of all remotely possible story material by television is so ravenous, that there is no time for a little soul to creep into the fare, only expertise and technical craftsmanship.

At the outset of this biography I had no notion that it would introduce me to a human being so dedicated and creative, so maddeningly contradictory, and so trouble-prone as Stan Laurel. It was news to me that Stan contributed nearly as much to the films of Laurel and Hardy as Chaplin did to his, the difference being that Chaplin had complete control and got the profits while Stan did not. It was something of a shock to discover Stan's conservatism, though his allegiance to the status quo is not hard to comprehend. It was one of the few things that stabilized him when it seemed every woman he had ever known was dragging him into court. Chaplin didn't need that; he had his millions.

So I was more than casually interested when Virginia Ruth Laurel, whom I first thought to be the widow, contacted me about a biography. It transpired that I was mistaken about her final relationship to Stan, but not in my decision to work with her as a primary source. Over a period of three years, we became close, caught up in the mutual task of trying to shake out the significant facts of her complicated years with Stan – they were married three different times – and to recall what Stan had told her of the years before that. Ruth Laurel had a remarkable memory. There were only a few lapses. This book would not exist if Ruth had been less thorough and co-operative. Getting all this down was the thing that held her to life long after her health collapsed. Unhappily, Ruth Laurel died in 1976 before the final manuscript was completed.

Ruth remembered most vividly the best parts of her years with Stan – the fun, the yachting trips, clowning around the bedroom. She was haziest about the calamities: the brooding silences that were often followed by abrupt departures, his obsession with his first wife Lois, his groundless fears about his sanity. Her marriages to Stan were disastrous for both parties, but time had filed down the jagged edges of certain events remembered.

Yet Ruth could supply only part of the story. A bridge had to be forged to the other side, to Stan's true widow and his friends in retirement, and in this respect I owe an inestimable debt to John McCabe, Stan's good friend, and for some time mine, and author of several valuable books on the team. Professor McCabe provided endless documents, letters and suggestions; he reviewed the manuscript itself and together we corrected errors, clarified details of events and leading characters, and curbed my tendency to form conclusions from a theoretical rather than a factual base.

Insight into Stan's often perverse sense of humour, his unpredictable loyalties and his eccentric and erratic behaviour towards nearly all of the women in his life came principally from close eye witnesses: former vaudevillian Alice Cooke and producer Joe Rock.

I was especially fortunate in spending an afternoon with Hal Roach who was, with the exception of Mack Sennett, the most significant maker of comedies in American films. Roach was guarded in discussing Stan Laurel. There was some old acrimony there and he was ambivalent in his feelings for the man he knew and the new folk hero. His position is analogous to Louis B. Mayer's whenever the subject of Garbo came up. Mayer was quick to take credit for her looks, even her face, and especially for the postures that deservedly passed for great acting even among film critics. Garbo herself, according to the Mayer version, was a lumpen peasant. According to Roach, Stan was "probably the best creator of gags ever", but yet he knew very well that in the production of Laurel and Hardy comedies, Stan was far more than a gifted gag-writer. Even at eighty-three – his age when I interviewed him – there was some residue of bitterness in him.

What was so remarkable about Roach was his vitality. One sensed that with Roach putting his weight against a door, you were safe from any outside threat. His eyes moved constantly, perhaps looking for some action. When he laughed, it was deep and about as masculine as laughter can get. He was tanned, steady-voiced, his eyes clearer than those of most men half his age.

Among the other friends and associates of Laurel and Hardy interviewed were Lucille Hardy Price, Hardy's widow – her friendship and that of her husband Ben Price have helped sustain the author through the difficult months and years of seeing the manuscript finished and into print – composer Marvin Hatley and his wife Jo, director Gordon Douglas, Booth Colman, Bert Jordan, Mrs Irma Campanaro, Bob Davis, Roy Seawright, Ruth Burch, Larry Byrd and Mrs Art Lloyd. My thanks to all of them, and to novelist Gilbert Phelps for giving me a special insight into the English character; to James Powers of the American Film Institute for giving me access to Peter Bogdanovich's *Oral History* interview with Leo McCarey; to the Library of the Academy of Motion Picture Arts and Sciences; and to the Lincoln Center Library of the Performing Arts, Paul Myers, Curator.

During my research, as might be expected, I encountered a cult of admirers. For a refreshing change, these men (there were only a few women) were not morbidly seeking mementoes of the team's passage through life, nor were they much interested in where they were buried. Indeed, someone's suggestion at a "Sons of the Desert" banquet I attended that Hardy's remains be moved so that the boys would be buried together seemed to plunge nearly everyone into embarrassment or shock. These dedicated fans convened in "tents" in various cities where there was always good food, a vintage Laurel and Hardy was shown, and toasts were drunk to Mae Busch.

For all of those delightful, mostly youthful "Sons", for dear friends Jack, Lucille, Ben, Joe, Marvin, Jo and Alice, for the Roach people from Hal on down, and for Dick Bann, who knows as much about the Hal Roach operation as anyone alive and who is responsible for most of the filmography, here is some part of Stan Laurel alive and quite a bit of Oliver Hardy as well. It is not intended as a tribute; it is the truth about a man of decent instincts to whom a number of devastating and amusing things happened, including fame. Here then is a man who, off camera, was too involved with living to whimper.

Lancaster County, Pennsylvania   Fred Lawrence Guiles

1 || Lancashire, 1900

It was Mafeking Night, Friday, 18 May 1900. After a siege of 217 days, Lord Baden-Powell and his band of Her Majesty's troops had been relieved, the ring of enemy surrounding that cattle town in South Africa was pierced in several places and dispersed. It was the turning-point of the Boer War and the Afrikaners had lost the most critical battle.

When word of the victory reached England, an excitement raced across the country unlike anything anyone could remember. Performances at all of the music-halls and legit-houses throughout the British Isles were halted and announcements made from the stage. Audiences rose to a man, roaring their jubilation. For a placid, apparently civilized people, the English can be thrilled by a battlefield triumph like none other. In North Shields, a small mill town in the north of England, owner-manager Arthur Jefferson gave out the exciting tidings from the stage himself.

A gala show was planned for the next day, and Jefferson's second youngest son, Arthur Stanley, was pressed into service as a bugle boy. Costumed in the wide-brimmed bush hat worn by the troops, cockily turned up in front, khaki shirt and trousers, and leggings, young Stan stepped on to a professional stage for the very first time that Saturday. He was not quite ten years old and, to him, wars were a kind of theatre on distant stages.

Stan's parents were actors; his father descended from the Jefferson family that had produced Joseph Jefferson, famed in America for his "Bob Acres" in Sheridan's *The Rivals*. Joseph Jefferson was touring in a dramatization of Washington Irving's *Rip Van Winkle* in 1862, the year of Arthur Jefferson's birth in Darlington, Durham.

Steeped in theatrical tradition, events outside the theatre were generally of little consequence to the Yorkshire – Lancashire Jeffersons. But Stan's father, known to nearly everyone as "A.J." or "Jeff", was fiercely loyal to Her Majesty as only a middle-class Englishman can be, and the celebratory pageant in all the Jefferson theatres (there were three of them scattered about that corner of England) was spectacular. The resultant front-page accounts of the performances in north-country newspapers did the Jefferson theatrical "empire" no harm.

Audience response to young Stan's appearance confirmed something he already suspected – that this was what he wanted in life, the warm, clapping "thank yous" of a thousand Englishmen. It was an uncomplicated relationship, audience with boy. The sight of him, a solitary bugle boy symbolizing the valiant and victorious troops on that South African front line, had stirred them to a thunderous ovation.

His father later wrote that Stan's "young mind was obsessed with the idea of one day 'following in father's footsteps'". Actually, the boy was soon looking beyond his father's provincial theatres. It was in London and the Midlands where the great Dan Leno, Little Tich and George Robey usually starred.

Of course, to a Lancashire boy, London was as remote as Samarkand. Most north-country natives had never seen it. A trip to Manchester or even Blackpool was a great adventure to Stan. Years later, he would be astonished by Hollywood film people running out to their ranches in Palm Springs for a weekend, a distance that would span all of England, east to west. Conversely, Londoners looked upon Lancashire and "the North" as almost a foreign country even though the natives spoke a kind of English. Scouts from the London theatres and music-halls would go north searching for talent, expeditions regarded as necessary hardships towards sustaining the life-blood of their trade.

In 1900, having servants, a comfortable town house and other middle-class appurtenances was new to the Jeffersons. On 16 June 1890, when Stan was born, his parents had been struggling actors unable to afford a home of their own. They lived then with Jeff's in-laws, the Metcalfes, in Ulverston, a small factory town off Morecambe Bay on the Irish Sea, about thirty miles north of Blackpool. A hilly town, its glories were a brewery and a paper-mill. Stan's playmates in Ulverston were the sons of merchants, never the children of the working class. The poor boys often worked themselves despite various parliamentary acts controlling child labour; they were employed in the mill or the brewery at less than adult wages or even in the nearby workhouse if there was no responsible parent.

Farms ran up to the borders of Ulverston, and the farmers peddled their vegetables and fruits from horse-drawn carts led through the streets. The Metcalfe home, made of stone, was one of a row of foundry cottages built for the workers by the foundry owner early in the nineteenth century. There was no visible landscaping; the houses were built right up to the edge of the pavement. A cheerless place, Ulverston missed having a view of the fabled Lake District by ten miles, and neither Coleridge nor Wordsworth ever mentioned the place.

But it was home to young Stan, not only during his first five years – later on, whenever there was a school holiday he would beg to go to Grandma Metcalfe's. He knew a security there that he was never to know again. It was the one true home of his life.

Grandfather Metcalfe, when he was sober, ran a shoe repair shop while his wife, always in a mob-cap, looked after the family, including Stan's older brother Gordon. A baby sister, Olga Beatrice, came along in 1895 just as the Arthur Jeffersons' fortunes were improving and the move to North Shields was being planned.

Jeff and his wife Margaret, known as Madge on the stage, were both handsome and talented. He had imposing features with a prominent nose and a shock of bright wavy red hair. Madge was a delicate brunette with a rich trained mezzo voice. The first song Stan ever remembered hearing was "Annie Laurie" as sung to him by his mother. Jeff and Madge were players in a tent-like theatre outside town at Spencer's Gaff. It had wooden sides and a canvas top, and Jeff doubled as company manager. Later, the structure was made more permanent when it was properly roofed and remodelled, becoming the Denville, where comedian Will Fyffe began his rise to fame in the music halls.

Within two years of Stan's birth, the more lucrative post at the Theatre Royal in North Shields was offered to Jeff, and the couple moved, Madge being taken on as the resident vamp. The children were left behind in Ulverston, although Gordon, the eldest, was soon to rejoin his parents. It was during those years that Madge Jefferson became nearly as successful as her husband in the role of femme fatale, a kind of Theda Bara of the North Country, travelling with companies formed by Jeff throughout Lancashire and Yorkshire. Her career lasted until halfway through her last pregnancy, when her health collapsed. The birth of their last child, Everett, known as "Teddy", was difficult and she struggled for another ten years, unsuccessfully, to recover her health. (A fifth child, Sydney, died in infancy.)

It seems more than pure coincidence that the two most beloved screen comedians to come from England, Stan Laurel and Charlie Chaplin, were almost exact contemporaries, and that they both had ailing mothers and philandering fathers. Chaplin was born a year earlier than Stan, the son of a vaudeville baritone who was only a visitor in their home and on the rarest of occasions. Chaplin's "home" was invariably a hovel in London's East End. Completely irresponsible, Charlie's father was to drink himself out of show business. So both youngsters, Charlie and Stan, were exposed to acute alcoholism. Young Stan used to look on in bewilderment as his grandfather Metcalfe crawled up the front stoop on his hands and knees from the corner pub and his grandmother rushed up the stairs in high dudgeon, slamming her bedroom door and bolting it, but Charlie suffered more keenly. Chaplin's father could not hold down a steady variety house engagement because of the bottle and the boy was raised by his mother with his brother Syd in a grim successsion of flats in the slums of London, where Mrs Chaplin's grip on sanity eventually loosened.

When success came to father Jeff around 1896, he was more than ready for it. He stepped into the role of impresario as easily as he had done into that of leading comic actor. He had a brief-case bulging with Victorian melodramas of his own devising, many of them already tested at Spencer's Gaff. They had sweeping epic titles such as *London by Day and Night, The World's Verdict* and *Dawn of Hope*. He soon acquired the leases for other north-country theatres, and he formed at least two acting companies to tour the provinces and even near parts of the continent, Belgium and the Netherlands. He had a fancy brougham for himself and his family and those who were not his close friends called him "Guv'nor".

Stan had inherited his father's shock of red hair, but Stan as boy and man was most casual about his attire while his father dressed in hand-tailored suits and traditional ties. Vainer than Stan ever could be, Jeff was a ladies' man, a fact which Stan discovered in boyhood. Budding actresses and *ingénues* were expected to be "nice" to their producers, an arrangement that Jeff exploited thoroughly. Once his wife Madge was too ill to work any longer, his affairs became less discreet. Stan's first knowledge of his father's amours came to him when he was eleven and he overheard tearful recriminations from his mother. He grieved for her and soon developed a conviction, which he held for years, that actresses were women of easy virtue, bed partners only a notch above prostitutes, women you might take as a mistress but never as a wife. His saintly mother was an exception, he was convinced, and he drew protectively close to her. It must have been a relief to his father that Stan was away at school for five days of the week.

When Stan was home at weekends, Jeff indulged his boy and permitted him to hang around backstage. There is some evidence that Stan never forgave his father for so grievously wounding his mother, but it is clear that the boy admired Jeff where it counted most with Stan – as a major show-business figure in that part of England. Even theatrical folk up from London sought Jeff out to pay their respects.

The first vastly popular music-hall performer Stan ever saw was

George Robey, who preferred the provincial houses to those in London. Robey had the most commanding presence of any comic on the boards. He would allow laughter to roll for a minute or two and then, as the king of mirth he would flash a warning finger and one word, "Desist!" and the house grew quiet. His audiences, nearly all working class, would pay sixpence to see him and the twenty or so other turns that evening. In the now demolished Manchester music-hall with its plush and gilt décor, Robey usually appeared in two guises – one of them was that of a slightly shabby man-about-town, a little bowler hat atop his domed forehead, fuzzy wig, arched eyebrows and a red nose. He carried a cane and both cane and bowler were later borrowed by Chaplin, who early idolized Robey and would follow him from hall to hall during a Saturday evening. Robey and other stars often played four or five halls between eight and midnight. Robey travelled from one to the other in his brougham, fifteen-year-old Chaplin on foot. Both Stan and Charlie later spoke of their mutual admiration for Robey, and once, in a boarding-house room that the two young Karno comedians shared, Chaplin sang all of Robey's "Clarence, the Last of the Dandies". Stan preferred his "dame", and Robey certainly did seem more richly verbose and more easily affronted by mankind in skirts and a mop-like wig.

2   There was very little family life for the Arthur Jeffersons. Stan's baby sister Olga Beatrice was sent to a convent school in Belgium which had been discovered by brother Gordon while he was taking a Jefferson touring company through the Lowlands. The Jeffersons were not Catholic but Madge was not physically or emotionally up to the demands of motherhood. Olga Beatrice moved from the Sisters' hands right on to the stage as an *ingénue*, where she remained for a number of years. Stan recalled: "We were very seldom all together. It was almost always either in boarding school or living with my grandparents in Ulverston where I was born, but still, strange as it may seem, we were always a close family."

Boarding school in the North Country for Stan meant Bishop Auckland, a town in north-east England about twenty-five miles due south of Newcastle. There in Bishop Auckland Stan discovered that he was funny through –

a certain teacher named Bates . . . Bates would come and take me into his private study where he and a couple of other masters were relaxing – with a bottle. Bates would then have me entertain them with jokes, imitations, what the hell have you – anything for a laugh. I must have been awful but they seemed to get a big kick out of it, and I played many return engagements there.

I can't remember now mostly what I did but I certainly had this talent for clowning right from the beginning, more or less. I don't think playing to Bates and the other masters helped my education any as I was given a lot of privileges – and a lot of my backwardness in class was overlooked which many times since I've regretted . . . those were happy days at Bishop Auckland.

Stan's clowning at boarding school remained his secret and his father, on Stan's weekends at home, knew nothing of this side of his boy. In the back of Jeff's mind, he was thinking that Stan might become a theatrical manager like himself. Son Gordon had already proved himself capable on the road.

As for the movies, they were at that time a novelty to be marvelled at, rather like a perpetual motion machine or a water clock. They were certainly not a rival to the halls or theatres. Jeff was intrigued enough, however, to look into them. He remembered "going up to London" (North Countrymen always went *up* to London rather than down, as any map of England indicates they should),

and while there I met a Mr Walter Gibbons. . . . He showed me a marvellous appliance that would project living moving pictures on to a screen. He called it the Randvoll and, having seen the miracles he had described to me with my own eyes, I bought it.

And so it came about that I took the first kinema projector to the North. And did the North like it? Not a bit! Not even when I put a singer at the back and tried to synchronize her with the film. And did Stan get excited? Not a bit. I don't remember a single display of enthusiasm on his part.

This did not surprise Jeff so very much, since by now and with much encouragement from Jeff himself, he was thoroughly stage-struck.

In that black box lay his future fortunes. And he was not even interested. I sold it in the end for a trifle to a man with whom I was having a drink. He started in the moving picture business with it. Today he is a leading film magnate . . . I sometimes see him arriving at his office in Wardour Street in his Rolls-Royce. Yes, that black box was to make rich and world-famous the little boy who was fooling around upstairs in the attic *(in a short-lived miniature theatre Jeff had built for Stan)*. But, whatever it was to do for my son, it was to kill my great love, the drama.

Stan resisted the growing appeal of the movies, which it could be said had grown up with him, for a very long time. There were no great performers on the screen at that time – no Robey, no Dan Leno. He said little to his father about his growing obsession with comedy since Jeff's own reputation as a performer was mostly based upon his flair for comedy roles. Jeff even had set down "Comedian" as his profession on Stan's birth certificate. Stan was so shy about revealing to his father his own studies of successful comic routines that his first comic stage appearance came as an overwhelming and delightful surprise to Jeff.

Stan's father never did get to know the boy very well. There was always a barrier between them despite Stan's insistence on the "closeness" that existed among the scattered Jeffersons. But Jeff was aware of his son's poor scholastic achievements at Bishop Auckland, so Stan was taken out of that school, away from schoolmaster Bates and the rest of his first enthusiastic audience, and placed in Barnard Castle Grammar School, known for its strict discipline.

That onerous régime was blessedly brief. During Stan's twelfth year, his father took over the management of the Metropole Theatre in Glasgow, more than a hundred miles north of their home base in North Shields.

Glasgow was a seaport and several times the size of Manchester, Leeds and Newcastle, the cities that Stan had visited with Jeff and knew best. It was not an attractive place. There always seemed to be an industrial haze over the city, even on the sunniest day and its slums were more extensive and decayed than any Stan had ever seen. The Jeffersons settled into a town house and Stan was enrolled that autumn in the first of two Glasgow schools he would attend, Queens Park. A year later, pursued by the same devils of inattention and mischief that had sent him from one school to another back in

Lancashire, Stan eluded total failure by being transferred to Ruther Glen School (known to its boys as "Rug'len"), where his education would end in his sixteenth year.

Jeff did not seem too concerned about Stan's academic failure; he had plans for his son to take over as assistant manager of the Metropole. He was still in the dark about his son's studies before his bedroom mirror with make-up borrowed from his father and a costume he was piecing together from Jeff's wardrobe, including his best frock-coat. Stan's ailing mother Madge knew of this ambition and encouraged it. Whenever Stan visited her in her bedroom, the conversation was about the stage – her past triumphs, and noted actors who had worked with her or Jeff, including George Arliss. It was to his mother that Stan first confided his fear that he could never act "because I can't talk right", but he could mug and caper and make people laugh.

Stan was aware of the perils of theatrical life. His grandmother, on his visits there, constantly reminded him of the uncertainties, possible starvation and the lack of a stable home life. During the Jeffersons' first year in Glasgow, brother Gordon had to cable his father for funds when a booking was cancelled in Belgium and they were stranded.

The Glasgow Metropole had formerly been the Scotia Music Hall, and it was there that Harry Lauder made his start. Jeff did not advertise this fact, since many a Scotsman detested Sir Harry for impersonating a stereotype who existed only in vaudeville. The Jefferson Company soon became known for its lavish productions. Among Jeff's leading players besides himself, John Clyde was the most impressive. He was a huge man, whose most successful vehicle was *Rob Roy*, a spectacular melodrama based upon the life of the seventeenth-century Scottish freebooter who was immortalized by Sir Walter Scott. There was a pillar to Rob Roy's memory standing in the heart of Glasgow. John Clyde was the father of Andy Clyde, later a stellar comedian who began playing doddering old fools in American movies while still in his thirties, and eventually getting his own series of two-reelers at Educational Films ("The Spice of the Program") that were real competition for Roach's "All Star" comedies of the twenties.

Queen Victoria died the year of the Jeffersons' arrival in Glasgow and the South African War ended eighteen months later. Edwardian Scotland was a congenial place for a young man to discover himself. Stan's problem was that he knew who he was but was wholly lacking in the confidence necessary to share this knowledge with the outside world or even his family beyond his mother.

A more permissive age had begun. Ladies' bloomers became the subject for comic repartee and were sometimes visible on a lady cyclist or a bather. A slapstick comedian named Fred Karno had recently become the reigning producer of comedies in London with several companies on tour. Karno's timing had been perfect. He was brash, he was vulgar and he knocked unmercifully everything that the late Queen stood for. He rode the Edwardian crest with a reckless disregard for any and all proprieties. To advertise a revue he called *Jail Birds* (the use of "Birds" in his titles became a sort of trademark), he hired a black maria to drive around London. Jeff saw the promotional wagon and did the same thing the following week in Glasgow to advertise one of his melodramas. Stan thought his father was very clever.

There is no evidence that Stan had any adolescent affairs, crushes or infatuations. He was consumed with a single passion – to create his own comic skit and perform it somewhere. *Anywhere*! He had been practising in his room for weeks and was sure that he was ready. As he lay sleepless in his third-floor bedroom, he saw himself as a successful mime already, Stan Jefferson, boy comic, convulsing audiences and moving from one engagement to another.

1906 . . . . Glasgow:

A small, working-class audience is gathered in the Panopticon, a tavern-sized auditorium in Pickard's Museum, watching indulgently as a skinny, coat-tail-flapping youth bounces on stage from the wings. He has the baggy pants, red nose and knotty cane umbrella of the popular music-hall hayseed comic. He wanted to appear in the guise of the great Dan Leno – there were several Leno characters to choose from, including Leno's celebrated drag – but that would be pushing idolatry to the point of impertinence. This outfit was inspired by Leno the rube, the jokes and songs from the likes of Nipper Lane, boy comic non-pareil; the entire act was squirreled from months of watching others, one chestnut after another.

Stan Jefferson is eager to please and the all-male audience is generous. They smile and even laugh. A few men in the adjoining penny arcade, looking for at least a glimpse of ankle in the penny flickers, hear the laughter and leave the machines. The boy's smile widens with innocent joy. Stan will not project total confusion until he is more sure of himself.

3   In Stan's seventeenth year, he left home to tour in Levy and Cardwell's Juvenile Pantomimes, a company of young actors performing parodies of well-known plays. Pantomime in the variety halls of England was not the mute performance we associate with Marcel Marceau. There was considerable dialogue.

Stan had won the role through his father's friendship with the producers, but the boy was talented and there were no complaints. Perhaps he was so readily accepted by the other boys because he didn't remotely behave like a rich man's son, and he worked harder than anyone else in the company to improve his craft.

Those weeks were a dizzying, exhausting whirl of performances in crowded variety halls, stinking with fumes of the patrons' cigars, pipes and cigarettes (it would take several horrible theatre fires around the world before smoking was limited to balconies or outer lobbies), and sweating bodies. There was the misery of enduring jeers and crude, noisy dismissals – Bermondsey was the worst offender – not meant in any hostile way, just high-spirited factory hands letting off steam. Sometimes a singer or a comic would have to yell or scream to be heard. Then someone like Marie Lloyd would go on and there would be an instant hush. How Stan longed to hear that silence while on stage in a crowded house!

On free Sundays, he often appeared in clog-dancing competitions, and on at least one of those occasions, in Sunderland, an ugly working-class seaside resort with industrial smokestacks flanking its southern end, he shared a stage with Charlie Chaplin, who at seventeen was an experienced juvenile actor and veteran clog dancer, having toured some years earlier as a non-sibling member of the acclaimed Jackson family of cloggers known as "The Lancashire Lads".

The Levy and Cardwell Company was playing in one of the northern industrial cities when Stan had his first taste of feminine treachery. He and two fellow actors went to a pub near the theatre after the Saturday night performance – pay night. There were two young women at the next table who asked them if they were on the stage. When they said they were, the young ladies pretended great excitement and spoke of "how thrilling" it was to be so close to live performers. It was Stan's first brush with celebrity and its rewards, or at least what he mistook as such.

One compliment led to another and finally one of the girls said, "If you boys will buy the groceries and the wine, we'll cook dinner for you." They pooled their money and bought everything the girls asked for. Then the boys were escorted down several side streets to a large block of flats. The girls left the "celebrities" at the door, telling them, "Our landlady doesn't allow us to have men callers so we'll go in and you wait. We'll give you the signal when we turn on the light. We'll flash it three times and you'll know the coast is clear."

Stan and his friends stood in the November chill, smiling expectantly into the pleasant silence of the darkened house. But the silence deepened and the darkness mocked them until finally Stan said, "Well, I'm going in to find out what's happened."

He made his way into a hallway lit by a single bulb, followed by his friends. Once inside, they were challenged by a landlady in night attire. "If you're looking for those women with the groceries, I saw them go out the back way." It was something to remember, that first night out with the ladies, something to roar about – but not that night it happened.

It was during Stan's first year away from home that Madge Jefferson finally gave up the ghost. During a second prolonged illness, Stan was summoned home from the road and she died in his arms. It was a shattering experience for him. From the sketchy details available, it is probable that she succumbed to a respiratory disease that was worsened by the industrial smog of Glasgow.

Stan was inconsolable for months. He later told his wife Ruth that he blamed his father most of all, that Jeff had killed her will to live through his habitual dalliances. But there was no rupture between father and son. Some of the family closeness, which Stan chose to believe had existed through the years, vanished and from that time onwards there was a sense of dutiful attendance at family gatherings, all a bit stiff-collared and unsettling. Stan had no interest in living at home ever again.

Professionally, Stan pleased his father enormously. Jeff caught his son's act whenever the company was playing nearby. He was convinced, with reason, that Stan had got his talent from him. Caught up in the notion that a gifted comedian had passed on the cap and bells to his heir, Jeff put aside his Victorian melodramas (the content of straight plays had not changed radically with the death of the Queen, although Shaw's work would begin to go public) and concentrated on writing a number of comic sketches to be performed on the Moss Empire circuit, a network of first-rank variety houses. One sketch, *Home from the Honeymoon*, concerned two bumbling drifters on the run from the law coming upon a vacant estate just before a young aristocratic couple arrive. The drifters pose as the maid and the butler.

Shortly after the sketch opened at the Birmingham Empire, Jeff got in touch with Stan and told him that he was having trouble with one of the players. Would Stan step in as understudy? He didn't hesitate for a moment and left the Levy and Cardwell troupe the following week. The troublesome actor soon quit the show and he found himself playing the role.

Moss Empire bookings were prestigious and led to other dates, but Stan had not yet found himself as a single. When there was nothing available in the halls, back he would go to one of the lesser circuits. He was having more than a little trouble surviving as he couldn't hang on to money after pay-day. He and several other young variety artists would lodge together in one boarding-house room on the road. Food was cadged, stolen or done without. There were many times when they were evicted and Stan and his fellow actors had to walk the wintry streets of London, paying a ha'penny for two hot potatoes which were put in their trouser pockets to keep their legs warm. A fierce pride, probably inherited, kept him from seeking subsidies from his father.

He was part of this world now, the world of the halls. There could by no prying him loose. To Stan, the music-hall was the only worthwhile thing the world had to offer. Food, girls, family; everything else was second-best.

The halls were to have a lasting effect on American film comedy, first through Chaplin and then by way of Stan. The halls were theatre, but they were considered by those who worked in them as

separate from straight playhouses. They traced their origins back to
the country fairs and carnivals rather than to the Globe. The halls
had evolved naturally out of the need for a roof over the heads of
their audiences, out of demand for sheltered entertainment. Sometimes they were converted stables. The more elegant early estab-
lishments were public baths, and aquatic acts were interlarded with
turns upon the stage.

The first building to be called a music-hall was the Canterbury,
which opened on 17 May 1852. A soubrette of that day, Emily
Soldene, recalled her first glimpse:

> Coming to the Canterbury was dreadful. I remember the shock I
> got when I went under the railway arch, down the dingy, dirty,
> narrow street, the greasy sidewalk, the muddy gutter, full of dirty
> babies, the commonplace-looking public house. I felt I could not
> go in; but I did. The people were very polite, and showed me
> upstairs; there was lots of sawdust. Soon I found myself in a long
> picture gallery, at the other end of which a rehearsal was being
> held . . . the smell of beer and stale tobacco smoke revolted
> me. . . .

Within sixteen years, there were over three hundred provincial
halls and about half that number in London alone. They began to
take on a look of elegance and vastness. Architect Frank Matcham
designed many of them and he had a taste for classic simplicity that
could be "scrubbed down" easily.

The industrial revolution had, in turn, fostered yet another revolution, that of trade unionism, and workers were no longer slaves to
the mill-owners. Once organized, there was a jingle in their pockets
and while most of it was used for the bare necessities, what was left
was poured into pubs and music-halls. The lower classes had
snatched most of their "dirty babies" out of gutters and placed them
in overcrowded tenements, but, as T. S. Eliot wrote in 1923:

> In the music-hall comedians they find the expression and dignity
> of their own lives; and this is not found in the most elaborate and
> expensive revue. . . . The working man who went to the music-
> hall and saw Marie Lloyd and joined in the chorus was himself

performing part of the act; he was engaged in that collaboration of the audience with the artist which is necessary in all art and most obviously in dramatic art.

Stan thought only of success in the halls. Besides Leno, Robey and Little Tich (who was noted for his sand dance and acrobatics in yard-long shoes), his gods were Mark Sheridan and Arthur Roberts. There was a particular niche in the halls for Stan – a youthful mime in shabby clothes who turned the pain of life inside out.

As he moved about the halls, Stan was surrounded by cockney costers, chanteuses, "skirt" dancers from Paris, dog acts, performing elephants and what were bluntly called "nigger minstrels".

Stan remembered one act that, like Robey, Leno and the other great stars, was in demand everywhere. It was called "Professor Duncan's Marvellous Troupe of Trained Collie Dogs", and it played as many as four theatres each evening. The manager of the Paragon on Mile End Road would obligingly put on the dogs – featuring one very brave collie rescuing a small child from a burning building – early enough for Professor Duncan to run the pack through the streets to the Royal West London on Edgware Road for another bold rescue a half-hour later.

What was carried over into the American movies from the halls was the particular emphasis upon fundamental, day-to-day coping with life. Landlords were the enemy of the hall comics; so were wives. "The Coster's Laureate" Albert Chevalier summed up the attitude of the halls towards womankind with his song:

They call me woman hater! – if they only knew the truth!
That somewhere, where the flowers are seen,
A white cross marks the spot I mean,
Who keeps a little grave so green?
A poor old bachelor.

2 || Fred Karno and the Uneasy Friends

1   It was in a small variety hall in 1910 that Stan was discovered by that most successful music-hall impresario of
the day, Fred Karno. In the decade and a half of his rise, Karno's
several troupes had become so beloved and famous that when the
First World War arrived, British armies sang about him in sometimes unprintable verses: "We are Fred Karno's Army" – the British
equivalent of the Americans' SNAFU (Situation Normal, All Fucked
Up). Even today, Karno's name is invoked when things begin to get
out of hand.

Becoming a Karno player did not mean any elevation in a performer's economic status. Karno was notorious for paying his
people as little as he could get away with. Still, for the prestige of
being part of the Karno acting family, it was worth sacrificing more
lucrative parts in riskier ventures. More importantly, no one knew
more than Karno did about what provoked laughter. Although his
patience was thin, his striving for just the right gesture, the appropriate pause, the heart-string tugging shrug would keep a company
in rehearsal all night, if necessary.

Charlie Chaplin was already in the Karno Company – he had
been scouted in the halls by the producer a couple of years earlier

while touring as the boy in William Gillette's version of *Sherlock Holmes* and was hired when Karno saw him in a juvenile sketch entitled *Casey's Court*. For that last job, Charlie had been paid five shillings a week and his board. Surprisingly, Karno paid him in guineas and quickly gave him the lead in *Mumming Birds*, destined to become the most enduring and popular revue Karno ever created.

Mumming Birds was a burlesque of sorts. It was composed of a series of noisome routines mercilessly panned by an "audience" (actually members of the Karno troupe sitting in a box on the stage). One of the "audience" members was an "inebriated swell" played by Chaplin and understudied by Stan. Although Stan was to play nearly every part in the sketch at least once, the plum role of the drunk was not one of them since Chaplin never missed a performance. Even though the slight lad from the Lambeth slums had suffered from poor nutrition throughout his boyhood and skipped countless meals, he was virtually indestructible as an adult and outlived Stan by twelve years.

The opening of *Mumming Birds* was a rousing tune in fortissimo: "Let's All Go to the Music-hall," which gave way to a waltz. An usherette showed a boy and his uncle into a box, then brought the drunk into another. Girls entered, dancing on stage in a dreadful, out-of-step way. They were followed by two comics with song, dance and patter, interrupted by cat-calls from both the boy and the drunk. A pompous actor then recited "The Trail of the Yukon", slogging stubbornly through a barrage of insults from the drunk and the boy. When Karno first described his idea for the revue to his actors, he told them that they had all suffered rudeness and abuse from audiences, no matter how fine their performances, "so we're going to give them the kind of performance such audiences deserve." And he did. As the evening unravelled, the drunk got out of his box frequently to chase an off-key quartette from the stage, and to take on an obese and inept wrestler, Marconi Ali, and win the bout. There were numerous falls on stage by the drunk, and when Stan took over the role after Chaplin was summoned to Hollywood, he claimed he injured his head in falling. He was to become very wary of comic falls and was constantly worried about a hazard common to boxing but not usually associated with the theatre, the possibility of "bruising his brain". He mistakenly believed that had caused the mental collapse of Dan Leno.

Dan Leno was born thirty years ahead of Stan – exactly a generation separated them. Very early in Stan's stage career, once he had discarded the boy comic routines, he began borrowing from Leno. They had identical physiques except that Stan was a little taller; both of them were slight, slender, with double lines around the mouth and surprised eyebrows. M. Willson Disher in a charming study of the nineteenth-century halls, *Winkles and Champagne*, describes Leno in performances as having "a perpetually startled look in his bright, merrily gleaming eyes, framed in semi-circular brows, and in his jerky movements; there is eagerness in every part of him from the disconcerting legs to the straight, strained mouth set in the curious double-rim formed by the lines of the cheeks . . . he pauses with his fingers over his mouth . . ."

Anyone familiar with Stan's screen image will recognize the borrowings – he retained them to the end of his long career. There were also other, more disquieting resemblances. Leno never relaxed. He had to be joking even off the stage. Gags abounded. No one felt really safe around him. Stan's behaviour off-stage and later off-camera was remarkably similar.

Leno had sudden bursts of anger and would rage at his friends, then abjectly beg their forgiveness within hours. His behavioural history reads very much like the charges against Stan in the three divorce proceedings in which he was involved.

Dan Leno did not "lose his mind on stage", as Stan frequently stated, but began giving away money and valuables to strangers. He set in motion a long-cherished ambition (shared by most comics) to play Shakespeare, pulling a company together and starting rehearsals. He begged Constance Collier to be his leading lady. Naturally enough, she declined, and he went to pieces, unable to perform again for months. When he did return to the stage of the Drury Lane, audiences were too fascinated by his recent instability to laugh. Instead, they stared uneasily at him. So Leno retired that year and died soon afterward.

If one believes in spiritualism, a strong case could be made for the influence of Dan Leno beyond the grave. He died in 1904, shortly before Stan's initial appearance on the professional stage in a panto revue. According to show business rumour, comedian Peter Sellers believes that Leno has also been orchestrating his career, and Sellers' international success followed Stan's by only a slight interval. There seems no doubt that Dan Leno's spirit is not at rest: his image has been seen in his old dressing-room mirror at the Drury Lane by a number of noted performers, including Noel Coward. Stan would have laughed at such phenomena and speculation. He was never a church-goer, although he was nominally a member of the Church of England, and he considered spiritualism a harmless pursuit of crackpots.

The fame of Karno's comedians crossed the Atlantic, and later in 1910, Karno was invited to send a troupe of them over. It was a significant journey. American films, just then becoming a serious business, would be enhanced considerably by members of the company, namely Chaplin and Stan; Karno comedy, as learned from Fred Karno himself, would be the principal ingredient of a long tradition of screen humour – comic catastrophe in which the comedian reacts with a wistfulness that produces just the right note of pathos.

The first Karno company played Hammerstein's Music-hall, the famous variety house in New York. Then a second company was formed by Alf Reeves, newly-appointed American manager for the Karno organization. Reeves escorted about twenty performers, including Charlie Chaplin, Stan, a clown known as Whimsical Walker, Edgar Hurley and his wife, and Muriel Palmer, from Liverpool to Quebec aboard the *Cairnrona* in September. The ship was evenly divided between passengers and cargo, and there was no first or second class. The Karno troupe had the run of the ship, more or less, although Chaplin was to say numerous times that they came over in steerage. During the voyage Stan spent a great deal of time with Whimsical Walker who had been a close friend of Dan Leno's.

Within seven years, Alf Reeves was to be hired by Chaplin as his studio manager. Charlie had become close with Reeves and his wife Amy during the crossing. The comedian maintained a certain distance from his understudy Stan, but for several reasons, the most important one financial, he joined Stan in seeking out a cheap back room in a West 43rd Street brown-stone house just off Times Square. Chaplin wrote, "It was dismal and dirty and made me homesick for London and our little flat. In the basement was a cleaning and pressing establishment, and during the week the fetid odour of clothes being pressed and steamed wafted up and added to my discomfort." Chaplin's description was graphic but slightly careless. He neglected to mention that he was sharing the room with Stan, and there is no discussion of Stan Laurel, however brief, in Chaplin's entire autobiography, an omission that suggests that Charlie really considered Stan as an equal and even as a possible threat to his eventual title as the supreme clown of all time. He had two ways of dealing with such threats; he would either ignore them or destroy them. The saddest and most terrible instance of the latter was brought to light after Chaplin's death.

In 1924, Chaplin had hired director Josef von Sternberg to direct his principal leading lady Edna Purviance in a follow-up to her critically-acclaimed *A Woman of Paris* (1923). It was left to von Sternberg to find a vehicle, so he wrote a screenplay from an old story of his about some fishermen on the California coast and their waiting women. Under the title *A Woman of the Sea*, the film was previewed once at a cinema near Hollywood, then returned to Chaplin's film vault. In February 1978, two months after Chaplin's death on Christmas Day, his actress daughter Geraldine revealed that the Purviance/von Sternberg movie had been burned, negative and all, by Chaplin "because it was too good". His daughter knew him well and sensed that he could not bear the possibility of the von Sternberg production being discovered after his death and hailed as a greater masterpiece than *A Woman of Paris*. Chaplin protected his genius in every possible way from his very early successes onward. Poor Miss Purviance, who was on the Chaplin pay-roll until her death in 1958, maintained a discreet silence for nearly thirty-five years. *A Woman of Paris* was to be her only bid for real stardom, and von Sternberg's name, like Stan's, was omitted from Chaplin's *Autobiography*. While Chaplin's misdeed might seem nearly unforgiveable, it is highly unlikely that the Von Sternberg film would have surpassed the vital, graceful and delicate charm of *A Woman of Paris*. Von Sternberg never became famous for his subtlety.

·   ·   ·   ·   ·

The second Karno company opened at the American Theatre in New York with an act, *The Wow-Wows*, which was a burlesque of secret societies and fraternal orders. Stories about weird initiation rites in college fraternities in America as well as shocking details of Ku-Klux-Klan ceremonies convinced Karno that *The Wow-Wows* was just what Americans would love. Chaplin once again played the lead, but the sketch was a dud.

Nevertheless, Karno's reputation and, beginning at about this time, Chaplin's own, were what had attracted the booking-offices. Very soon after their arrival in New York, the company was booked for a six-week tour on the Percy Williams circuit. They were a hit, and the Sullivan and Considine booking-office signed them for an additional twenty weeks in the west. On tour, they switched to the dependably funny cruelties of *Mumming Birds*, changing the title to *A Night in an English Music-hall*.

It was American vaudeville's heyday. Major feature films had not yet destroyed the big time and the two a day. Shuttling about the country, chiefly by rail, were one-legged dancers, two-legged dancers usually in pairs, mind readers, hypnotists, sharpshooters, bird acts and educated geese, minstrels, jugglers, magicians, contortionists, "girl acts", dog acts, and even one troupe of harmonious cats and rats, featuring a big, black rat walking on a tiny platform carrying the American flag.

The Karno troupe played two a day with music supplied by an eight-piece orchestra. Audiences on the big-time circuits were loyal, coming back again and again to see their favourites. Headliners sometimes changed when a new celebrity was born – the boxer, Battling Nelson, for example – and it was at about that time that the brilliant female impersonator Bert Savoy made his first big splash, an act much admired by Stan.

The vaudevillian was a breed apart. His loneliness was often acute and after hours, there was the constant search for companionship, usually in some bar. Although Chaplin has recalled those days with a stately melancholy in his prose, a mood quite appropriate to the vaudevillian's sense of alienation, he continued sharing cheap boarding-house rooms with Stan while on tour. They sought out cheap restaurants together and Stan remembered many a meal cooked on a gas-ring, an art Chaplin had learned from his mother.

Since Stan did not cease refining his craft in his room at night, Chaplin proved to be a brilliant critic, for which Stan was lastingly grateful. But Stan was reluctant to get too close to Chaplin, and there is no evidence that Chaplin would have allowed it. Stan never told interviewers of their experiences together on the road; he told his wives. There was a fierce ambition in Chaplin, greatly exceeding Stan's own, that coloured all of his relationships with others.

Before they left England, Chaplin had turned down the title role in a Karno production entitled *Jimmy, the Fearless*, and the part had gone to Stan. Chaplin then sat out front for a week watching Stan's performance and liked what he saw. On the following Saturday, he informed Karno that he had changed his mind and would accept the role. Stan was fired from the production that weekend, although he was kept on as a regular member of the company. He never forgot the incident. It made him keep his guard up for a while after their arrival in America, but Chaplin was simply too gifted to be anything but admired.

When the Karno company reached Los Angeles, only the sight of the Pacific Ocean afforded any excitement. The roads leading to the beaches were nearly all unpaved. Hollywood as a movie centre did not yet exist, although some scattered film-making was going on in the area and D. W. Griffith had established a custom of going there to continue with his one- and two-reelers for Biograph every winter. Stan fell in love with the hills and open countryside at once. By the time that he settled in as a permanent Californian some years later, when he was making his comedies with Oliver Hardy, there were many more houses and most of the streets were paved, but it was still essentially pastoral, and much of the charm of those early films of Laurel and Hardy lies in the fact that they were photographed in what appears to be a country village.

A Night in an English Music-hall doubled back across the country after its tour of California and began a week's run in Colorado Springs. In that era, vaudevillians usually had to pay their own travelling expenses. If they were frugal they might just manage. But it was hard to save anything, and for Stan it was impossible. He was careful about food and lodgings, but whatever was left over was spent in bars. They had more than six weeks of tour ahead of them and he was broke. He approached Alf Reeves for a rise. The request was passed along by cable to Fred Karno in London, and the answer came back with impressive speed: "No rise for Jefferson." Having no other option, Stan wired his father for the fare home.

Chaplin, too, had been denied a decent salary by Karno, and the producer attempted to conceal from him his growing popularity. Karno, called, like Stan's father, the "Guv'nor" by nearly everyone, believed that his name on any show was a guarantee of success. "Any fool can engage a star at a couple of hundred quid a week," he said, often enough. Karno was approaching millionaire status at about this time, but neither generosity nor even fairness was in his make-up. This ruling monarch of British comedy was rude and inconsiderate to his performers, stingy with his profits and beastly to his wives.

2 On his way back to England, Stan conceived a sketch, a knockabout routine set in Rome before its fall. He called it *The Rum 'Uns from Rome*, and it was suitably pointless. While with Karno, he had seen how effortlessly gag ideas were joined together to create a new sketch. Sometimes, he had suggested something himself to Karno, and the Guv'nor had listened. If it was truly funny, it might even be used. Karno was tough, but he listened to anyone with an idea. The only suggestions he rejected were those that called for the audience to think before it laughed. He knew better than anyone that the audience's mind was in suspension while in the variety hall.

In *Rum 'Uns*, Stan played a Roman soldier. A chariot drawn by a burlesque horse utilizing two performers, one playing the head and forelegs and the other, the rear end, was driven by Arthur Dandoe, another Karno casualty who had played "The Magician" in the American company.

Dandoe climbed down from the chariot and on to a platform, presumably in a forum, booming out: "Gather around!" Stan was anticipating a key element in his eventual screen character by more than a dozen years as he began walking dumbly around the speaker – "gathering around" – while Dandoe looked on in growing annoyance and perplexity, finally staring so ferociously at Stan that the latter stumbled to a stop. Then Stan, believing the stare to be the prelude to an attack, suddenly swung at Dandoe with his battle-axe.

Dandoe escaped into the forum column, one of the few props in the work. When a dummy head, made to look like Dandoe appeared from behind the column, Stan swung and sank the axe into the head. Such a "harmless" act of violence almost always provoked the audience into explosive laughter. The prop head disappeared and Dandoe stepped from behind the column with a similar axe sticking in his head, dripping with "blood". More laughter.

The carnage seen nightly in the music-halls – although it was not real – was part of "their money's worth". In Edwardian England, real violence was *felt*; a street mugging or a bloody accident aroused genuine compassion. Concern for others remained constant outside the music-halls until the early nineteen forties. Then, as the statistics from Hitler's charnel-houses filtered in, nearly everyone's sensibilities were dulled self-protectively. Beyond Hitler's holocaust lay Stalin's purges, the wholesale slaughter and torture of political juntas, and Vietnam. It affected screen comedy. By the nineteen seventies, there were far too many people who didn't really know how to laugh spontaneously and one wondered if it was an atrophied mechanism of the body that was at fault or the times. Many millions of television viewers were programmed to laugh at minimal "humour". It may be that by the seventies there was a comedians' ice age with Woody Allen standing alone at the thawing end. Allen's *Annie Hall* (1977) is intellectualized Chaplin with peripheral gags borrowed from Sennett and Roach (i.e. the abuse the rented car has to take at Allen's hands). Leading lady Diane Keaton is Allen's Purviance or Goddard. It is very nearly an occasion for dancing in the streets.

As the twentieth century moved into its second decade, the arrival of trade unionism and some paralyzing strikes had taken the working classes a long way out of bondage. But the lid was still on tightly, suppressing any real violence against the ruling industrialists. The prize ring, where the Irishman, "Gentleman Jim" Corbett, had been the hero at the turn of the century, and the music-halls were rivals in giving their patrons the release they craved in gory exhibitions of the punishment of human flesh. It was Fred Karno's foundation for humour and, through him, it became Stan's. When asked, both men would say that humour was basically cruel. Indignities, extending from plain humiliation to bodily assault, underlie many of their gag ideas. Survival as a comic in the halls and variety houses required an ability to "take it".

Among the comics and their producers, there was a continuing struggle to remain "nice" away from the theatre. Apparently Karno didn't even try. His two wives, one of whom had been his mistress and had shared in humiliating the first wife, bore the brunt of his vile temper. Wife number one was permanently scarred by the heel of Karno's shoe. Stan, a more gentle character, was decent and good-natured with friends, but this veneer wore off quickly with his wives, except for the last.

Rum 'Uns opened successfully in London, and Dandoe was promptly signed up on the strength of his performance by another producer for more money. The role of the imperious Roman victim was not easy to cast, and Stan, finding no satisfactory replacement had to abandon the sketch for a time. Then, while playing in *The Wax-Works* for Charles Baldwin, he found another suitable "Roman" in Ted Leo.

This time, the sketch was booked into the Royal Victoria Hall in Lambeth, but they came perilously close to not opening when they found that there wasn't enough money between them to hire a van to take their props to the theatre. In desperation they hired a push-cart, which they trundled along the streets themselves, heckled all the way by urchins.

At that time, Stan was living on the thinnest edge of survival. Even a small success was crucial. While audience reaction at Royal Victoria Hall was enthusiastic, as happened occasionally with Stan, *Rum 'Uns* was killed off by applause. A variety hall colleague of Ted Leo's, Jim Reed, came backstage to offer both men jobs in a new act he was putting together entitled *Fun on the Tyrol*. Reed told them that he had bookings in Holland and elsewhere on the continent. There was an additional incentive to perk up the deal, a bonus of food and drink beyond the actor's usual "doorstep", a slab of bread and butter (sometimes with jam) and a cup of tea. The booking agents in Holland owned the equivalent of a pub, where the cast could run up tabs. Stan and Leo could not resist.

They were to open on a Sunday in Rotterdam, which had a reputation for being a great town for comedy. Then the rains began.

That wouldn't have mattered anywhere else but in Rotterdam at the Circus Variété, where the tattoo on the wooden roof muffled all sound within. Performances had to be cancelled during a downpour. Unfortunately, as the rain continued into the week, credit at Pilcher and Dekker's saloon dried up. On the following Sunday, sunshine finally broke through a mackerel sky and *Fun on the Tyrol* made its début. The Dutch found its coarse humour to their liking, and a decent run seemed assured. On Tuesday, however, the rains began lashing that roof again and by mid-week, the booking was cancelled. Stan, as close to starvation as he ever would be, actually stole a loaf of bread from a delivery man, who carried baked goods on his head. But this was consumed at once and when the *Fun* company moved on to Liège, Stan was so weak from hunger on the opening night that he collapsed during a stilt-walk routine, knocking down all the other walkers in the company like so many dominos.

Somehow he got back to London, where his brother Gordon was managing Prince's Theatre (now the Shaftesbury) and living in a handsome flat in Holborn. Stan had to walk from Waterloo Station to High Holborn, a distance of perhaps two miles, because he lacked even a penny for the tram. Finding Gordon out of his apartment, he walked the few blocks to the theatre, where Gordon was standing out front in evening clothes. Stan, in soiled, shabby garments, his face smudged by travel and gaunt from hunger, waited several minutes till Gordon was alone to spare him the embarrassment of acknowledging such a scapegrace brother.

Gordon studied Stan for a moment, then took him up to his office for a lecture, which he concluded by predicting that Stan would never make it in the theatre as a comic. Stan was so convinced that the very next day he accepted a job from Gordon as a walk-on in the current production, Dion Boucicault's *Ben Machree*.

As Stan saw it, an actor's fate was in the hands of a diabolical headsman. One would achieve some stature and then be cut down, time and again – it was at moments like this that he began to lose his belief in justice. It made him into a stoic, which he remained until very nearly the end of his life.

Then his luck changed again. Alf Reeves ran into Stan in Leicester Square, told him that *A Night in an English Music-hall* was returning to the States for a second tour, and offered him his old role as understudy to Chaplin. Much to Gordon Jefferson's astonishment, Stan would be getting four times what his brother was paying as Fred Karno had met Stan's demand for a raise this time around. It was very nearly a decent salary – six pounds a week or more than thirty American dollars.

There was a week of frantic clothes-buying and rehearsals, and then the company was off, but this time aboard the faster *S.S. Olympic*, which sailed direct from Liverpool to New York. Stan did not know it, but he was not to see England again for twenty years, not until he returned there in triumph with Oliver Hardy in 1932.

3 New York City had changed between 1910 and 1912. Gone were the horse-drawn trolleys; they had been replaced by the clatter of iron of the first subway trains. The Woolworth Building, a sky-scraping tower of some sixty stories, was under construction. W. C. Fields was starring in the *Ziegfeld Follies*. But Stan had only a few days to sightsee in Manhattan before the company boarded a train to Cincinnati, where they opened at the Empress.

Stan realized almost immediately that the reputation of the Karno troupe had risen enormously since their last visit. Audiences were expectant, easily amused, warm and responsive. It was apparent, too, that people were coming to see the young man with the funny walk. Word of Chaplin's artistry preceded them in each city, helped along by an advance man who trumpeted the little "drunk's" popularity as though he were a star.

While they were playing at the Nixon Theatre in Philadelphia, Alf Reeves received a wire from Adam Kessel, one of film-maker Mack Sennett's chief backers:

IS THERE A MAN NAMED CHAFFIN IN YOUR COMPANY OR SOMETHING LIKE THAT STOP IF SO WILL HE COMMUNICATE WITH KESSEL AND BAUMAN 24 LONGACRE BUILDING BROADWAY.

Reeves turned the wire over to Chaplin, saying that it must refer to him, and Chaplin hastened to New York. There he was offered $125 a week to star in screen comedies for Sennett – three times what Karno was paying him. Predictably, Karno made no effort to meet the Sennett offer. There is no record of his ever having attempted to retain a principal actor by becoming involved in a bidding match with a rival producer. He believed to the end that it was Karno comedy which brought in the audiences, and that they would continue to come no matter who was in the company. He was wrong, and by the late nineteen twenties he was finished as a leading producer.

When Chaplin left the Karno troupe for California, Stan was not surprised. He knew that Charlie had reached a point where mime becomes art, where audiences felt they were in the presence of a wonder and were left more awe-struck than convulsed. Not until audiences were distanced by his celluloid image thrown upon a screen would they feel free to roar with laughter once again.

While Stan had seen a number of one- and two-reel comedies by then, mostly in theatres where he was part of the live half of the bill, until Chaplin was summoned West, he had never thought of the possibility of a screen career. Yet, with reason, he thought their destinies were linked: there was too much in their backgrounds that had been the same despite the economic differences. They had both admired the same music-hall idols and had been exposed to the same grooming in the hands of Karno. From the time Chaplin left the company, Stan became a keen student of movie comedy, trying to see everything available. Meanwhile, he stepped into the role of the drunk, giving a flawless impersonation of Chaplin.

If the management of the Nixon Theatre had been able to foresee the enormous drawing power of even an imitator of Chaplin within three of four years, they might not have been as unhappy as they were with Stan. In their contract with Karno, it was specified that Chaplin himself would appear. Without him, they were not interested in continuing with the act. Others in the Karno troupe besides Stan had for some time recognized Chaplin's brilliance and hypnotic hold upon audiences, but it came as a great shock to all of them to discover that he was the primary reason for their bookings. They had believed in Karno's own vast popularity, and his nearly insufferable egotism seemed not misplaced to them. But that was in England, and Karno was never to have a great success in the States again.

Stan's time had not yet come. It would not come for another dozen years. It was not that he was a victim of imperceptive booking offices, producers and audiences; he was one half of a whole yet to be realized. He would be nearly middle-aged before that whole was achieved – thirty-seven years old – by which time Chaplin was three-quarters of the way through his career.

At the last moment there in Philadelphia, Alf Reeves persuaded the Nixon management to accept the leading comedian from the London company, Dan Raynor, as Chaplin's replacement. There was a wait of three weeks before Raynor arrived in America and reached the troupe. When he finally opened, the reaction was cool. American audiences watched Raynor in mute bewilderment. Chaplin was universal; Dan Raynor was provincial music-hall gone big-time. Business fell off alarmingly and the booking was cancelled. One wonders if the booking could have been saved, had Stan been allowed to continue. He knew where Charlie's laughs were, knew every shrug and movement.

In an unexpected, magnanimous gesture, Karno offered to pay for second-class boat tickets for those who wanted to return to England. But this time Stan decided to stay on in America and pick up jobs where he could find them. He said later he felt himself a failure when he was not allowed to take over the role for which he had been understudy for so long. Perhaps he didn't relish the ignominy of knowing he was a little farther down on the ladder to fame than he had been on his home ground before leaving for America. He teamed up with two other Karno casualties, Edgar Hurley and his wife Wren, and the threesome went by train to Chicago. They opened in small-town houses, often playing split weeks, with *The Nutty Burglars*, a routine created by Stan. In Stan's words, there was "no plot, just gags, anything for laughs". It was not a time to impress movie scouts; it was a time for survival.

Still, *The Nutty Burglars* was funny and earned them a big-time agent, Gordon Bostock, who with his brother Claude had the reputation of handling only "class" acts. Bostock suggested changes in the gags and even costumes to bring the Jefferson-Hurley act up to big-time calibre. The Three Comiques, as they called themselves, were on their way.

The Bostocks were to become extremely influential in Stan's life. He seemed utterly incapable of managing his own affairs, and he was in constant trouble with finances, with the ladies and eventu-

ally, with his fellow performers. He welcomed anyone who could
come in occasionally and clean up the mess, and both Bostock
brothers did so frequently, with Claude eventually taking over and
managing Stan in every area of his life. Claude and his wife even
suggested that Stan rid himself of a wife of whom they did not
approve sometime later.

Gordon Bostock booked *The Nutty Burglars* into the Poli circuit,
where they first worked out the minor snags in the act in Poli's
"family time" theatres, doing three or four shows a day in tandem
with movies, and then went on playing similar vaudeville dates all
over New England, Pennsylvania and New York.

In 1915 they were playing in Toronto on the same bill with Alice
and Baldy Cooke. Alice Hamilton Cooke, like Stan, had been raised
in a prosperous theatrical family. Her father, William Cranston
Hamilton, had founded the old San Francisco *Star*, but had
won lasting fame in show business annals by being circus owner
James A. Bailey's chief press agent.

When Alice was seven years old, her parents took her to Paris,
where her father was managing Buffalo Bill Cody and his Wild West
Show. Cody had won the immediate affection of the Parisians with
his rousing spectacle of dozens of bareback-riding indians, covered
wagons, and frontier soldiers engaging in mock "massacres". Back
in New York City, Alice grew up rather as Stan had done, surrounded by theatrical impresarios and actors. At the age of sixteen,
also like Stan, she left school and then fell in love with a young man
named Balderston (later Baldwin) Cooke.

"Baldy", as everyone called him, although he had a handsome
head of wavy hair and a profile like those of young men in Leyen-
decker's drawings, had no perceptible talents. But Alice placed
rapture above everything. Once having met him, she cared about
nothing except marrying Baldy.

So marry him she did, and sooner than her father or anyone close
to her expected. There was now a sudden interest in where Baldy's
talents might lie. It was discovered that he had a fine baritone voice,
untrained but, in Alice's words, "just gorgeous". She announced to
her new husband and her family, "We're going into vaudeville",
and together with her younger sister, Florence, and a second man,
went out as a four-man act.

Unhappily, acts with more than two in the cast were hard to book in the "dumps" where beginners were launched. These houses belonged to no *time* at all, time being the vaudevillian's term for *circuit*. They were just a step up from the recently abandoned nickle-odeons. Baldy spent his mornings scouting in neighbouring cities and lining up future bookings in Albany, Troy and Saratoga Springs.

3 ‖ The Keystone Trio

1 By 1915, Alice and Baldy had ditched the other half of their foursome and become a duo. Prospects immediately brightened and they began to move nearer the big time. In Ontario, they were on a bill with an act called *The Keystone Trio*. They watched the routine, which had no plot but was simply a clever pantomime burlesque featuring a remarkable likeness of Charlie Chaplin and cruder but still identifiable impersonations of Chester Conklin and Mabel Normand.

The Chaplin impersonator was of course Stan, the others Edgar and Wren Hurley. The act had been Bostock's idea and was not original at all. There were perhaps a hundred similar take-offs touring various parts of the world at that moment. But Bostock knew the act was bookable, and he especially knew that Stan Jefferson was probably the best of all "Chaplins", having studied the routine and timing with their creator. Edgar Hurley was a fair carbon of Conklin, and Wren, relying more on make-up than on talent, was still able to suggest Normand.

When the Cookes met Stan, the first thing he did was to complain about the Hurleys' shortcomings. He said he was ready to quit them cold and that Bostock agreed with him. It was a clear case of perfectionism versus loyalty, and the Cookes understood it as such. But when Stan proposed that Alice and Baldy take the Hurleys' place, Baldy quickly refused, telling him, "That would be too unprofessional. We couldn't do that." Baldy did leave the door open, however, saying that Alice and he would be happy to become a part of Stan's act "if you and the Hurleys split up of your own accord and you still want us". Stan took Alice's mother's address in New York City and they parted.

The foregoing account is Alice Cooke's version of the events that led to the Cookes' close association with Stan. Her portrait of Stan is persuasively human and in line with that recalled by others who had intimate contact with him. Stan's own recollection is a bit different and a trifle self-serving. He said that Edgar Hurley wanted to play the Chaplin role, but,

> he wasn't qualified to do so. Hurley quickly copyrighted the act, not telling me about it, claiming it as his material as a means to stop me from doing the act with another couple (*the Cookes*). He replaced me in the act with another fellow, Ted Banks. Then the theatre managers discovered I was not in the act, and it had become an inferior act anyway. They couldn't get further bookings and *The Keystone Trio* folded forever.

The Hurleys were not unaware of Stan's conversations with the Cookes about replacing them and clearly took whatever measures they could to hang on to the act and survive. The rupture between Stan and the Hurleys was, as expected, permanent. Since the Cookes themselves would be abandoned by Stan after an intimate friendship and professional association of several years' duration, we are faced with a hero of shifting loyalties, whose eye was on the main chance and whose nimble feet were moving heedlessly over a number of dead bodies. Some of the same callousness that stained Chaplin's character throughout his career had crept into Stan as well.

Stan's perfidy could not be forgotten by the Hurleys. There were to be other temporary "victims" who learned to be more forgiving. And yet nearly everyone who did not get closely involved with him would remember only his charm and gentleness.

· · · · · ·

Summer was an off-season for vaudevillians. If an act survived the torrid months of late June through August, it had to be very good or performed by headliners. Most small-time vaudeville houses shut down entirely for all of July and August because there was no such thing as air-conditioning. In a few large cities, there were big-time houses or movie palaces (then just beginning to open their Moorish or Italian Renaissance doors around the country) that relied upon "air cooling", an uncomplicated system of blowing huge fans over blocks of ice to make theatre-going tolerable.

Alice and Baldy had gone home for the summer, but had then somehow managed to get a booking in a large cinema in Brooklyn. One evening in July, as they walked into their Brooklyn hotel, the desk clerk told them, "A great friend of yours came to see you and wanted to know if he could wait in your room." The Cookes were mystified; they had given up on Stan weeks earlier. But Stan it was and he was full of plans and enthusiasm. He told them he had an idea for a new act and even a name for it, *The Stan Jefferson Trio.*

Stan seemed light-hearted and foot-loose. He said that he hadn't had a vacation since he was a small boy on holiday in Ulverston and suggested that they find a summer cottage somewhere. On a trip to Atlantic Highlands, New Jersey, they rented a little house on the beach.

Their plans to rehearse outside had to be abandoned because of the gnats, but the cottage itself was ideal for the purpose. They threw ideas at each other, cooked their own haphazard meals, consumed a great deal of whisky, and slowly began putting an act together. Alice remembered that summer as the happiest time of her life. "We were all happy," she recalled.

They agreed to pool their earnings and draw on them for expenses and "fun". Much of their off-stage time was spent in saloons, their favourite spot in New York being Dowlings. Alice pretended, at least, to have a large capacity for alcohol, and Stan calling her "Alice, the Bar Fly". Baldy, after putting away a few Scotches, often became drunk. It would take Stan longer to reach that state. There is an art to drinking, as there is to all civilized matters, and the Jefferson Trio seemed to have mastered it. There was no coarseness, no hostility. Instead, they became elaborately polite to one another. Bowlers were tipped decorously to ladies if they were out on the town; flowered and fruited hats were admired, the more outrageous, the more effusive the compliment.

Thus *The Stan Jefferson Trio* moved into 1916, guided by Claude Bostock, who had taken over much of the supervision of bookings and promotion from his brother. There were tricky moments, as when they crossed into Canada with bottles of whisky hidden in a wardrobe trunk and several boxes of props, but they were never caught.

It was a transitional time for vaudevillians. There was no longer any clear-cut distinction between the big-time vaudeville house and the top film-houses in the major cities. No one on the circuits, except perhaps the management back in New York and Chicago, knew that vaudeville itself was entering its final decade and that by 1928, there would be literally nothing but films (talking pictures had arrived) and "six big acts on the stage". But Claude Bostock had pushed them ahead on to the major circuits, the Fox for one, and for the first time in his career, Stan seemed content with each day as it came along, usually in the company of the Cookes and perhaps an attractive female performer on the same bill. In the west, they were on the Pantages time, not the most prestigious of bookings since that circuit was called "the Siberia of vaudeville" by many troupers. But it was a living and no one in the Trio was straining for recognition anyway. They were frittering away their days and occasionally one of them would see their situation with some clarity. Once, Alice told Stan to buy a new suit before he went to see Bostock again. "You look a little seedy," she told him, but with great love. He bought the suit.

Another season rolled around and, by 1917, they were earning $175 a week, and spending it all, certain that there would be more money the next week. When there wasn't, Bostock would give them an advance. They finally decided that this was even astute on their part as it gave Bostock an incentive to get them a better booking in order to get his money back.

They were in Philadelphia when everything fell apart. An act known as *The Hayden Sisters*, who weren't sisters at all, had played the theatre the previous week, and the two women, who had an open week (no booking), dropped backstage every day for their mail. One of them was more highly-coloured than the other with sharp features, probably well into her thirties – her name was Mae Charlotte Dahlberg. Her dancing "sister", Cissy Hayden, was paler and prettier, but quite unremarkable. When Stan saw the tall, pre-possessing Mae Dahlberg (actually her name was *Mrs* Mae Dahlberg Cuthbert and she was married to an Australian actor), his reaction was immediate. Thereafter his eyes never left her, while she, with utter transparency, played the shy coquette. Alice, watching the performance from a few feet away, nudged Baldy and whispered, "Just watch that! That Mae is trying to grab off Stan. I can feel it. I just know it."

Stan saw Mae Dahlberg on every possible occasion during the week in Philadelphia. Since Alice and Baldy still dined with him regularly, they also saw far more of Mae Dahlberg than they cared to. The affair didn't go down very well with Alice, whose feminine instincts were sending up alarms over Mae's "rapaciousness". Baldy agreed that Stan didn't seem to know the first thing about such women. Stan flirted, twittered, giggled and attempted to charm the lady while the Cookes knew that *he* was the prey. Alice was surprised that Stan had fallen for someone "that homely" and "so much older". Mae was also heavier, but, as the Cookes later discovered, Junoesque women appealed to Stan. Two of his wives would be nearly as stately as Mae and despite Alice's opinion, she was not unattractive.

Stan agreed that she was no great beauty and soon began calling her "the old hag" behind her back. This was when he was sober, of course. Whenever they were at their favourite pastime in Dowlings or elsewhere, then she was "the Australian beauty".

On the mornings after these occasions, Alice was usually sick with dread when she realized that Stan's relationship with Mae would not end in Philadelphia. In a month or less, much of the fun drained out of Stan's alliance with the Cookes. Gaiety changed to brooding and forced jollities. Dinner became a strain on all of them so that more was drunk than eaten. It must have been a relief to Alice and Baldy when Stan finally announced over an evening meal that he was pulling out of the act. The stinger was, as all of them knew, that Stan was its sparking-plug.

But Stan was reassuring! His farewell was peppered with compliments about the laughs Baldy was getting and Alice's marvellous timing. The next day, he was gone, but he had left a letter for the Cookes backstage in which he said that he was giving them the act, *The Crazy Cracksman*, and recommended another comic, Billy Crackles, to replace him.

The Cookes were not wild about Billy Crackles. For one thing, he drank more than the three of them put together; for another, he could not get Stan's laughs. After a few weeks of performing a sketch that no longer seemed amusing to anyone, including the audience, Alice and Báldy decided to confront Stan and tell him what they really thought.

Stan was staying in New York with another English comic, Harry Cutler and his wife, Florrie. This led the Cookes to believe he was working up a new double act for Mae and himself. They were mistaken, as they were to discover.

They found Stan at home and as warm towards them as he had ever been. He embraced both of them, and in minutes had disarmed them totally. There was something so completely guileless about Stan that Baldy hesitated to bring up their very real grievance. Still, he forced himself to do so and told Stan that Alice and he didn't think Stan had treated them fairly. But Stan, as he had done before, declared how confident he was of their ability to carry on. He was pouring them drinks and laughing about old times. The Cookes' trip to New York, so difficult to undertake, seemed about to turn into a holiday.

In an hour or so, full of good alcohol and with their mission apparently scotched, literally and figuratively, the Cookes had to leave to catch the train back to Pennsylvania. They said their good-byes. Stan stood in the doorway, waving to them as they went down the hall but halfway out, Alice burst into tears. Baldy tried to comfort her but saw that it was hopeless. She would gasp for breath and then more convulsive sobs would shake her. Her tears seemed to sober Baldy. Suddenly he turned, went back to Stan and began shaking him by the collar, like a cat with a mouse. "You see that girl crying?" he asked. "Well, Stan, you're going to pay for every tear she's shedding." At last the Cookes departed, never expecting to see Stan again.

At that moment Stan probably thought he would never see the Cookes again either, nor get back his Chaplinesque shoes and cane that he had asked them to send. Alice and Baldy tried to forget Stan as they took *The Crazy Cracksman* to Toledo, still saddled with Billy Crackles.

A number of props were needed for the sketch, including fly paper. The day of their arrival, as they were listing their needs to a stage manager, they saw the theatre owner coming at them in a rage. "What do you mean by coming in here with the same act I just closed last night?" he exploded. "You're asking for the same music and even the fly paper!" What had happened, as the Cookes quickly discovered, was that, instead of going out in a new double act with Mae, Stan had put another man in Baldy's place and Mae in Alice's and was continuing with *The Crazy Cracksman*. By the following week, all of the Cookes' future bookings were cancelled by managers who had heard that Stan had replaced them.

Baldy was nearly beside himself. He had very little to fall back on. Suddenly, Alice remembered Stan's letter in which he had clearly stated that he was turning the act over to them. They showed the letter to Gus Young, a booking agent.

Young knew that vaudeville teemed with pirates. Comedy acts were choice booty. If a comedian was original, whether he wrote his own material or bought it from others, he soon found himself the victim of thieves. In Fred Allen's words, "Good gags spread like bad news." When acts split up, the performers often took on new partners and both teams continued to do the same act. But Gus Young thought that Stan's letter to the Cookes altered matters. It clearly put Stan in the wrong, and it was impossible for two groups to perform the same act on the same circuit.

Young arranged for the Cookes' previous bookings to be reinstated and Stan's act cancelled. Stan made no effort then or afterwards to apologize to the Cookes, although in a few years' time they would become closer than ever and for keeps. Alice saw nothing caddish about Stan's behaviour and never blamed him for their humiliation. "He was hooked on Mae," she explained.

2   When George Burns was touring vaudeville's *Siberia* with Billy Lorraine, he recalled that Stan and Mae were on the same bill with him – they were number four while Burns and Lorraine were number two – and that Stan was:

in drag very ratty and funny – possibly playing his wife's mother (*Mae was now calling herself Mrs Stan Jefferson*). He cried a lot in the act and got pushed around, taking many comedy falls. . . . He had the type of thing that you loved . . . You wanted to take him home – you always wanted to take him home. . . . They seemed to be fighting day and night . . . and with the thin-walled dressing-rooms on the Pantages circuit, they could easily be heard all over the theatre. . . . When the dressing-room door would open, they would both be smiling at each other as if nothing were going on. But the minute the door was closed, the battle would begin again . . . she had the voice, he had the talent.

What their incessant quarrels were about nobody ever knew, though Mae was tagged as jealous, ambitious and vain. For his part, Stan could not easily control his temper, nor his principal weakness after drinking – his incorrigible flirtatiousness. He took nothing seriously, which made him dear to his backstage friends and accomplices, but scarcely qualified him as a stalwart lover-companion.

In the skits he devised for "Stan and Mae Jefferson", Mae was always the aggressor, whether Stan was impersonating another female or not. She was taller than he and usually pretended a ludicrous dignity in the later mode of Margaret Dumont of Marx Brothers fame. Stan's drag appearances drew their inspiration directly from his memories of Leno, using the same mop-like wig and frumpy clothes with outrageous stockings slipping down.

As they became better known, Stan began leaving Mae's name out of the billing and the annunciator (the lighted billing-card holder on one side of the proscenium arch) would read "Stan Jefferson" only. Before long, however, that name began to worry him because it had thirteen letters in it. Actors have always been extremely superstitious.

Almost unconsciously, Mae began searching everywhere for a new name – on billboards, in magazines and newspapers, and even in telephone directories. Finally, as she recalled shortly before her death in 1969:

I was in the dressing-room . . . looking at an old history book that someone in the previous week's show must have left. . . . I opened it up casual like, and I came to an etching or a drawing of a famous old Roman general, Scipio Africanus Major. . . . Around his head he wore a laurel, a wreath of laurel. I learned later that laurel leaves are really bay leaves. . . . That word stayed with me. I said it aloud, Laurel. Laurel. Stan Laurel. Stan looked up from what he was doing and he said, "What?". . . . "How about that for a name?" He repeated it aloud, too. "Stan Laurel. Sounds very good."

4 || Stan Laurel in Hollywood

1 In 1917, Stan and Mae were playing the Hippodrome Theatre in downtown Los Angeles. The theatre was owned by Adolph Ramish, who had many friends in the mushrooming film industry and occasionally investigated new talent for them. By that time, Stan and Mae had been touring together for more than a year. Their act seemed fresh, though it was the refinement of a routine they had been using for a number of weeks, and their timing was as smooth as a Tissot watch. They were a joy to see and terribly funny.

Ramish saw movie potential in Stan at once. Audiences were riveted by his every vulnerable move. There was something lovably helpless about him, an underdog with grace. Then, too, Stan had a lean, English handsomeness, redeemed from juvenile good looks by a long chin – that also counted for something. It is perhaps worth noting that nearly all of the silent comic leading men were handsome; Chaplin, Lloyd, Keaton, Langdon, Charley Chase and even Fatty Arbuckle had attractive features. Of course, the line between handsomeness and character projection cannot be made too rigid. Stan would later use clown white make-up and comb his red hair straight up in an extra long crew cut to mask his basic good looks, just as Keaton froze his leading man features into an unsmiling sobriety.

Ramish asked Robin E. Williamson, a comic star in his own right and director for Kalem Studios, a film company recently headquartered in Florida, to prepare a story for Stan and Mae to be filmed in Los Angeles. The finished one-reeler, a slap-dash affair about a mental patient who escapes from an asylum wearing a business suit and a Napoleon hat, went out as a Nestor release entitled *Nuts in May* (1917).

The comedy was previewed at the Hippodrome in Los Angeles, a huge cinema centre featuring vaudeville, and Ramish rounded up some key film men for the screening, including Charlie Chaplin and Carl Laemmle, the diminutive head of Universal Pictures. There was much discussion in the lobby afterwards; Laemmle spoke approvingly of Stan's ease before the camera and asked about his availability. Chaplin also seemed interested. He said to Stan, "Come and see me." Stan waited several days for a word, thinking that Charlie would call him and set up an appointment. Finally, he decided that Chaplin's casual suggestion called for some action on his part, so he went to Levy's, a deli in the heart of Hollywood where actors congregated. Stan sent a message through a waiter, "May I see you now?" But Chaplin sent back word saying, "I'm sorry, but I'm just tied up at the moment. But we'll get together." Stan didn't have the aggressiveness necessary to pursue the matter further.

Understandably, Chaplin was not eager to bring a comedian with a background identical to his own into his newly-formed company, then under contract to Mutual. This wariness may explain why he never once offered to assist Stan's film career in any fashion or suggested that the team of Laurel and Hardy should come into United Artists with their own production unit, a move that would have made both men millionaires, added to the Chaplin coffers, and probably slowed down the eventual decline of the team. Chaplin was never known for his generosity in dealing with rivals. Since boyhood, he had learned to beat down all competition.

Would Stan have been as tough-minded had their roles been reversed? The record indicates that he would certainly have taken the risk and helped Chaplin. Stan was an egocentric, unconsciously so, but never ungenerous. Alice and Baldy Cooke, Harry Langdon and Fred Karno all benefited from their friendship with Stan at one time or another. As the years rolled on, the only thing that set a limit to Stan's reckless open-handedness was the financial chasm beneath him that became a little deeper with each divorce.

It was Universal that now signed up Stan. Mae seemed to accept being overlooked by their talent scouts and even joked about being a "lady of leisure". Knowing her mercurial moods, Stan never felt that Mae's gracious acceptance of his going it alone was genuine. He remained wary.

Stan's contract was to run a year, during which time he would be launched as a bumpkinish chap named Hickory Hiram in a series of three one-reelers. With the release of the films his luck ran out. *Hiram* was an error in judgment by studio head Laemmle. Hardly anyone wanted the comedies. Rural humour was being banked in silos against the day when Will Rogers would be brought out from Ziegfeld's *Follies* and Chic Sale made his first short. Chaplin's *Little Tramp*, Harold Lloyd's *Lonesome Luke* and Mack Sennett's *Keystone Kops* were all city types. Stan said much later that the aborted series was released "to all the very best comfort stations".

But Alice and Baldy Cooke had seen one of the *Hickory Hiram* films while on tour and thought it pretty wonderful. Alice had told their mutual friends with awe in her voice: "Stan's in pictures!" The Cookes were being booked by the Wether-Fisher-Newton circuit of Chicago, who booked theatres all the way to California. The Hippodrome in Los Angeles was included in the Cookes' itinerary, and they were thrilled by that prospect.

Still, Alice was not about to forget what Stan had done to them. That still rankled. On the train west, Alice and Baldy were discussing these past troubles with Stan with other vaudevillians on their bill. One of them asked Alice what she would do if she saw Stan in Los Angeles. Alice insisted that she "would haul off and punch him right in the nose".

During the middle of their run at the Hippodrome, one afternoon Alice and Baldy left the theatre for a stroll. "Oh, Baldy!" said Alice, "look who's coming." It was Stan, and he threw his arms around Alice, and they hugged and kissed, Stan reaching out to pull Baldy into the embrace.

When the Cookes returned to the theatre, they mentioned that they had run into Stan. "Well," someone asked, "did you punch him in the nose?" "No," Alice said, still inexpressibly touched by the warmth of Stan's greeting, "I kissed him."

Much to their surprise, Stan had no contract for any more movies and he and Mae were in worse shape than they had been when the Cookes last saw them. Stan's suit was threadbare and Mae had apparently pawned the last bits of jewelry she possessed. That was one of the ways vaudevillians appraised another's solvency: if the rings, bracelets and watches were gone, they were in trouble. It was very disillusioning to Alice. She had thought that with vaudeville slowly collapsing, the movies would prop up sagging careers and bank accounts, but here were Stan and Mae stuck in a seedy boarding-house, unable to leave because they owed several weeks' back rent.

There was no love lost between Alice and Mae, but Mae was so obviously devoted to Stan that the Cookes made an effort to accept her. And in important ways, they noted, Mae had changed. She no longer seemed brash and over-zealous, trying to attract male admirers. If anything, she was subdued, even frightened. She had endured days without decent food, humiliating scoldings from hotel managers and boarding-house landladies calling for the rent, and nights alone when the shouting matches had driven Stan to the streets; above all she had seen the failure of his movie series. Perhaps most dishearteningly, she had forced herself into a semblance of domesticity, dreaming of a home base somewhere with Stan. She was ready to put down her roots and was convinced that a permanent apartment or a house would have a steadying influence on Stan, while he considered such aspirations tedious. Hotels and boarding-houses were fine with him. In fact, he *preferred* them to any of the homes he would ever have and wound up his days in a motel suite, which was just the man's style.

A home was important to Mae. She had left Australia with her son by Jack Cuthbert and had been forced to place the child with foster parents in New Jersey when she had first gone on tour with Cissy Hayden. There was no way she could reclaim the boy when she and Stan reached the big time if they had no home. To that end, she later claimed that she and Stan had gone through a common-law marriage ceremony in New York on 18 June 1919. This is an unusual claim and apparently meant that vows were exchanged in the bed-room. Since there had not been any witnesses at the ritual, Stan never felt it could pose a threat to his peace of mind or his finances. He was mistaken.

About one thing there is no doubt at all. Mae and Stan lived and travelled together as husband and wife for nearly a decade. Though she clung to him with ferocious tenacity, Stan had come to need her. She was stronger-willed than he and she gave him an imperishable gift – his name – not a trivial gesture when one is bandying around such names as Laurel and Hardy. She had involved herself com-pletely in his professional career – even the Bostocks deferred to her. And despite the ill fortune that seemed to dog Stan, he *had* climbed several rungs up the ladder of recognition while Mae was his part-ner. Carl Laemmle didn't cast comics in comedy series, even aborted ones, unless he saw film material in them. Much of Stan's financial troubles came from the depression that was slowly killing vaude-ville itself, causing circuits to fold, straight vaudeville houses to close, and enforcing wage cuts. Smart and sometimes ruthless cir-cuit operators were getting out and moving into films or the legiti-mate theatre.

Then there was a dramatic turnabout in Stan's fortunes, the consequences of which would ultimately rend his relationship with Mae. In 1918, he was called back to Universal and made nine short comedies, enough of them with Mae to suggest that her influence on his career might not be completely beneficial. Mae's years of troup-ing, her marital woes, the absence of her child and the shouting matches with Stan had etched unattractive lines in her face. Exhibitors began protesting about the things that Stan and Mae did in their one- and two-reelers. Mae was still using affronted dignity as her comedy prop, but it emerged on the screen as unalloyed vulgarity. As producer Joe Rock recalled: "They'd climb over a fence or through a transom and he'd put his hand under her dress and she'd react – outraged, you know. They did that all the time and people complained." There would now be awkward pauses when Stan told movie executives, "My wife always appears with me."

The situation was aggravated by internal strife that came close to shutting down the studio. While several factions were struggling for control of Universal in December 1919, the company was reorganized and all contracts were cancelled. But Carl Laemmle, a tiger when aroused, won out over his cut-throat rivals and eventually built a splendid new studio in the San Fernando Valley. He immediately renewed all contracts with his major stars and even with a few of the not so major ones whose work held promise. Stan was not among those renewed.

Still, there were others in the industry with an eye on Stan. In early 1918, Stan's act had been seen by Gilbert M. ("Broncho Billy") Anderson, the first "name" performer in silent films, who had appeared in Edwin Porter's *The Great Train Robbery* in 1903. Anderson had founded the Essanay Company with George K. Spoor in Chicago, and had then moved their operations to California. One-reel westerns starring himself had made Anderson the first cowboy star, even before William S. Hart. When he scouted Stan, Anderson was preparing a series of comedies under the name of Sunkist (or, alternatively, Sun-Lite) for release by Metro. Comedies had overtaken westerns in audience appeal. Anderson was a city boy himself so the fare didn't matter to him – he was guided by whatever the public chose.

Impressed by audience empathy for Stan (like everyone else, Broncho Billy was aware that they rooted for Stan at Mae's expense), Anderson hired him to star in a two-reeler with the title *Lucky Dog*. It was filmed at the old Selig Zoo a few years before Louis B. Mayer began his career as a producer using those same facilities. Stan played a young man who was tossed into the street for non-payment of rent.

This theme was popular among vaudevillians. Always aliens in strange cities, now many of them were destitute as well. The plot line was made to order for Stan. The young man, homeless and alone, befriends a stray dog, which he carries in a satchel. When he sets down the bag, the dog pokes his feet through the bottom and runs off down the street. In one of the funniest moments, Stan chases the satchel past bewildered pedestrians. He catches up with the dog at a corner, where an overweight, moustachioed robber is waving his gun at a victim. The robber backs up to Stan, who is picking up the dog, and unwittingly puts the loot in Stan's pocket, then waves the victim away and spins about, his gun pointed at this unexpected stranger – Stan. He begins thrashing Stan until Stan empties his pockets and, to their mutual astonishment, finds the wad of bills there. As Stan is handing over the money, the robber prods him again and says, "Put 'em both up, insect, before I comb your hair with lead." Stan, angered by the manhandling and feeling he has nothing to lose, kicks the villain in his immense rear and runs down the block, through a hole in a fence, where the overweight bandit gets stuck in pursuit. Seeing this, Stan climbs back over the fence and gives his assailant a final, tremendous kick in the same spot as before and runs off.

Stan catches up with his dog, enters him in a dog show, and wins first prize. Then the rightful owners show up and accuse him of dog-stealing, although this accusation is withdrawn when they see what an innocent Stan is. We fade out on a quiet chuckle. All's well with Stan's world.

But audiences didn't care very much. Anderson's director, Jesse Robbins, had succeeded in capturing for the first time some of Stan's ultimate screen appeal – that of a helpless and much-put-upon soul with all the odds against him. The dénouement showed Stan emerging a winner by dint of dumb luck. It was right for Chaplin, but wrong for Stan. A character peg for Stan had yet to be found.

The double-chinned menace who threatened to part Stan's hair with lead was also a harbinger of the future. His name was Oliver Norvell Hardy.

2   Hollywood in 1918 was still semi-rural. On Hollywood Boulevard just below Gower, there was a wooden bridge over a creek. The boulevard itself ended at La Brea and beyond that there was nothing but fields and groves of citrus trees. In the middle of La Brea stood an oil derrick pumping day and night. For amusement, there were the gambling casinos and the race track at nearby Tiajuana, which was quite civilized with a splendid hotel and night club and, for the less affluent, a local track where the Beverly Wilshire Hotel now stands. The advent of the studios had brought a real estate boom, and there were billboards advertising "Wilshire Boulevard Frontage, $95.00 a foot. It'll never be any lower!" – a considerable understatement.

Stan began talking about settling in Los Angeles even though his act with Mae kept them on the road most of the time. This was no aberration in his character; he thought of "settling down" in furnished rooms or a hotel suite. He just liked the place, which was not an uncommon love affair for Englishmen. The novelist Christopher Isherwood stayed there, finding a tonic in what other writers found soporific. In 1918, Stan and Mae again were booked into Los Angeles, this time at the Main Street Theatre.

Hal Roach was then four years into a career as a producer. He attended a performance at the Main Street and liked Stan sufficiently to go backstage and chat with him about the movies. It was the beginning of an odd association that brought together two men who were as contrasting in natures and opinions as the two statesmen clashing in the nation's capital at that moment – Woodrow Wilson and Senator Henry Cabot Lodge.

Roach had gone into "partnership" with actor Harold Lloyd to form an independent company named Rolin Films. It was not a real partnership; Lloyd had no status other than that of an actor. But when they met as fellow actors on the set of *Samson and Delilah* at Universal, it was forcibly brought home to Roach that Lloyd was an actor of some training and potential, while he always felt a bit phoney as a performer and much more at home with all the business that went on behind the camera.

Roach was blunt, a muscular stevedore in appearance, with a deceptively bright, agile mind. He could talk about brahmin bulls with cowboys and they *knew* he was one of them, and of tracking shots and ingenious new dissolves with cameramen. Lloyd was slender and much tougher than he looked: he had been a boxer for a brief time. He was versatile; he could play everything from menace to romantic hero and get laughs in between. Since comedies were very much in vogue with the success of Chaplin at Essanay and the entire comic crew at the Mack Sennett Studio, Lloyd wanted to be a funnyman, too.

Roach had little business sense at that time, but a contagious belief in himself. During the shooting of *The Hoosier Schoolmaster* (1914), Dan Linthicum, who was financing the film, came around to see how it was coming along, but the director was too busy to talk with him. Instead, he spoke with Roach, who had advanced himself to assistant director. Roach informed the money man that he was "the best undiscovered director in the business." Such self-confidence in a man as vigorous as Roach impressed Linthicum so much, he bankrolled Roach in making a series of one reelers with cowboy actor Roy Stewart, leading lady Jane Novak and Harold Lloyd as comedy relief.

Lloyd's first alliance with Roach was broken off when Lloyd asked for the same pay as Stewart was receiving – ten dollars a day. Roach, pinched for cash as he struggled to build up a stable of comedians, balked, and Lloyd went over to Keystone. Meanwhile, unscrupulous distributors were cheating Roach of rental monies due him and he was forced to throw his modest inheritance into the company treasury. But he learned the business side of the movies rapidly and accepted an offer from Pathé to release his pictures through them. That same year (1916), Roach was asked by Pathé to get Lloyd, Stewart and Novak together again at any reasonable figure. Stewart and Novak were committed elsewhere, but Lloyd came back at a starting salary of fifty dollars a week. Lloyd's first comedy series was a blatant plagiarism of Chaplin, a baggy-pants misfit with a thin moustache called "Willie Work".

The series was not a great success, but it enabled Roach to hang on in those very early Hollywood days, becoming as much of a "Founding Father" of Hollywood as Mack Sennett, Cecil B. De Mille, Thomas Ince, Sam Goldwyn and Carl Laemmle. He equipped a ramshackle, primitive forerunner of what was to become one of the most enduring of all the independent studios. In those early years, it was held together mainly through the sweat of Roach, Lloyd and a handful of overworked comedians.

The evolution of Lloyd from "Willie Work" through "Lonesome Luke", a tougher, more aggressive clown, to the self-effacing, bespectacled but always triumphant "average American" everyone remembers took less than three years. During that transitional period, more than sixty "Lonesome Luke" comedies were made. Those years carried Roach and Lloyd from gag comedy of the broadest, crudest sort to two-reelers with attention paid to story values and some attempt at characterization. Roach's growing success with Lloyd took him from those rudimentary facilities on Sunset Boulevard to a new studio on Angel's Flight, next door to Chaplin's own studio, built for him by the Mutual Company.

Thus it was that in 1917, Harold Lloyd became the first silent comic to look like a well-tailored bank teller (Charley Chase was the second); the glasses were visible in *Over the Fence*. A dark-haired beauty of eighteen, Bebe Daniels, was brought in as his leading lady, bearing a strong resemblance to Sennett's incomparable Mabel Normand. Soon Roach was running an independent studio with the verve and productivity of Sennett, if not with the latter's eccentricity. There was no soaking in a huge tub in front of a large window to oversee what was happening below on the lot for Roach, as Sennett often did in his studio penthouse in Edendale. Roach, too, practically lived on the lot, but he was hopping from set to set, so intrusive that his stamp was far more identifiable on every film than that of any of his individual directors or comedians.

The remarkable thing about Roach was that despite being the biggest busybody producer ever until David O. Selznick came along, he had a most tranquil disposition. He could have been managing a hardware store, but instead of checking the inventory of pails or shovels, he wondered if there were enough laughs in the particular two-reeler he was finishing. Less astonishing was his vitality. This was a constant in all the major film-makers of the day. Mayer, Lasky, Goldwyn, Schenck, Jack Warner, Laemmle, Sennett and Roach were all men of awesome energy and physical durability. There was not much internal fighting in most of those early companies, Roach's company being the exception; they had to be united to survive.

Roach and Sennett had similar backgrounds. Life had toughened both of them at an early age, Sennett as a pipe-fitter in a boiler factory in Connecticut, and Roach as a roustabout teenager throughout the northern half of the American continent. At eighteen, Roach was in Alaska on the Richardson Trail, working a pack train. Making his way south to Seattle, he became a truck driver; then in Los Angeles, a gang boss for a construction firm.

Roach was the least given to "moods" of any of the studio heads. He very quickly evolved a system that guaranteed an amusing film, walking about the lot to observe what was happening on each comedy in production, viewing the rushes with the directors and stars, and making sure that everything on screen "worked". He listened carefully to the comment and noted all reactions at sneak previews in Pasadena or Glendale, and he decided on those bases what should be left in and what changed. Although several major companies begged Roach to come in with them – comedy makers were being courted then – he elected to remain independent and to continue to have his films released by Pathé, a distributor who left him alone.

One of Roach's earliest stars was Toto, the famed circus clown. A "Toto" series had been launched in January 1918, with *The Movie Mummy*. Like Stan, Toto was an eccentric comic under the clown white. In his first-released comedy, he played a worker in a plant that made dummies for the movies (to fall out of buildings, off trestles etc.), but the job was getting to him and he felt compelled to escape. Deciding the best exit was as a dummy, he filled an order with himself, and in the second reel he was tossed, tugged and knocked about in a manner just short of annihilation. Toto felt very much out of his element as a screen clown. He craved live audiences and the delighted shrieks of children. After several more comedies, seven in all, he left Roach in the middle of his contract and returned to the circus.

At the suggestion of Alf Goulding, an Australian whom Roach had coaxed over from Fox, Roach attended that Main Street vaudeville performance of Stan's in Los Angeles. He was desperate to find someone to step in and complete the Toto series of which five were still unshot. Backstage, he found Stan eager and quite willing to turn his back on vaudeville forever. American stage shows were not the halls, they were just a way of surviving and Stan knew quite a bit about screen comedy. He had seen numerous Roach one- and two-reelers, including the "Luke" series with Lloyd, some with character comic Snub Pollard, and even one with Toto. To Stan, they had the brawling vitality of the halls. They maintained their rapid pace by having one gag follow another in machine-gun fashion. There was also cruelty, as film historian William Everson points out, with, for example, Luke "kicking his opponents (or innocent bystanders who had the misfortune to be in the way), sticking knives, forks, and other sharp instruments into them, or wiping his sticky hands on their beards." It was precisely the sort of comedy Stan had learned under Karno.

Mayhem aside, Roach was fairly unique in Hollywood. He had

come from a provincial community, Elmira, New York. The grip of morality and family was still strong upon him. The sleazy behaviour so often encountered in film moguls appalled Roach, at least at that point in time. He sought to maintain a high standard of morality within his own studio, and soon looked upon himself as the proxy father to his grab-bag of comics and staff. It was a feeling he shared with Lloyd, his star comic who was so circumspect in his private life that it was not until he was dead that anyone but his closest friends knew he had had a mistress for many years. And once a year the Roach lot was festooned and bathed in the sentiment of Christmas, culminating in one huge party with presents for everyone. Secretly, Stan loathed Christmas. Jeff had forced the family through all the rites of "Christmas at home" following their mother's death and Stan had hated every moment of it.

Roach didn't learn for years of Stan's "strangeness" about Christmas, but he still had the quick perceptions of a gang boss about everyone in his crew, and by the time Stan had finished the five "Toto" comedies, the stories and telltale evidence of his bouts with the bottle and with Mae had made his position with Roach untenable.

If Roach had found the right formula for Stan, his off-screen problems might have seemed less reprehensible. Stan was cast first as an innocent tramp *(Just Rambling Along)*, then as a misfit prisoner *(No Place Like Jail)*, and finally in his first domestic comedy *(Do You Love Your Wife?)*. The films had little impact with audiences or booking offices, for Stan's screen image kept changing and no one could remember him from one comedy to the next. It is an undeniable principle of screen comedy that no comic can succeed unless he remains consistent from film to film. That is why W. C. Fields as "Micawber" looked and sounded exactly like the Fields we know and cherish in the movie version of Dickens' *David Copperfield*.

Stan was paid little more for his first sustained screen work for Roach than he and Mae had received on the stage. When the stint was over, within weeks Stan was broke again. But he now had allies and, in a sense, patrons: Broncho Billy Anderson, a comedy director named Percy Pembroke and his wife Gertrude Short, producer and former comedy stuntman Joe Rock, and Alice and Baldy Cooke, who had just about decided to stay in California. Roach did not tell

Stan that he had hopes for him beyond acting, as a writer and gag-man; he felt that his private difficulties made him too grave a risk. As for the comedies themselves, he said that Stan's eyes were too blue to photograph properly and that this was a handicap that no cameraman could surmount. "He looked like he was blind, and therefore people *(audiences)* felt sorry for him."

Roach's compassion for Stan was not bottomless and never would be. In the years of great success which were six years away, Stan Laurel and Hal Roach would spend far more time talking to their respective lawyers than they ever would to each other when off the set or away from the writing department.

3 Vitagraph was one of the first film companies to set up operations in the United States. The Vitagraph studio was originally in Flatbush, Brooklyn, but before the First World War was over, the company moved to new quarters at Hillhurst and Prospect Avenues just off Sunset in Los Angeles. Roach and Chaplin were about two miles away in Boyle Heights, although Roach would move into a modern plant in Culver City in late 1919, where he remained until the studio was closed permanently in the 1960s.

In 1918, Vitagraph's biggest comedy star was Larry Semon, an actor nearly forgotten today but who had had his own company of players and an enormous following. Semon was short and athletic, famed for his breathtaking spills and leaps, which were actually performed by his double, Bill Halber, since Semon was considered too valuable to do any of the stunts himself. Halber would jump from a bridge on to a moving train, and the marvellous thing was that the matching shot that Semon did was always perfect. Semon would match himself in the air with Halber's descent so that his double could be cut out of the finished print halfway down. From that point on, Semon would be falling, hitting the ground and rolling over. A few years later, Stan would perform similar falls, using his double Ham Kinsey.

Based at Vitagraph at this time there was also what was surely the earliest film comedy team in a long-running series, Rock and Montgomery. Joe Rock and Earl Montgomery were not very funny as comedians, but there were good visual gags in their one-reelers, usually involving stunts with motorcycles. Like Semon, Rock and

Montgomery were obliged to make twenty-six comedies a year in Vitagraph's effort to keep up with the insatiable appetite for humour of almost any sort that Americans had developed in the immediate post-war period.

Salaries for top comedians were high, pushed into the upper brackets by the huge audiences who were now paying fifty cents for the privilege of seeing their favourites, by Chaplin's ascending financial requirements, which made his rivals more valuable as their studios promoted them, and by the intense and often heated competition among the leading comedy studios themselves – Sennett, Roach, Al Christie and Vitagraph. Joe Rock was making $1500 a week and Larry Semon somewhat more when Stan Laurel went to work for Vitagraph in 1918.

Although he had been starred by Roach and Broncho Billy, Stan was hired to appear in several Larry Semon films merely as a supporting player. Such were the vagaries of those early years. If Stan had his dark moods and fits of depression when permanent success finally came to him, it was less the ghost of Dan Leno haunting him than the memories of those unstable years which had begun with his association with Karno.

Despite the lower billing, Stan was getting exposure on the screen. Vitagraph's comedies were booked eagerly throughout the country, which in itself meant more than being the star of the unlamented and largely unseen *Hickory Hiram* series. Stan did three Semon comedies in one year: *Huns and Hyphens*, *Bears and Bad Men*, and *Frauds and Frenzies*. Apparently, the title man at Vitagraph was on an illiterative binge. In the first of them, Stan played with Pete Gordon, a former vaudeville acrobat who was to become a fixture in Stan's life when Stan later hit his stride with Roach, the short and leather-faced tumbler being employed as part of Stan's personal staff (read *hired crony*).

Beyond being seen by millions of film-goers, Stan's work on the set was being observed by another Vitagraph star, Joe Rock, who had known Stan and Mae in vaudeville. Joe was close enough to Stan to see his frustration, to sense that he was only waiting for someone who would know how to utilize all of his talent. Joe was reassuring; he would do something about Stan's situation.

Meanwhile, fresh gag ideas poured from Stan's brain in profusion.

His mind was a fount of variations on a thousand themes he had seen or done in the music-halls, of his own troubles transmogrified into whoopers. Semon used a few of them, but like Chaplin, he seemed to have felt threatened and uncomfortable in Stan's presence and did not encourage a friendship. When Stan was dropped by Vitagraph, it was only with the vaguest promises of more work.

The final one-reelers that Stan had made earlier for Hal Roach were released in 1919, but he had been paid for them long ago. Yet audiences must be seeing them and surely they were laughing. He waited for some word from Roach that the comedies were doing well in release and he might resume work for the Rolin Studio. None came.

All through 1920, Stan and Mae trouped in vaudeville. They opened in Waco, Texas, in late January, and a month later they were doing a week at the Fulton in Brooklyn. It was a hard grind, and Stan was drinking heavily again. His quarrels with Mae were no longer material for domestic comedy, they were abusive, and Mae was not above striking back physically. As she was bigger-boned and stronger than Stan, he began to be a little afraid of her.

Stan only did one two-reeler during all of 1921. It was *The Rent Collector*, and its title called to mind one of several threats to his sanity and survival. Chaplin's *The Kid* had been released in January; it was his first feature-length comedy, although it was filled with pathos and heartbreaking drama. The big men behind the scenes in New York, Nicholas Schenck and Adolph Zukor among them, were insisting that it was the *drama* in *The Kid* that was drawing such huge audiences. That was a portent. It was becoming the biggest smash since Griffith's *The Birth of a Nation* (1915) without the controversy and booking problems of that film, and it had made a star of a seven-year-old boy, Jackie Coogan.

The Kid's success was demoralizing to Stan. He was not envious; he rarely was. He was simply flattened by the world's response to a man whose background was Stan's very own, when he and Mae were having difficulty meeting their rent. Still, he admired Chaplin more than ever for facing the problem of feature-length films so brilliantly, for getting into his comedy certain things that were much deeper than one would think that simple Tramp character could manage. Stan attributed this finally to that quality they had learned under Karno – getting the wistfulness under the laughter. Karno had realized that there were little pockets of melancholy inhabiting all great comedy. Later Stan expanded on his feelings about *The Kid* and said, "You know really the kid was Charlie, and Charlie was a kid all his life. Jackie Coogan was really Charlie Chaplin when he was a little guy." Commenting on a scene where Jackie throws rocks at the windows and then Charlie comes by, Stan remembered that that had been an incident in Karno's own life. Fred Karno had broken windows when he was a very young man hoboing around England. Someone had taught him the art of the glazier; he had then broken windows surreptiously and knocked on doors to ask if the owners wanted their windows repaired. So Stan knew that much of *The Kid* was drawn from real life. "To be able to get all of that humanity packed in", Stan said, "is just marvellous."

Then in 1922, Stan's undaunted first producer, Broncho Billy, found the money to do a number of films. Unbeknown to Stan, ever since Anderson had produced *Nuts in May* five years earlier, he had been talking about Stan to anyone who would listen. Broncho Billy had been struck by Stan's innocent befuddlement on screen and was convinced that it could be parlayed into a hugely profitable series.

Anderson had dozens of ideas filed away in his head by the time the financial backing appeared, but the first two he filmed were typical gag affairs – *The Egg* and *The Weak-End Party*. The third was more ambitious. Rudolph Valentino had just had a great success as a bullfighter in *Blood and Sand*, and Broncho Billy suggested a parody of this to be called *Mud and Sand*. Although Mae again insisted upon having a role in the film, the burlesque was a success. Probably prompted by the length of the latest Chaplin films, it ran to three reels.

One scene of *Mud and Sand* called for Stan, in the role of Rhubarb Vaselino, to be chased down the street by a bull. Before the action was completely shot, the bull caught up with Stan and threatened to toss him.

Broncho Billy told him that the camera had failed to get the action and that the scene would have to be repeated. Stan balked, then laughed louder than anyone when he realized it was just a studio prank. This is the only film of Stan's in which his natural good looks are enhanced rather than played down. He wears a slick pompadour and is convincing as a sexy bullfighter, which makes the bull chase all the more amusing.

Audience response to *Mud and Sand* was such that another film parody, this time of a Marion Davies spectacular (*When Knighthood Was in Flower*, 1922) was put into production and released as *When Knights Were Cold* (1923). Stan said of this comedy that it had "one beautifully funny sequence that I've never seen in movies, either before or since. We had an army of knights in a chase sequence. There were over three hundred of them working with basket horses – the circus-clown type horses, with the men's legs extending beneath the little papier-mâché horses built around them. It was hilarious . . ."

After five comedies for Anderson, all profitably released through Quality-Metro, Stan was suddenly a "hot property". Anderson made further, more ambitious plans. He began seeking the best writers he could find to work on stories of greater length, tailored to Stan's peculiar blend of timidity and tentative audacity. It seemed to be the beginning of a whole new career for Broncho Billy on the business side of the camera.

In the meantime Harold Lloyd had left Roach to form his own company. It was a staggering blow to Roach as with *Grandma's Boy* (1922), Lloyd had begun to rival Chaplin in popularity. Since he was far more prolific than Chaplin, averaging two features a year through most of the twenties, Lloyd very quickly became the richest actor in Hollywood, surpassing the great Charlie in earnings, his thirty-two room Italian Renaissance home, Green Acres, becoming a showplace more glittering than Pickfair.

Lloyd's great success had done more to make the Roach Studio the largest and busiest comedy factory in Hollywood than anything else. The earnings from his films had allowed Roach to expand in several directions at once. In 1922, he had launched the *Our Gang* series, which had become so popular so quickly that Roach could nearly forgive Lloyd for his defection. There is some evidence that Roach actually encouraged Lloyd in his decision out of his profound regard for the man and for what he had done to build the studio. Pathé was to become the first distributor of the Lloyd independent features, the first being *Girl Shy* ((1923); they were, of course, distributing the Roach films at that time.

Upon Lloyd's departure, Roach signed up the Ziegfeld lariat-spinning, homespun comedian Will Rogers for two series of twelve films each, and he beckoned to Stan once again, offering him more than Broncho Billy could possibly afford, one hundred and seventy-five dollars a week. Broncho Billy Anderson, the man more responsible than anyone else for bringing Stan back from the edge of the abyss and launching him finally as a bookable screen comedian, was unable to keep his fledgeling company going and retired from films, becoming anonymous Max Aronson again, slipping back into the obscurity from which he had drifted with *The Great Train Robbery*.

Previously having discounted Stan's "look of a blind man" (panchromatic film had been discovered for one thing), Roach now shot two series of twelve films starring Stan, their production extending over a period of seventeen months. They were all gag comedies and one-reelers (*Under Two Jags, Gas and Air, Short Orders, Oranges and Lemons, The Soilers*), but Stan, charged with the adrenalin of the prospect of sustained success, kept the wit bubbling throughout.

In 1923, Stan was sent to Catalina Island with cameraman George Stevens (exactly a decade before Stevens' debut as a director of comedy with *The Cohens and Kellys in Trouble* and twelve years before his dramatic classic with Katharine Hepburn, *Alice Adams*), director Ralph Cedar, and chief grip Byron "Bones" Vreeland to do a one-reeler entitled *Roughest Africa*. They had no story, only a vague character, a big game hunter (Stan), and certainly the wrong location. But Roach was convinced that he could find or duplicate any location in the world in Southern California. The desert between the city and Palm Springs became his Sahara; Laurel Canyon his Scotland; the streets of Los Angeles his Chicago; and rear projection (actual footage of Switzerland or Spain, for example, projected behind the live actors) his everywhere else.

While at the St Catherine Hotel in Avalon, Stan suddenly burst into laughter, and everyone in the crew looked at him hopefully as they had been there for more than a day and hadn't yet come up with a clue for the picture. "Why not", Stan wondered, "have me shoot my gun into the air, just straight up without aiming, and a dead duck falls out of the sky?" Everyone thought that this was at least one good gag, which they could build on, so Bones Vreeland was dispatched to the market to buy a dead, unplucked duck.

Bones found a duck, and, as a possible alternative, an unskinned rabbit. He took the game back to the "jungle" location, where he had rigged up a platform resting on two, tall ladders about ten feet in the air, out of camera range. Stan moved into position, casually stuck the shotgun skyward as Stevens' camera turned, and pulled the trigger. Caught up in the surreal illogic of it all, Bones tossed down the dead rabbit. When the long-eared creature fell at Stan's feet, Stevens was able to capture his genuine amazement. With such controlled madness, this and other comedies were completed on schedules of gratifying brevity.

Stan stimulated everyone to be on his mettle. His belly laughter when something reached just the right peak of hilarity became a familiar sound around the Roach lot, in the writers' wing and in the screening room. It was only at home with Mae that he was seemingly insensitive and turned off. He had begun the habit of walking out when her tirades began. Now that he had money, he would check into a hotel, carrying a little overnight bag bearing his name in gold letters.

Stan's films of the mid-twenties met with moderate success, possibly because a number of them were genuinely funny and Stan had been sufficiently seen on the screen by audiences to trigger a recognition factor. But the pace was not yet right – it was much too fast, and Stan's screen character had failed to jell.

Before he let Stan go again, Roach added Charley Chase to his stable of comedy stars. Immediately before Chase's advent, Roach's "Our Gang" had posed the most serious threat yet to Chaplin's and Lloyd's supremacy at the box-office. With "Our Gang" and Chase films emerging from his studio in successful monthly releases, it seems inexplicable that Roach could not find a suitable format for Stan, with whom he had flirted professionally for six years.

But Roach's relationship with Stan was an extremely complex and delicate one. Though he greatly admired Stan's talents, he moved cautiously in making a permanent place for him in his company. And there is no doubt about Roach's real reservation concerning

Stan – it was Mae. She was not his wife and this was 1924 when major comedy stars could not pass off their mistresses as their wives with any certainty of success. It was unthinkable to make such a living arrangement public at that time. After completing *Short Kilts*, Stan was dismissed without a commitment for further work.

Years later in a court of law, Stan would insist that he had never been emotionally involved with Mae. But he had to have been to have allowed her, as sheer dead weight, to drag him down in this fashion. Doubtless for years, between tirades, she had pampered his sensitive ego and kept him intact. But no one pins medals for past achievements on an incubus. The trick is to remove it, surgically if necessary.

Fortunately, Stan's weaknesses gave him an endearing sort of helplessness which attracted samaritans. Percy Pembroke, who had directed one of Stan's last films for Roach, *Rupert of Hee Haw* (1924), was one of these. When Stan and Mae could not meet their rent after the last salary check from Roach had been spent, Pembroke, known to his friends as "Perce", and his actress wife, Gertrude Short, took them in.

Once Stan became a star, he never forgot the generosity of the Pembrokes, as well as of the Cookes and most others who had helped him. His assistance to a small army of down-on-their-luck vaudevillians and washed-up film players continued until nearly the end of his life.

1. Stan Jefferson during a vaudeville tour, Peoria 1918

2. Stan dressed u[...] as Charlie Chaplin in *The Stan Jefferson Trio*, 1916
3. Charlie Chaplin's first autographed photo, sent to Alice and "Baldy" Cooke, 1915
4. Arthur Jefferson Stan's father
5. Alice and "Baldy" Cooke, th[...] rest of *The Stan Jefferson Trio*, 1916

3 4

6

7

6. Laurel and Hardy clown on the studio lawn, 1929
7. Stan and Ollie in a formal portrait for Metro-Goldwyn-Mayer, 1932
8. Stan, "big Lois" and baby Lois with their St Bernard, early 1929
9. Stan looks fit and prosperous in golfing togs, 1927

8

9

10. Virginia Ruth Laurel poses beside her brand new Ford V-8 sport coupé, 1934

11. Stan and wife Ruth stroll on Catalina Island, 1937

12. Stan and Babe in a rare get-together on the golf course. *Front, l to r:* chewing gum tycoon P. K. Wrigley, Stan, Ollie. *Back, l to r:* Myrtle Hardy, Mrs P. K. Wrigley, Ruth Laurel and orchestra leader Jan Garber

13

14

13. The Laurel mansion in Cheviot Hills, Stan's first excursion into the good life. He made it into the only one-bedroom house in the neighbourhood, 1935

14. Ollie and wife Myrtle stroll along the boardwalk at Santa Monica, 1933

15. A London party, 1932. Stan and Babe on balcony: Joan Crawford and husband Douglas Fairbanks Jr. below Babe

15

16

16. The irrepressible Illiana Laurel, who turned Stan's life inside out for eighteen months, taken before her troubles with the Beverly Hills authorities, 1938
17. Stan carries daughter Lois down the studio back lot street, 1935

17

5 || Lady Albatross
       Number One

1   Joe Rock, who had admired Stan's work at Vitagraph,
     was an intimate of the Pembrokes. When Joe felt that
he had accumulated enough capital from his savings as a comedy
star and famed daredevil to go out on his own, he left the team of
Montgomery and Rock and set up an independent film company,
Joe Rock Productions, to produce comedies. Pembroke urged Joe to
consider doing a series with Stan.

But Joe, too, had his doubts, and none of Roach's solid financial
footing. He couldn't afford to gamble. He discussed the matter with
Earl Hammond at Educational Films and Elmer Pierson at Pathé.
Both men were discouraging, although they liked Stan's work as a
comedian and "an athlete". In those distant days, a comic's capacity
to run, fall down, get hit on the head, sail through the air, and
otherwise show skills that were more gymnastic than comedic often
determined whether he was hired or not. Pierson said he doubted
very much that Rock could keep Stan sober. Stan's reputation for
closing the Los Angeles bars with Mae was now famous. And all of
the distributors were agreed that Mae was poison to Stan's pictures.

Joe had seen in Stan the same unique clown that had excited
Broncho Billy. Stan's marvellously mobile face was unlike any other

on the screen; like Chaplin and Langdon (in that year being scouted in vaudeville by Hollywood), his image was that of a loser, but he was not so far away from the norm that he lost empathy. He was neither infantile nor a bum, but seemed almost to be the chap next door, the only difference being that before his films were over, you thanked God he was not.

Joe needed a fresh approach to comedy if his new company was to succeed, and almost against his better judgment, he decided to take a chance on Stan to provide it. This was a calculated risk, of course, much like Joe's practised leaps from one rooftop to another in his films with Earl Montgomery. But Joe always had a mystical faith in his survival. When he was playing basketball in the early years of this century and his team beat another on the latter's home ground, the winners would get pelted with bricks, jumped on and mauled, and often seriously injured. So much for sportsmanship in the early 1900s. But somehow Joe was never touched as he scrambled through the back window and raced to the subway. Two years after the Wall Street Crash destroyed Joe Rock Productions overnight and wiped out his wealth, his home and his standing as an important independent producer, Joe was producing major features in England, where he had settled with his wife Louise and his children in an English manor house with a chauffeured limousine. In retirement at eighty-four, Joe, carrying a mountain of laundry to a corner laundromat, was run down by a truck. He brushed himself off, stayed in bed for a week and then resumed his normal activities.

So Joe Rock was not easily intimidated by employing Stan and signing him up for a twelve-episode series. Besides, Joe had begun production on three Jimmy Aubrey comedies, which provided a slight hedge.

Once the decision had been made, Joe Rock hurried over to the Pembrokes' home to give Stan the news. "Now, Stan, look," he said. "I'm going to give you $1,000 towards a series. There can't be any slip-ups because I must deliver twelve films. And you know Mae will not be in them."

Stan desperately wanted to make the films. He needed more than rescue. He needed reassurance that his stubborn faith in what made people laugh, in his own clownish self since that was the repository of that faith, had not been misplaced. Then he thought of Mae, whose will was so much stronger than his own. He winced and told Joe, "Mae wouldn't stand for that. She said . . ."

"I don't care what Mae said! She's ruining your career. I'm sticking my neck out as it is. I'm going to make one picture with you to start off."

Everything was ready for the action to begin at Joe's studio space at Universal. He operated out of the "bull-pen", an area usually rented to independent producers such as Edward Small, but loaned to him for the cost of the lights only because of Joe's close friendship with Carl Laemmle. He was allowed to use the magnificent standing sets on the Universal lot, authentically recreating the streets of London, New York and even Shanghai for nothing. One day, close to the date set for shooting to begin, Stan entered Joe's office and there were deep red scratches over his face.

"Migod!" exclaimed Joe. "What happened?"

"You know that cat we have?"

But Joe cut him off short. "You mean Mae?"

"She wants to be in the film, Joe."

Joe Rock studied his star, possibly ill-chosen, the scars of domestic battles, his sense of hopelessness. This was the clearest signal he would ever have that Stan's weakness – a fatal attraction to bitches that could prove impossible to deal with – might permanently hobble him. "We're not going to use her, Stan. That's out and you know it. The sets are built and the cameras are ready."

Stan simply sat there. He had been doing everything he could think of to pacify Mae, to keep her frightening meanness in check. His nerves were shot from the apprehension. He never knew when she would strike out, although her wrath was guaranteed over Joe's intransigence. He sank deeper into his chair, holding his head.

When Joe saw Stan's agony, he picked up the phone and called Mae. "Stan says you haven't got your costume yet," he told her. "Come over and we'll talk about it."

The ruse may have been a little unfair, but Joe felt no shame about it. Mae was a woman who would use any weapon handy to keep Stan in line. In an old photo that Mae showed newsmen later, she looked like a lady lion-tamer, and she could have been a most successful one.

When Mae arrived – in about ten minutes – Joe said, "Stan tells me that you haven't got your costume and that you're going to be in the film. Who told you that you were?"

Mae's composure cracked only a little. She was in the big cage, but Joe was an unpredictable lion, certainly no pussycat. Her words sounded aggressive, but there was fear behind them. "Well, I *am*!" she said.

Stan glanced at Joe to see if he, too, would cringe, but Joe was unruffled. Something had caught Joe's eye. He was staring at Stan's worn-out shoes, his threadbare suit. Where had the advance gone? Back rent? That seemed impossible. Then he noticed that Mae had come dressed to impress him. She wore a well-designed new summer frock with a diamond clip, and there were small diamond earrings in her pierced ears. Her jewelry had come out of hock.

"Mae," Joe said as gently as he could, "you are *not* going to be in the film. That was the understanding I had with you, with Perce (Percy Pembroke had been signed to direct), and with Stan."

Mae's self-possession crumbled. She blew her nose. Joe thought tears were about to flow. "Well," she said, "Stan can't work without me."

Joe saw that civility was getting him nowhere. "Mae," he began, and his tone had an edge, "you are a stone around Stan's neck. He can't get a job. *He* is the comedian people want to see, not you. You are a good *character* actress . . ."

The cruel words struck home and Mae was visibly shaken. For her, Joe was one of the numerous foe, those who were trying to break up her relationship with Stan. If Stan and she didn't work together, they had nothing. Neither of them ever once discussed the possibility of her being a homemaker. Perhaps if they ever got far enough ahead, she would be able to fetch her son from New Jersey, but that dream now seemed remote. Stan refused to discuss it.

Joe's voice modulated to a placating tone. "You are even a *great* character actress. I can put you into any picture we've got as a character actress and you would be as good as anyone around. That is your *forte* . . ."

Mae glanced at Stan, her common-law husband who, back in her native Australia, would have thrashed this man for impugning her attractiveness. Stan slid further into his shoulders and thrust his hands more deeply into his pockets.

"Are you going to let Stan work, Mae?" And Joe's eyes were defensively alert, the wide-awake eyes of a former champion athlete. Mae said nothing. Stan remained silent as Joe handed him back the contract for the series, Mae watching in disbelief.

"Stan thought you were his friend," Mae said.

"I *am* his friend, and I have nothing against you, Mae."

"I'll sue," she said as they prepared to leave.

"On what grounds?" Joe asked. "I have no contract with you. My contract is with Stan. If you want him to work, fine, but stay out of his professional life."

Then Mae, sensing that her years of drifting from one engagement to another with Stan, sometimes poor, sometimes more than comfortable, might be ending, played her last hand. Leaning against Joe Rock's door, she let the sobs shake her. She could not have known that a nearly identical scene had been played out in front of Stan by Alice Cooke weeks after Mae had moved into his life. Joe was relieved to see Stan unaffected by Mae's performance, as he had been by Alice's. Stan told Joe that he would report to the studio the following day, and Joe knew that he meant alone.

2 In those two-reelers for Joe Rock, Stan Laurel was at last on his way to becoming a significant film comedy star. If his private life was a tangle of relics from the past – Mae, the bottle, no real home of his own and not even a decent wardrobe – his career was now finally in the ascendant. It would be up, up, up for years.

Joe Rock's films were distributed by Standard Cinema-Selznick. Lewis J. Selznick, the father of David and Myron, had risen from being a lower east side jewelry merchant to become the most controversial movie mogul of them all. He had sneaked into Universal during the power struggle and appointed himself general manager, each warring faction thinking that one of the others had engineered his elevation. When Laemmle finally won control, he believed Selznick was an enemy and got ready to oust him, but then Selznick snared the silent superstar Clara Kimball Young, and later Norma and Constance Talmadge. No longer needing Laemmle or Universal, he inaugurated a franchise booking system in the major cities, a daring innovation that worked.

The films that Joe Rock made for Selznick with Stan were again one-situation comedies interlarded with gags and shot by Perce Pembroke from a rough outline. It didn't matter that Joe Rock's production budget was miniscule. What went on to film and finally emerged in a two-reel comedy as a Selznick release had major studio class stamped all over it. In the first of them, *Mandarin Mix-Up*, in which Stan played an English bobby trying to protect the honour of what appears to be a Chinese call-girl, the set was a Limehouse background on Universal's back-lot.

Stan and Mae remained with the Pembrokes during the shooting. Perce, who had become a sort of father-confessor to Stan, lent a sympathetic ear to Stan's complaints about Mae and was able to control his drinking most of the time. Perce told Joe Rock that the situation was heartbreaking: Stan no longer loved Mae but felt an obligation to her that seemed deathless. It was not just that he was soft-hearted – he and Mae had gone through such hell together. He remembered the times when they had gone into a town with a booking only to hear the theatre manager say, "There must be some mistake." Stuck in some God-forsaken backwater and no fare for the return trip! And those long, exhausting train rides! They had been comrades through too much together. Stan realized, he told Perce, that she may have been too brash at times. Their characters were almost always in conflict, but he knew that she loved him profoundly, still loved him. They both knew that his first love was getting on to a stage or before a camera and making people laugh. Mae had come to accept that and no longer seemed to resent it. And the laughs they had shared! How many wives or lovers had Mae's sense of humour? It had been a rough life, and Stan felt he owed her a great deal for sticking with him through all the disasters and come-downs.

With the second comedy, *Detained*, Joe Rock switched Stan to the opposite side of the law as a prisoner in a jail-house riot (incongruously wearing the bowler that soon was to become his trademark, even though it was appropriated from Chaplin). Another, more ambitious two-reeler in the mould of Stan's *Mud and Sand* was a parody of Valentino's recent success, *Monsieur Beaucaire*, which was titled *Monsieur Don't Care*. The Selznick organization found the exchanges about Stan very enthusiastic by this time, so Joe Rock decided to try still another burlesque, *West of Hot Dog*, a parody of the cowboy hit, *West of Pecos*.

After more than half a dozen pictures, it appeared that Joe's gamble was paying off. Perce Pembroke and Joe were giving Stan warm support, Joe telling Stan of the excitement these comedies were stirring around the country. The drinking subsided. Even Mae subsided as she responded to the friendly solicitude of Gertrude Short, Mrs Pembroke.

As audiences grew and profits rose, Joe was able to spend more money on each succeeding Stan Laurel film. With *The Snow Hawk*, he moved out of Universal's back-lot to take his company on location to Arrowhead, a mountain lake. Stan as the star, Pembroke as director and Joe each had a private bungalow near the lake, while the other members of the crew were housed in a rustic lodge. For the first time, because of the circumstances, Mae was allowed near a production, although she was barred from the actual shooting.

All went well for a week – the larger budget had increased the shooting time on each film, too – until one day when Joe was crossing the snow-drifted area in front of the bungalows on his way from location. He was intercepted by Stan, who seemed quite disturbed. "Joe", Stan said, "I wouldn't have believed you would do such a thing."

"Come on, Stan," Joe said. "What is it? What's the problem?"

"What did you try to do to Mae yesterday?"

"Mae? Yesterday? I saw her. I talked to her. But nothing happened to upset her. I was with Louise. . . ."

"With *Louise*?" Stan seemed astonished by the fact of Joe's wife's presence. "Mae said you were trying to get her into your bungalow."

"Stan, would you believe such a thing of me?"

"No, Joe, I wouldn't. But she told me . . ."

"What would you have thought or done if Louise hadn't been here?"

Stan fell silent and moved off. If the situation was as Joe described it, then Mae was not only a problem but dangerous as well. It should be added that a decade later, in a conversation with Ruth, Stan expressed some doubt about Joe's version, saying he did not want to cause a breach between himself and his producer so accepted his story. But whatever he really believed, Stan now clearly felt that Mae was no longer worth all the heartache.

Early in the spring of 1925, immediately after the completion of *The Snow Hawk*, Stan played his first sailor, a role he came to love. He would play a "gob" of one kind or another seven more times during his career. During the shooting, the crew of a Japanese destroyer visited Universal and soberly lined up for a group photo with Stan and his leading lady, Julie Leonard (later the wife of director Norman Taurog). Stan was becoming a minor celebrity on the lot.

He was also becoming a problem again: he started to be late on the set; he forgot his routines; his face was drawn. Pembroke said that he could no longer control Stan's drinking away from the camera.

At the same time, Joe Rock was beset with other problems. Lewis Selznick had gone into bankruptcy. As of that moment, there were 1050 prints of the first seven Stan Laurel comedies in danger of being lost in the assignment of assets. Joe hurried to New York and arranged to have the films handled by F.B.O., then headed by Joseph P. Kennedy.

While filming of the series was temporarily halted, Mae began urging Stan to create a new duo act for them so that they might return to vaudeville. This was madness, of course. Vaudeville was on its way out, but then so was Mae. She was now aware that the movies were certain to take Stan away from her. Stan told her he was determined not to leave Los Angeles at such a critical moment. He said nothing of the clause in his contract which gave him fifteen per cent of the net profits on each film for Joe, an unusual particular, given Stan's erratic career. Such was the backdrop of a non-stop quarrel that kept Stan from sleep, drove him back to the bottle, and was seriously affecting his performance in *Dr Pyckle and Mr Pryde* when shooting resumed.

Joe believed that getting rid of Mae would solve all of his problems with Stan and proposed that they arrange to get Mae deported back to Australia. Unfortunately, the U.S. Immigration Office evinced no interest in such a project, even though Mae and her son had entered the country illegally. Then Joe decided on bribery – not of the Immigration Office but of Mae.

"We have to make sure she's willing," he said. "I want to have a talk with her, find out what she wants in the way of money, clothes. I'll arrange it. . . . She'll go back on a one-way ticket. I'll pay for it. What else is involved?"

"We've got some more jewelry pawned somewhere," Stan said. "It's really mine, but if she wants it, I'll let her have it."

"I'll see what there is against it," Joe said, familiar with the language of the pawn shop.

When he finally had his talk with Mae, he learned that she was amenable to going back to Australia under certain conditions. So surprisingly easy was her acquiescence, Joe realized that her unhappiness must have been nearly as deep as Stan's. As the "deal" was worked out in Stan's presence, Joe agreed to pay $1000 for Mae's one-way transportation from San Francisco, buy her a new wardrobe, redeem the jewelry, and give her about $300 in cash. However, the cash and jewels were to be delivered aboard ship by the purser one day out of port.

Mae protested against this last detail. She thought that she should be trusted to take the jewelry along with her new wardrobe. The discussion was painful to Stan. He did not seem to feel personally guilty about the situation, just fearful of inflicting any more pain than was necessary.

Joe was firm about the jewels, telling Mae that the deal was not negotiable, and at last she came round. "I'm sending you home a lady," Joe said, with a bit of triumph in his voice. He paid the ship's purser $10.00 to handle the transaction and send him a telegram from the ship confirming its execution. Afraid that Stan might try to contact Mae in remorse, Joe placed his brother Murray as a watch over Stan until Mae was safely at sea.

On the day of Mae's departure, Murray took Stan to the Hollywood home of Lois Neilsen, a minor player for Joe Rock who had been Joe's girlfriend before his marriage. Lois was a honey blonde with a winsome attractiveness and an apparent agreeableness quite in contrast to Mae. Stan was downcast upon his arrival, his mood not helped much by the weather, which was stormy that afternoon. But he brightened perceptibly when he saw Lois, and there was a log fire burning in the fireplace. The scene had been carefully stage-managed by Joe, who had arrived earlier.

Lois brought the men hot toddies and returned to the kitchen to supervise the dinner. The smell of pot roast and gravy wafted in as she opened the kitchen door. Then the phone rang and Joe answered it. He began reciting the telegram as it was read to him: "Everything taken care of on ship."

At that, Stan leapt into the air, clicking his heels together and yelling, "Yippee! Yippee! I'm free!" When he landed, he grabbed Joe and then Murray and hugged them. "You're the best friend I've ever had!" he told Joe. "I'll work for you for nothing." Those words would ring hollowly in Joe's mind within a few months.

Lois joined them again. Stan sighed deeply, then laughed, and they all had drinks. After another round or two, Joe got up and said he had to get back to the studio. Murray, a bit too readily, added that he, too, had an appointment. Just as the stage-managing threatened to become obvious, Lois convincingly asked, "What am I going to do with all this food?"

"Well, Stan will stay, won't you?" Joe said.

Stan not only stayed the afternoon; within weeks, he had moved into Lois's apartment there on Florence Avenue.

During his first week with Lois, Stan phoned the Cookes and invited them over. Alice and Baldy had left vaudeville and were now living in Hollywood on earnings from occasional picture work. Lois had an attractive sweetness of manner, but under that façade there was a gritty practicality. She was cautious in her relations with the Cookes. She even ventured an opinion that they drank a great deal, encouraging Stan to drink more than usual. Alice noticed that she sat out for most of the rounds.

Perce and Gertrude Pembroke visited often and, on special occasions, Joe and Louise Rock also came. Everyone who knew Stan agreed that he was becoming more relaxed. Once, on a night out with the boys, he confessed that Lois had limited his poker money to $5.00, but he added that they were saving to get married so no one teased him about it.

Stan would probably have been quite happy to have gone on living with Lois indefinitely, much as he had done with Mae. But Lois would have none of that. Stan's roving eye was disquieting. She wanted marriage, and despite the thousand alarms that such an ultimatum must have set off in Stan, he proposed formally early in 1926 and was accepted.

Stan asked the Cookes to act as witnesses for them and set the date for the civil ceremony on a Saturday. A few days later, Alice and Baldy had a call to work at the Roach Studio and as they drove up to the gate, they met Stan and Lois.

"They looked kind of sheepish," Alice recalled. "And we said, 'What's the matter with you two?' And they said, 'Well, you know we wanted you to stand up for us. You don't have to because we were married this morning. We went off for some breakfast rolls and decided to get married while we were out.'" Alice remarked, "You've done us out of a good job," and everybody laughed.

They had completed the second year's series of comedies five months ahead of option time, but Joe's financial arrangements allowed him to release these last two-reelers only one at a time every thirty days even though Stan was paid his advance as each film was finished. This meant that for over five months in 1925–26, Stan would have no income even though he was tied to a four-year contract that had two years to go.

Lois was, under all her agreeableness, a shrewd businesswoman. She was now married to a successful comedian who was not making any money. When she mentioned the matter to Perce Pembroke, he agreed that something had to be done. Meanwhile, as Joe Rock recalled: "I knew Roach was talking to Stan. The world of film comedy was a pretty small one, and I kept hearing rumours that Stan was being approached not only by Roach but by a lot of the major studios as well. They all knew that with Mae gone and Stan happy, things were looking up for him."

Perce Pembroke, in the temporary role of Stan's agent, approached Larry Darmour, the financier who had backed Joe Rock, and said that Joe had broken his contract by failing to move ahead with the next comedy series so that Stan would have an income. Darmour told Perce that Joe Rock's agreement with Stan was still valid and that he and his banking colleagues could not negotiate with anyone else.

Word then reached Joe that Stan was *writing* at Roach's, and, in Joe Rock's words: "that he was also going to make some appearances in front of the camera as well. I called him to my office and told him that I did not object to his writing or directing, because I was not paying him and he had a right to earn a living, and that he could act as well, as long as he was not the star. That could compete with my *Stan Laurel Comedies*, since five or six were still not released. I reminded him that he had a fifteen per cent interest in the films, though, of course, no profits would accrue until all costs were recouped. This meant nothing to him, Lois or Perce, because they never believed the percentages would ever amount to anything.''

To keep Stan with him, Joe then promised to raise his advances when the option for the next series was picked up. But this only prompted Stan to say he didn't want to make any more films and had decided to go back on the stage – a response which surprised and angered Joe. He couldn't believe it; Stan had been far too elated when Mae was successfully removed from the scene and he knew he was free to move forward as a screen comic. Nevertheless, Joe said that if Stan was sincere about it, he could not prevent Stan from making live appearances. He asked Stan to put what he said in a letter which Joe could show the bankers to get him off the hook.

Stan wrote the letter, but within weeks he was under contract to Roach to write, direct and occasionally appear in films. Joe then furiously wrote to Roach and four other producers of comedies who might wish to borrow Stan (from Roach) saying that he had a contract with Stan as a star in films for another two years. A long, legal controversy was begun with Stan represented by Benjamin Shipman, the lawyer who had ties to the Roach Studio and would eventually become lawyer-manager for both Laurel and Hardy. In July 1926, Shipman filed a suit against Rock in Superior Court, asking for a quarter of a million dollars in damages. As Joe understood this complaint, he had allegedly impinged upon Stan's freedom to walk out on a contract. Ben Shipman's usually mild disposition was suppressed long enough for him to bludgeon Joe Rock into idleness. Joe could not move forward with another comedy series starring Jimmy Aubrey since the banks had frozen all his capital until the case with Stan was settled.

Briefs flew back and forth and the case dragged through the autumn and winter. The irony was that Stan was kept busy in the writing department throughout the legal action by Roach, while Joe Rock could only fume at his desk. In January 1927, at Stan's request, Shipman petitioned the court to dismiss the case. The dismissal allowed Joe to return to production, moving ahead with the Jimmy Aubrey comedies and a brand new series called *The Three Fat Men*.

Hal Roach, who had been waiting for Stan to become more responsible, thought the moment had now arrived. From their earliest association he had known that no one in the business was better at creating gags than Stan. He had seen Stan's recent comedies for Joe Rock and had begun to discern, if dimly, a comic image that could be sustained through a series. Harry Langdon's *The Strong Man* had been released, and everyone was hailing a new comic genius, or as its director, Frank Capra, called his star, "the man-child whose only ally was God". Roach saw something of Langdon in Stan, as well as a bit of Chaplin. Roach was not altogether a tough-minded realist. He played hunches. Movie-making was that kind of game.

At thirty-six, Stan was a very slow starter in the race for stardom. The inroads of age would be visible before he retired from the screen after only twenty-five years as a leading comic. It had been a long, slippery climb. There had been too much heartbreak, too many rows and setbacks. Stan stood at the threshold of fame feeling no excitement whatsoever.

6 || Laurel and Hardy Are Born

1   It was the twilight of the silent years in Hollywood, but in 1926, very few were aware that this was so. The production of feature attractions was at its peak; some forty or fifty of them were emerging from each of the six major studios annually, not counting the front-rank independents such as United Artists and the "ten-day schedule" producers on Poverty Row, then including Columbia and Tiffany.

One out of every three of these features could be called a comedy of some kind, which meant that at least a hundred feature-length comedies and several times that number of two-reelers were being made in Hollywood that year. The source for this enormous laugh-making machine was just about everywhere movie-makers could find a funny idea: the stage, magazines, books, and sources right on the lot – a strange breed of "idea" or gag-men only to be found in the film capital, some of whom were unable to write a line of dialogue or action. These men considered Stan a colleague and he felt more comfortable with them than with most other performers.

Every well-known comedian from vaudeville was now in the

movies. If Roach had not snared Stan during this mad scramble for funny-men, another studio would undoubtedly have signed him up, and Laurel and Hardy could never have come into being.

A number of the comedies being made at that time were important, lasting classics. Chaplin was in the early production stage of *The Circus*, not his finest feature by any means, but an enduring one. Harold Lloyd's *The Freshman* had been released late in 1925 and was still doing phenomenal business. Buster Keaton, who now rivalled Chaplin and Lloyd in international appeal, was involved in creating his greatest film, *The General*, based upon an actual incident during the Civil War when a platoon of Union raiders attempted to steal a Confederate locomotive and nearly succeeded.

Stan had yet to meet Buster, the film star, although their paths had crossed in vaudeville. In Buster's days of glory, he lived in an Italian villa with wife Natalie, one of the Talmadge sisters, a lifestyle which was completely alien to his ebullient spirit. He and Stan would not become close until nearly ten years had passed, when Stan was among the most successful movie clowns ever and Buster was divorced, his great career destroyed by sound and by the consequent necessity of taking any job he could get.

As Stan's own star began its rise, his friends were nearly all old vaudeville partners and friends like the Cookes and a few Roach writers. He had discovered that the Roach staff, including most of the players, had a strong loyalty to the company. So, too, Stan would be loyal now that the ground beneath his feet was stable. Loyalty was a virtue that Stan really prized, and his friends soon learned that their own loyalty to Stan could amount to total commitment. Nothing could plunge him into the depths of melancholy faster than the seeming perfidy of a friend.

The Roach Studio was, despite the relaxed atmosphere, as industrious as any of the majors. Roach was to sign a distribution agreement with Metro-Goldwyn-Mayer in late 1927, making him in effect a part of the largest studio in Hollywood. Still, he remained on his home ground, which was just two blocks away from Metro. And the comedies rolled out, one every few days – from the "Our Gang" company, Max Davidson, Charley Chase, The Boy Friends and Clyde Cook. Enhancing most of these series were cuties like Viola Richard and Dorothy Coburn. For a little hauteur, there was Elinor

Van Der Veer (a prettier Margaret Dumont). Thelma Todd would come in for a long run in the late twenties, becoming Queen of the lot. These resident beauties were used as screen wives, sweethearts and "tootsies" and as unlikely targets for custard pies. Off-screen, they were also girlfriends on occasion. The philandering that occurred (and how could it not?) was stage-managed in such a way by Roach and other executives that marriages had longer runs there than elsewhere in Hollywood. But Stan would not allow Roach to get close to his private affairs and, as a possible consequence, ran through three wives and as many mistresses during his years there. Babe Hardy, however, permitted Roach to tidy up his alliances and kept them down to two marriages (not counting the pianist) and one mistress.

Cameraman Art Lloyd's widow recalls that the studio was "wonderful because if they had a party or anything like that, everyone came. It wasn't a star system. Everybody was in on it, and it was such fun." Film editor Bert "Eddie" Jordan remembered "there weren't quite as many restrictions as at some of the other studios. People were most free and easy. Before the union finally went in, sometimes we'd work at night, too, no extra pay for it. I remember I worked on Christmas Eve to get a show out. I stayed there all through the night until Christmas morning."

There was a family feeling about the place, and perhaps it was rather exaggerating that point when Roach brought his parents on to the lot to live and keep an eye on things after hours. His father was also the paymaster. The elder Roaches shared a building with the writers; Stan, McCarey, Charlie Rogers and Roach would leave story conferences upstairs and have to walk through flapping laundry on the lower porch to get to the pavement.

Roach made a genuine effort to keep everyone happy. Although there would be quarrels with Stan later, he scrupulously saw that much of the profits flowed back to his stars, players and crew, so much so that outside union officials considered the Roach Studio to be almost impregnable.

The studio was crowded with brilliant character comics, men like Snub Pollard and Max Davidson (who had their own series for a time), Eugene Pallette, Tiny Sanford, Charlie Hall, those two "terrible tempered" slow-burners Edgar Kennedy and James Finlayson, and the combustible fat man, Billy Gilbert.

Oliver Hardy was there on a "per diem" basis at first. Stan was directing a Comedy All Stars two-reeler, *Get 'Em Young*, and Ollie or "Babe", as he was known to everyone on the lot, was playing a butler in the film. He had done a long line of butlers, crooks, anything in fact that required a bit of heft and an intimidating out-thrust chin or chins. One day, in the midst of production, Babe phoned in ill. A gourmet cook at home, he had scalded himself the night before while basting a leg of lamb. The injury had been serious enough to call for medical attention and he would be unable to work for an indefinite period. Roach asked Stan to step in and take over the role.

Stan was enjoying directing and was much distressed by the request. But Dick Jones, who was one of Stan's greatest boosters at the studio and a creative production supervisor whose opinion Stan placed even above Roach's, prevailed upon him. Roach clinched it by offering him a pay rise, and he did the role, "a *whimpering* butler", Stan was to tell John McCabe, "the first real mannerism that definitely became a part of my later character when I teamed with Hardy."

Stan had been hired by Roach in the spring of 1926 to write and direct, with the proviso that he would appear on screen whenever a suitable part appeared. The association with Roach now seemed a durable one, as such matters go in Hollywood. He had joined an impressive team of dependably funny men: Leo McCarey, who had been there four years; Charley Chase, who had begun his career as an actor in Chaplin's early Sennett comedies and whose Roach contract, like Stan's, allowed him to work on both sides of the camera; a witty elf from England named Charlie Rogers; Robert McGowan, who spent most of his working hours devising fiendish delinquencies for his "Our Gang" to perpetrate; and Roach himself, who contributed many of the story lines for all the other comedies on the lot.

The ambience of the place suited Stan perfectly. Sentiment, which he always avoided in performance, was frowned upon. There was something idiotic in the everyday working world outside the studio walls, and the Roach people considered it their mission to set it all down, every last absurdity. Roach's working-class origins were the touchstone. If you knew that he was a former truck-driver, then you understood at least part of the man and something of the tone of his films. The point of view of a Roach comedy was invariably blue collar or – as in the case of the Charley Chase comedies – low-rung white collar.

Roach had a shrewder story sense than Mack Sennett; his gags usually had a motive behind them, so he was prepared when the revolution in sound brought with it the built-in necessity for sequential dialogue, as Sennett was not.

Babe Hardy recovered from his burns within a few weeks. Meanwhile, Roach had decided to cast him with Stan in the film version of Arthur Jefferson's music-hall sketch, *Home from the Honeymoon* (now retitled *Duck Soup*) with Stan pretending to be the maid, a monument of ineptitude and foolish demeanour, and Hardy assuming the role of butler. The film barely suggested the great potential of the team, yet there was a glimmer of it, enough to warrant a series. While it was, naturally enough, Stan's idea to make the film, he was unhappy with the result and remade it in 1930 as *Another Fine Mess*. Then it was made with sound, including what was to become the most quoted fade-out line in movie history from Ollie to Stan: "Here's another nice mess you've gotten us into!"

The chemistry between the two comedians was apparent at once to both Roach and Leo McCarey, but McCarey watched their development with increasing dismay through *Slipping Wives*, *Love 'Em and Weep*, *Why Girls Love Sailors*, *With Love and Hisses*, *Sailors, Beware!*, and *The Second Hundred Years* (all 1927). Except for their stupidity and Stan's cry, for which Roach took all the credit, there was no distinguishing set of characteristics to make them unique other than the obvious contrast of their shapes. In describing the evolution of Stan's whimper, Roach said "That was a thing that had been done before, but (here) it was my idea. . . . Laurel and Hardy, they're children, really. And their whole attitude is well, when people are little, a baby falls hundreds of times. They fall off every damn thing. The first thing that parents do is try to laugh them out of it, if they can, you know – 'Oh, ho, ho, ho, Johnny fell down!' You know. If Johnny fell down and is hurt, that's a different thing.

Then he cries. A little kid gets attention when he cries. So the mother says 'Johnny, what did you do in the kitchen?' And he knows he's caught but that if he cries, nothing happens to him. So he starts to cry. You know he's not hurt, he's not scared. He's just crying. Well, Laurel never cried when he was scared. He never cried when he was hurt. Laurel only cried when he was confused, which is exactly the reaction of a kid." It is certainly possible that with Roach's phenomenal success with "Our Gang", he would see Laurel and Hardy as grown-up counterparts of his little rascals. But that was stretching it a bit, since Spanky, Farina and the other kids were mental giants alongside Stan and Babe.

Leo McCarey began to pull the boys together in his mind as a team that was totally different from everyone who had preceded them. Sometimes Roach had Babe in a beard; that was wrong, thought McCarey. Roach was casting them *together* in a series of comedies, a stroke of genius in itself, but McCarey knew that this would not pay off unless they made some changes in pace, and in the way they looked and behaved, that would remain consistent from film to film. Roach had come to respect McCarey as the most talented comedy hand in the business and he asked him to take over the supervision of all future Laurel and Hardy production, an association which began with *Putting Pants on Philip* (1927). It was during the filming of *Philip* that McCarey suddenly came up with the bowlers as an integral part of the team's image; subsequently, *Hats Off* was the first McCarey production to reach the theatres.

That was the way the partnership began in 1927. Charles A. Lindbergh was the world's hero and America was ecstatic. "Lindy's" historic saga was followed by that epic movie of the skies, William Wellman's Wings.

With the whole world marvelling at America's skill at defying gravity, Leo McCarey's and Hal Roach's counter-movement was launched quietly in Culver City, California. Laurel and Hardy were to demonstrate in reel after reel that what goes up must fall *down. More significantly, the point was made that disaster or at least trouble lurked in that much-vaunted sanctuary, home and hearth. It was safer to be out of it than curled in its treacherous bosom.*

Within a very short time, they had become folk figures, their images as recognizable as Huck Finn, whose philosophy they advanced in nearly every foot of film on which they appeared. While there was no trace of social comment in their films, no one was safe from their irreverence – employers, college deans and professors, wives, girlfriends, grandmothers, policemen, truck drivers, members of fraternal orders, the Army, husbands, criminals, society matrons, tycoons, Scotsmen, primates and eventually Jean Harlow suffered at their hands. Humourless feminists writing today are outraged by their "abuse" of women.

Stan Laurel, as the creative half of the team, must share with McCarey the credit or the disrepute engendered by the choice of targets. And just as Chaplin's Little Tramp *– quick, shrewd, assertive – seemed to reflect the life experience of his creator, Stan's final screen character, that of the befuddled outsider with a genius for achieving the least life can offer, bore the imprint of the man who played him.*

Forever making frontal assaults on that invisible wall that separated him and Ollie from even a small success, Stan Laurel seemed to be a bit of every man except the insensitive. Stan felt *perhaps more than most of us. There was a nervous apprehension in him as he rapped on a stranger's door or ventured a comment in court about a savage criminal ("Aren't you going to hang him?"). While never very bright, he took stands, took in children and stray dogs. Quite often, he went on secret flings away from domineering wives and sometimes got drunk. Audiences were with him all the way because they often did the same and got away with it. Stan on screen never got away with anything.*

McCarey's first instinct was to slow the boys down. As he remembered it: "Comics had a tendency to do too much. With Laurel and Hardy, we introduced nearly the opposite. We tried to direct them so that they showed nothing, expressed nothing, and the audience, waiting for the opposite, laughed because we remained serious. For example, one day, Babe was playing the part of a maitre d' coming in to serve a cake (in *From Soup to Nuts*, 1928). He steps through a doorway, falls and finds himself on the floor, his head buried in the cake. I shouted, 'Don't move! Just don't move! Stay like that!' Hardy stayed still, stretched out, furious, his head in the cake . . . you could only see his back. And for a minute and a half, the audience couldn't stop laughing."

There was one great difference between Laurel and Hardy. Stan's technique and screen character grew out of a tradition that went back long before he was born. Hardy came from small-town America with no show-business background anywhere in his family history. He acquired everything as he worked. In the end, Oliver Hardy was the consummate film actor, aware of the intense concentration of the camera, of the way it picked up even the lifting of his pinkie. There was a mastery of film technique in Babe that was only discernible in a handful of actors – Chaplin, Keaton, Brando, Tracy. Before her death, Carole Lombard came close to this absolute unconsciousness of the camera as a presence, yet intense awareness of its capabilities; so did Marilyn Monroe in one film, *Some Like It Hot*.

Stan was more aware than anyone of Hardy's extraordinary naturalness. It was something that was there, an asset to be used. And it was, again and again.

Babe never thought of himself as a comedian. He was an actor first and foremost, a *screen* actor. During their later personal appearances, some of the subtleties of his performance would be lost, while Stan's broader music-hall approach never failed. Babe rarely made the slightest effort to be funny. He simply *was*. It was the edge that Laurel and Hardy had over later teams such as Abbott and Costello and Martin and Lewis. (The same technique is used today by Woody Allen. Allen's apparent dead seriousness makes his comedies all the more hilarious.)

Once a set was shut down for the day, Babe walked away from it, got into his car and forgot movie-making altogether. That was the essential and critical difference between them as working partners. Stan would sit through the rushes, insist upon retakes, and worry over some fairly inconsequential bit of business. He remained at the studio long into the night, often making a party of it and frequently asking a few girls to come over for some laughs in the projection room. Other members of staff pretended blindness as they saw a giggling redhead being led by a laughing Stan up the stairs into the screening-room. Wives were not as blind, but Stan would also take his work home with him, waking up in the middle of the night to act out some new gag that had struck him as being right and funny, with a wife as sole audience. It was hard to stay mad at Stan. He was too gently disarming.

When Stan discovered the excitement of being able to create off the set as well as on, in the cutting-room, in the gag room, *there* was his life, at least all he felt that he wanted from it, in blazing focus. He was performing *and* helping to pull the ideas that had come from him or McCarey into a structured whole, and those ideas were being perfectly realized on film by a partner like Babe Hardy. It was a boon he never dreamed could come his way – a partner who was a performing genius yet had no interest in putting the film together so that he alone had that joy. In no way could Stan possibly have been more deeply satisfied professionally. There existed strong artistic camaraderie among the three of them, McCarey, Babe Hardy and himself. That was what made them such a flawless team and gives us a strong clue to their lasting appeal.

2 Throughout the nineteen-twenties, Sennett and Roach reigned supreme as comedy-makers, though as the end of the decade approached, it was fairly evident that Roach had overtaken Sennett, whose decline paralleled the chronology of the fall of his first employer in the movies, D. W. Griffith. Still, Mack Sennett comes first to mind even today when one thinks of the "custard pie" era, and he figures more prominently than Roach in most movie histories.

There is a reason for this. Sennett brought Chaplin into films and more than a dozen other major talents, including Gloria Swanson and Carole Lombard. He created an enormously popular comedy group, The Keystone Kops. His Bathing Beauties were legendary. His romance with his star Mabel Normand has become a part of the basic Hollywood myth. He was more colourful than Roach by far.

But the Sennett comedy formula did not mature, so while the Sennett legend survives, far fewer Sennett films than those made by Roach are in general circulation or even available today. For Roach, the leap from *Willie Work* to *Sons of the Desert* (1933) seems far greater than the nineteen years separating them. While Sennett knew what was funny, Roach could supply the components of a comedy, often including the story idea, and he acquired the services of some of the finest comedy writers and directors ever to enter the movie business. Most of Sennett's writers, stars and directors, including the great Frank Capra, went on to greater fame with the major studios. Few left Roach. So a substantial number of creative men stayed long enough at Roach to alter the shape of the films made there and contribute to their durability. Foremost among them was Leo McCarey.

Thomas Leo McCarey was born in Los Angeles in 1898, the son of a boxing promoter, "Uncle Tom" McCarey. After college, he attended law school and at twenty, he was a practising attorney, disastrously, according to a death-bed interview granted director and film historian Peter Bogdanovich. His youthful appearance worked against him, and he lost nearly every case.

Moviemaking had become one of the largest industries in Los Angeles by 1920, when Leo was forced to step down from the bar. Director David Butler gave him a job as "a script girl". Because of his legal education, he used big words and impressed studio heads thought he was brilliant. Although he had gone on to his first film a long way down the totem pole, "at the end of the picture," he recalled, "they were measuring me for jodhphurs!" But his first directorial effort was a dismal affair.

While Leo was working with Tod Browning on *The Virgin of Stamboul* (1920), which was not quite on the same level of horror as Browning's *Freaks* (1932), Hal Roach overheard him recounting some other personal misadventure at the Los Angeles Athletic Club and told him, "If you think you can be funny, I'll give you a job." *Funny* was, naturally enough, Roach's favourite word. He usually wanted to know if a performer could "act funny", or a writer could "write funny", and Leo decided that, given his grievous background up to that moment, there was no reason why he couldn't "be funny". But it took two years of further débâcles with other producers before the half-cowed McCarey turned up at the Roach Studio and asked Roach if the offer still held good. He was given a job creating gags for the first "Our Gang" comedies.

Leo established himself with Roach as the most capable moulder of comic images in Hollywood. In 1926, he was assigned to find a comic formula for Charley Chase, who had been signed up following a distinguished but unspectacular rise as a supporting comedian with Chaplin and Mabel Normand at Sennett and a recent stay with Famous Players Lasky, where he had begun to write and direct. He was a slender comic with a long face, thin moustache and the gold-rimmed glasses of a bank teller. He was, in Roach's words, "a work horse", a man of boundless energy, much like Stan, who bounced around the lot, looking in on everything that was shooting.

Chase excelled at playing ordinary chaps with extraordinary problems, usually domestic, surmountable only by strenuous and often surrealistic measures. Leo contributed the stories and central ideas, while Chase added humanizing touches that went a long way towards establishing his final screen character. In their first two-reeler, *Mighty Like a Moose*, he played a luckless husband with a very big nose married to a wife with buck teeth. They had to go through embarrassing contortions in order to kiss. Each of them decided to have plastic surgery and they parted for a month, with separate flimsy excuses for going away. One day they met on the street and didn't recognize each other but a romance was again ignited, more passionate than ever this time. Eventually, Chase was furious because his wife dared to deceive him with another man, not considering that he was also being unfaithful. Philandering was to become a key element in the plots at the Roach Studio, reflecting the changing sexual mores in America during the twenties. It was to become such a commonplace in nearly all Hollywood films of that period that it made virtue a refreshing change, launching the career of Janet Gaynor and sustaining that of Mary Pickford longer than any sophisticated movie-goer thought possible.

Stan brought many of the movements, gestures and *look* of his screen character with him from the stages of variety houses and music-halls. There was a great deal of Dan Leno, something of Chaplin, and much else picked up along the way. Very early on in his stage career Stan had made an interesting discovery: he found that audiences laughed at him before he ever said or did anything. It had something to do with the good intentions that were inherent in his smile, a trap to catch everyone off guard. It had even more to do with the way he looked at people. There was no eyeball contact. He could have been looking at a herd of seals or a cage of primates. His blink was slow, in some dim hope that comprehension might be there when he opened his eyes again but it was forever beyond him.

Babe Hardy was quite different. He *saw* what he was looking at with clear, unblinking vision. It was only later we would discover that his miscomprehension was, if anything, even greater than Stan's.

There was another essential difference. Not having had any stage experience, it could be expected that, like so many screen actors, he would pretend that he was recreating something close to everyday life and his gaze would ignore "the fourth wall" of the camera or audience. But at least as early as the first Laurel and Hardy comedy supervised by Leo McCarey, *Putting Pants on Philip*, Babe used the camera (and thus the audience) as confidante.

Philip was our first clear view of the pair as a film team – Stan the innocent with a curious slow-wittedness, and Ollie his stout and inept guide through the perils of life. Ollie, as Stan's "Uncle Piedmont", takes charge of him during his trip to America from his native Scotland. Stan as "Philip" naturally wears kilts and a tamo'-shanter, and Ollie is so embarrassed by this that he orders Stan to walk behind him rather than by his side. Ollie's small town conservatism – and its vulnerability – sparks much of the plot of this delightful film.

Hardy's manners, his "courtliness", were based upon those he had acquired as a boy growing up in Harlem, Georgia, where he was born on 18 January 1892. Like Stan, Hardy grew up in the comfort of one of the best homes in town. The Hardys were not in show business; his father practised law and held a number of political offices.

While the boy was still at grade school, his father died, and moderately hard times set in. His mother Emily Hardy was a woman of determination, tempered by a warm humanity. She sold their home and they moved to nearby Madison, where she bought and operated a hotel. It was there in the hotel lobby that young Norvell (as his family called him) began "people watching", a habit that enriched his knowledge of human quirks and gave him a broad grasp of characterization as an actor.

As the most beloved fat man in history, in or out of show business, Oliver Hardy eventually came to terms with obesity, ignoring it until the last years of his life when his doctor ordered him to reduce. But his weight was a problem almost from infancy and he was embarrassed about it all through childhood. By the age of fourteen, he weighed two hundred and fifty pounds and nearly wept with humiliation whenever someone called him "Fatty". His last wife, Lucille, explained that much of his difficulty resulted from a hearty appetite. He was actually a handsome boy, even cherubic, and he early developed a fine singing voice, heard too infrequently on the screen, enabling him to spend several years in a church choir and, briefly, as a wandering boy minstrel celebrated for hitting top C.

He never wandered far, however, since he suffered from chronic homesickness until he was nearly grown. When family finances improved, he was sent off to military school, then to the Atlanta Conservatory of Music as a voice student, and finally to the University of Georgia, where he planned to study law.

Dropping out of school at eighteen, he opened his own cinema in Milledgeville, where the Hardys then lived. On the side, he umpired local baseball games, and his half-sister (Elizabeth Sage) recalled that "they used to close the banks to see Norvell umpire." When he called an unpopular decision, some of the crowd would yell out "Fats" and Norvell would threaten to go home, but he never left a game.

Thoroughly filmstruck, he sold the cinema and set out for nearby Jacksonville, where Kalem and Lubin had studios at the time. He worked for more than a year there, usually playing heavies, despite his youth, because of his size and a way he had of making his eyes into sinister slits.

In Jacksonville, twenty-year-old Hardy met a pianist and singer named Madelyn Saloshin, who was touring the cinema circuits and earning as much as $300 a week. Madelyn found his careful manners a refreshing change from the rowdiness of most of her friends and her audiences. He had acquired the nickname "Babe" by that time; (it had been) given to him by a jolly barber who loved to shave and powder his several chins. Babe and the slightly older pianist married in 1913 and they attempted to make a go of their partnership with a series of boarding-houses and hotels.

But Madelyn's success was more than Babe could handle. Although she was instrumental in getting him any number of small film roles through her connections, Babe couldn't abide being paid ten dollars for a day's work when Madelyn was commanding three times that amount just for pounding out popular tunes on a piano. They both decided that his big break could only come in New York, where Biograph and Edison and nearly all the studios except for Essanay (Chicago) and the Florida minor league were located. California was not yet a serious contender since only Thomas Ince, who founded the first important Los Angeles film company, and Cecil B. De Mille, who followed him, were working there on any significant level. There was no divorce at the time, and Babe agreed to send her thirty dollars a week when he finally got steady movie work, if we are to believe a legal complaint lodged against him in the early thirties by Madelyn.

Babe was still in New York and working in a comedy one-reeler at Fort Lee, New Jersey, when America entered the war in April 1917. Unlike Stan, to whom wars were something quite alien, Babe was consumed with the notion that he had to be a part of the fighting. He headed for the nearest recruiting office, and, as his widow Lucille remembered the story: "The officer in charge . . . gaped at Babe for a moment, looked him up and down and yelled into another office, 'Hey, Sarge, come look at what wants to enlist!' The sergeant came out, looked, and the two doubled up with laughter. This was followed by a number of remarks intended to be funny. . . . He was terribly hurt and embarrassed – and this finished him with New York. He completed the job he was doing and then went back to Vim in Florida and a night job at the Burbidge Hotel cabaret there." But he avoided Madelyn.

Babe Hardy's roundabout route to Hollywood made him a familiar face and type to nearly every casting director on the East Coast. He was becoming known more for his availability than for his versatility. He would do and did anything before the cameras. Perhaps he became inured to bodily abuse on camera since it was to become as much a part of his character as Ollie as the tie-twiddle – he would fall into pastry, mud and water, get ink in the face, a piano on his back, fall through a roof or down a long flight of stairs, get frozen stiff, all as a star.

Suddenly, Babe had more offers for character roles in comedies than he could accept. He worked with Billy West, the most successful of the Chaplin imitators, with Earl Williams, Jimmy Aubrey and Larry Semon. Finally on the coast, William Fox kept him steadily employed as a villain in features and comedies up to 1923. For ten years he stood before cameras at nearly every American studio, but had not a single opportunity to put his legs apart and his hands on his hips in an attitude of incredulity at how far simple-mindedness could go. He specialized only in menacing looks and steely purpose, and no one even bothered to ask if he could dance. Hardy's grace under pressure preceded Hemingway's by at least six years when it was at last made visible.

Although it took Leo McCarey and Stan to bring all of those dormant talents into focus, Babe Hardy learned a great deal while he was jobbing from one studio to the next. His eyes were open. He noticed what worked and what didn't. By the time stardom came, he knew instinctively where to stand, when to move. He became a director's joy. There was very little to teach him about film acting.

Fourteen years after stepping in front of his first movie camera, Oliver "Babe" Hardy was placed on a weekly salary of one hundred fifty dollars by Roach; Stan was raised to slightly less than three hundred. Cheap for the fastest-rising comedy team in the world, but these were men who had known disappointment and ignominy too well and too long to quibble.

7 || The Fun Factory, 1927

1   1927 was an extraordinary time in America. The biggest business boom in history was cresting. Coolidge was in the White House – a man who kept a pet raccoon named Rebecca in the presidential mansion had to be more complex than his place in history suggests. Street crime was down; gangland warfare was up. The mob saw that raids on speak-easies were infrequent, and the best-run places were always tipped off in advance.

It was a heady atmosphere there at the Roach Studio in Culver City in the late Twenties. There were gifted cameramen working there such as George Stevens (later the acclaimed director of *A Place in the Sun*, 1951), and they were given one order by Roach: forget arty shadows and make it as clear as possible. This in itself was almost revolutionary in a Hollywood intimidated by Griffith, von Stroheim and Murnau. Leo McCarey and Roach himself were supervising things and Roach also directed occasionally. One of the better known directors working for him at that time was George Marshall.

Roach had three series that were guaranteed success before release: *Our Gang, Charley Chase* and *Laurel and Hardy*. Audiences began laughing as soon as the names appeared on the screen.

Stan and Babe did not expect such spectacular success so soon after the formula for their films had been codified by McCarey, and, in truth, apart from the huge bags of fan mail, some of it addressed to "Laurel and Hardy, Hollywood, U.S.A.", they were not aware of its true dimensions. Superstardom came late but rapidly in 1928 with the release of *Two Tars* that marvellous tale of two maladventurous sailors with its sea of wrecked cars. They had moved without fanfare into the ranks of Chaplin, Lloyd, Langdon and Keaton. Since they had become a team, they were unique. There were others who were teamed at the time: Marie Dressler and Polly Moran, George Sidney and Charley Murray (*The Cohens and the Kellys*), and, on the Roach lot, Thelma Todd and Zasu Pitts (with Miss Pitts being replaced by Patsy Kelly in 1930 when she became one of the most sought-after supporting actresses in Hollywood). But Laurel and Hardy were playing "themselves" in a world that fell somewhere between the real one that we know and that of Kafka.

Roach had the boys turning out one two-reeler every month throughout 1928, and even then he could not keep up with exhibitor demand. There was no problem of over-exposure. The public could not get enough of them.

Stan did not at any point sit back as Babe did and enjoy his success – he was afraid to. He wanted to savour every moment of it. If something wasn't happening around him, he felt compelled to create a little action. From the moment when their films began to catch on, he believed that neither a comedy team nor a comedian could last too long because times change as does the public and its taste. Sometimes, when talking about the pitfalls of great fame, he was more specific. He said that, excluding Chaplin, most screen comics have a peak period of no more than ten years.

Despite this fundamental stoicism, this was not the Stan whom Mae had known. He seemed renewed by this sudden, overwhelming recognition. It was more than that. When he and Lois entered a restaurant, even his peers and their bosses lifted eyebrows in surprise the moment they saw who it was. Sometimes that moment was slow in coming; off-screen, Stan was handsomer than the skinny man in the ill-fitting clothes and he even had a slight paunch.

Roach was surprised and delighted. When he lost Lloyd in 1923, he had concentrated on building up a huge stable of comedy stars

("All Stars", he called them), never quite believing that beyond "Our Gang", which was more a concept than a group of star performers, lightning could possibly strike him again. When it did, "Keeping the boys happy" became the watchword on the Roach lot. Fortunately for Roach, Babe Hardy had been signed up on a long-term contract more than a year after Stan had been. This meant that their contracts would expire at different times and they never would be in a position to refuse *together* to renew with Roach. It was pure chance that it had worked out this way, but eventually Stan would see it as a sinister plot against him. In all other respects, they were the Lords of the lot, deferred to at every turn. An entourage grew around Stan. He called a few of them "idea men" and they got on to Roach's pay-roll. It was a small price to pay, as Roach saw it, to keep Stan content.

Babe had married an attractive brunette, Myrtle Lee, in 1921 after divorcing Madelyn Saloshin Hardy. Myrtle was a sloe-eyed exotic beauty, not in films, who had followed Babe loyally through a succession of boarding-houses, cheap apartments and hotels. Now they settled into more permanent quarters, a small estate on North Alta Drive in Beverly Hills.

Not to be outdone, Stan and Lois found a rambling brick English colonial house with a servants' wing and a nursery at 718 North Bedford Drive, less than a mile from the Hardys and just across the street from Marie Dressler's mansion. A cook was hired and little ex-acrobat Pete Gordon came to live with them as general factotum.

Despite his elevation, Stan remained himself. He was perhaps the most democratic major star of all time. An Englishman born at the height of Britain's colonial empire, astonishingly, he had no sense of caste or even of movie status. Everyone was on the same level as him and he mingled equally with the stars, his own hired cronies, the studio crew, delivery men and chauffeurs. He had no social aspirations whatsoever. He and Lois would often entertain a studio grip or an assistant cameraman simply because they liked him. Lois was a warm, thoughtful hostess and only grew cool when the drinking threatened to get out of hand.

It is possible that Lois found Stan's plebeian tastes useful. Rather than waste money on a chauffeur, she bought him a bicycle for his journeys to the studio. The sight of the most important star wheeling in became a joke around the Roach lot. He said he needed the exercise, which was true enough as his weight was becoming a challenge to cameramen Lloyd, Stevens and Powers who needed to keep him looking thin.

In assessing Lois's role in Stan's life, most of their friends thought she was "good for Stan" and all agree that she sought to protect him, to create a quiet sanctuary for him in their home. Hal Roach wishes he had stayed married to her and is convinced that the future of Laurel and Hardy would have been different had he done so. She did not know when they married that Stan found any and all attempts to keep him out of harm's way both meddlesome and suffocating. Danger and risk were as necessary to Stan as breath itself.

He had thought when they first met that there was a sense of daring about her. She told him about a comedy she had done for Joe Rock in which she had worked with several lions and felt no fear. Several men wearing black face-paint were supposed to turn "white" at the sight of them: this was the principal gag in the scene. Stan often spoke of Lois and her lions with considerable pride.

But under her bravado was a bustling homemaker whose constant preoccupation was the curbing of Stan's improvident ways. He loved her so much that for months he tried to please her. She even began handling his money and doling out what he needed.

Lois could not have known that her role in Stan's life was untenable. The marriage seemed to be going well, and she was unaware that the two paths open to her in Stan's life were dead ends. She could become his partner in the frenetic activities surrounding him as a star who was also his own producer in everything but title – attending previews, screenings, helping with the refreshments on poker nights; or she could do what she in fact did and become a stabilizing influence in Stan's life. She drank in moderation at first and, finally, when she saw that alcohol was one of Stan's problems, not at all. While Louise Rock and Mrs Hal Roach found her sweet and endearing, Alice Cooke and some other lady friends felt that she didn't wear very well, that her sociability was strained. Apparently, she began to feel that she needed allies more than friends and, despite the recent lawsuit, both Joe and Louise Rock grew very close to Lois Laurel during this period.

18. Stan's prison porridge seems to have sailed on to a guard during this mess hall riot in *Detained*, produced by Joe Rock in 1924

19. Charley Chase, Roach's most popular comedy star in 1926

20. Studio head Hal Roach holds two simian members of his acting company, 1926

21. Stan, as an inept buck private, begins to take on a delightful and distinctive dumbness in *With Love and Hisses*, 1927

22. The dentist's chair was a favourite setting for Laurel and Hardy's calamitous humour. Here Stan is forced to take a little gas in *Leave 'Em Laughing*, 1928

23. The chef in the Culpepper mansion loses his patience with waiter Stan who seems about to lose his head. Ollie winces at the thought of all the gore to come in *From Soup to Nuts*, 1928

24. Not everything they filmed reached the screen. This shows a scene that director Leo McCarey deleted from the final cut of *Habeas Corpus*, in which they try to persuade an ominous-looking night watchman to admit them to a cemetery in the middle of the night, 1928

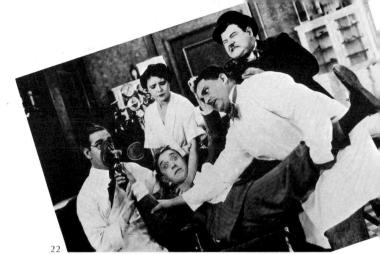

25

26

27

The Hal Roach Company poses for its [por]trait (without Hal). Far *l* is director [Jam]es Horne, next to him financial [wiz]ard Warren Doane, animal trainer [Tony] Campanaro with drum, fat Joe [Co]bb and Gordon Douglas (with horn) [beh]ind drum, composer Marvin Hatley [nex]t to Douglas, all of "Our Gang" lined [up] next to Joe Cobb including Pete the [do]g, director Bob McGowan with cake, [cam]eraman Art Lloyd right of [Mc]Gowan, Babe Hardy between them, [the] boys' lawyer Ben Shipman behind [Llo]yd (with glasses and shock of white [hair]), Stan next to Lloyd and Hal Roach [at] right of Stan, 1928

Mrs Hardy (Kay Deslys), Mrs Laurel [Is]abelle Keith) with bellicose Uncle [Ed]gar (Edgar Kennedy) and family dog [are] stalled on an outing by car trouble, [ma]rring their *Perfect Day*, 1929. Ollie and [Ed]an prepare for a scrap.

The end of the economic road: selling [Ch]ristmas trees in July in California. [Th]is study in futility was called *Big Busi[nes]s*, 1929

A movie-house ad during the heart of [the] depression when you could see a [m]ovie on screen and Laurel and Hardy [on] stage for a little over a quarter.

Jean Harlow got her start in films [do]ing bit roles for Laurel and Hardy in [the]ir silent *Liberty* and *Double Whoopee*, [19]29

28

29

30

30. Stan loved
play in drag, just
did his idol D
Leno. Here he pla
"Mrs Hardy"
Ollie can retain
claim to the fortu
which he will o
day inherit from
uncle. *That's*
Wife, 1929
31. The boys, es
cially Stan, seem
have found a tr
friend in *Ang*
Love, 1929

31

32

The boys deliver
racehorse named
lueboy'' to a mil-
naire whose
inting of Gains-
rough's famed
e Boy has been
len. The mil-
naire, without
king down from
upstairs suite,
ls them to bring
e lost treasure into
e house and put it
the piano. *Wrong
ain*, 1929

Stan, Fred
rno and Hal
ach, 1932. Karno,
e music-hall
presario, had just
ned a five-year
ntract with Roach
an associate pro-
cer. He lasted
ven months.

33

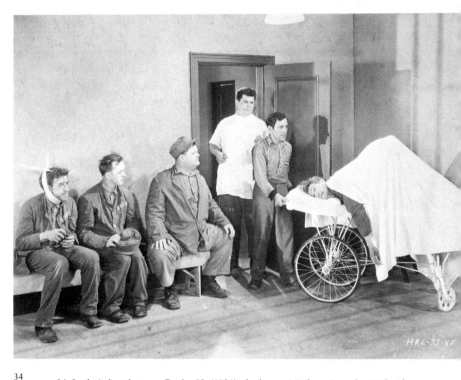

34

34. In their first feature, *Pardon Us* (1931), the boys visit the prison dentist but have second thoughts after a patient, whom they saw before on his feet, comes out on a hospital cart *in extremis*.

35. Mrs Hardy (Daphne Pollard) and Mrs Laurel (Betty Healy) catch up with their men at the local pub in *Our Relations*, 1936

35

When she became pregnant late in 1927, Stan seemed pleased, but having a child was an event of considerable consequence. Stan was fiercely domestic; he preferred to drink at home and frequently did so. He chose to eat at home whenever possible and he accepted party invitations with some reluctance, but he was a poor candidate for fatherhood. Small children made him extremely nervous; he could take them in only the smallest of doses.

Understandably, Lois insisted that Stan be with her when he was not at the studio. She had all the usual anxieties of expectant mothers, plus the added one of being the wife to an actor of a most mercurial nature. Stan would get so restless sitting around the house that he often disappeared without a word.

Lois kept these aberrations to herself for a very long time, but eventually word of Stan's behaviour at home reached Roach. Roach had known comedians by the score, and he found that the great ones were always the most difficult to deal with. He had come to believe that the process of being abused and laughed at on camera eventually got to them, and that after years of it, they inevitably became bitter and demanding. They would try to even the score by asking for more forbearance at home than most women could afford and more money at the studio than Roach thought they were worth. Roach always felt that he was as generous as he could possibly be, and he knew that resentment over his rejection of salary demands would be carried home, where the wives would get it again.

Alone with Lois, Stan became increasingly turned off. For days he made no effort of any kind to be even politely congenial. The routine of bourgeois marriage probably bored him. In any case, when he left the house now, it was frequently not just for a night out with the boys.

It was sometime in 1928 that Alyce (sometimes spelled *Alice*) Ardell came into Stan's life. She was auburn-haired, sophisticated, witty and beautiful. What intrigued Stan most about her was her French accent, which in Hollywood did not necessarily mean that she came from France, but it made her terribly desirable to him. Stan found a French, Russian or Viennese accent in a woman impossible to resist.

Alyce had been a minor player in films of Joe Rock, Hal Roach and, occasionally, the major studios, including Fox. Like other attractive young women in the film colony, Alyce enjoyed a good time but was not interested in marriage. In her way, she respected Lois, as she later did Ruth. She had no respect at all for Illeana, Stan's third wife, and that was to lead to a near-fatal encounter.

Stan's relationship with Alyce, lasting more than a decade, was not sustained by money. Quite often, when they were together, Stan would be broke for one reason or another – it was not an infrequent occurrence. That made no difference. Alyce had many admirers in the film community, some of them producers, and she was always comfortably set up in an apartment or residential hotel. For Stan, she was an island, a refuge. When life with Lois or Ruth or Illeana became too much for him, he went to Alyce's.

On the surface his domestic life continued to appear tranquil, though signs of strain were visible to the perceptive. With so much going for him, one would think that the insecurities and the self-doubts that had plagued Stan for so many years might be kept at bay. Yet, as his fame soared, as his voice around the Roach lot became more and more assertive and respected, he would fall into long silences at home. He and Pete Gordon would go into the library and drink as Stan tried to pull out of the depths.

Lois, now unable to go out of the house as the baby was expected within weeks, sat numbly in the background. Life with Stan was getting out of hand.

A little girl was born in 1928 and they named her Lois, Jr. "Little Lois" was plump and hale, resembling her delicate-featured mother except around the eyes. She also had the sober gaze of her father that made his humour so devastating.

For a time, Stan became a doting father. He carried little Lois to the studio, where she was duly admired. Believing that every child should have a dog, he bought her a huge St Bernard, and big Lois (for so his wife began to be called) had one more thing to fret about – keeping the two-hundred pound animal from stepping on her baby.

2   Leo McCarey remained in charge of the team's fortunes on the screen for four years or until *Hog Wild*, which was released in May 1930, and the tone remained consistent throughout – disciplined, even predictable lunacy. They had reversed reflexes;

unreason ruled their every move. Audiences came to love their ineptitude, and a certain amount of compassion spilled over into our feelings for their termagant wives, their stern bosses and the dumb-founded cops. They all deserved it.

Ideas for their comedies were inspired by just about anything that was in the air at the time. Following the controversial long count in the Dempsey-Tunney fight in Chicago when Jack Dempsey lost to Gene Tunney in the seventh round, Leo McCarey created *The Battle of the Century* (1927) for the boys, with Stan as the contender and Ollie as his manager. In McCarey's words: "Stan had knocked his opponent out, but he wouldn't go to a neutral corner, and the referee started to count, and he saw Laurel standing over him and he stopped counting and said, 'No, you've got to go over here.' Well, Stan in his stupid way couldn't understand, so they had to get a rule book out. All the time, the fellow was on the ropes, uncon-scious . . . after a lot of byplay . . . Laurel finally complies with the referee's request and the other fellow got up and knocked him for a loop."

It was during the production of this film that the wholly incidental arrival of a pie wagon near the set at lunchtime inspired one of the most memorable comic moments in American film. They decided to add a pie-fight sequence, and it quickly became so spectacular that the audience forgot about the Dempsey-Tunney fight and 'The Battle of the Century' became the battle of the pies.

Today, all that remains of this prime example of the Laurel-McCarey improvisational process is the pie-fight. It typified what was described so aptly by John McCabe and others later on as the principal of "reciprocal destruction". That principal works in this fashion: Stan slips on a banana skin and falls on to a city pavement. Ollie opportunistically grabs another banana and tosses it, hoping that eventually Stan will really be injured and he can claim on an accident insurance policy. Unfortunately, the first to slip inglori-ously and fall is a cop on his beat. While the banana peel is still on the ground, a pie baker (that magnificent comic foil, Charlie Hall) comes out of his shop and slips. This leads to a pie tossed by Hall into Ollie's face. The battle escalates as literally dozens of pedestrians, male and female, and merchants, rush to Hall's pie wagon to seize ammunition for the fray. A society matron in her chauffeured car gets one full in the face and preserves her shocked dignity for one awful moment; a young woman slips and lands in a pie. The joy of watching this sequence comes chiefly from the sense of release; no one is immune to the orgy; everyone is a target just as everyone is a pie-thrower.

By late 1928, every large cinema across America and in parts of Europe and the Orient was wired for sound. Roach was preparing Charley Chase for his sound début – his Baltimore accent was to enhance his comedies. "Our Gang" had acquired a sound track and Spanky McFarland's deliberations about what they should perpe- trate next could finally be heard, making him more of a real little boy and less of a smart aleck (as the title writers had been forced to make him previously). Laurel and Hardy were the last on the Roach lot to make the transition. Both Roach and Stan hesitated to change the style and format of the series since the boys relied so markedly on mime. Like Chaplin, they were masters in the art, and, as nearly everyone knows, Charlie did not speak any dialogue on the screen until 1940.

In October 1928, Roach, Stan and McCarey all conferred one afternoon about the possibility of adding sound to the team's latest comedy, *Liberty* (released in January 1929). They knew that sub- titles had been kept to a minimum in Laurel and Hardy films because there was little that was verbal in any of them. This fact possibly provided a challenge to a title-writer H. M. Walker as the few titles were sprinkled through their comedies were as laugh- provoking as anything in the action.

Finally, it was decided to dub sound effects into *Liberty* and add a musical score. The comedy was significant historically in one other detail. Its leading lady was an unknown platinum blonde named Jean Harlow, who had arrived on the lot more than a year earlier. Roach had spoken with her then at some length about her pros- pects. In the back of his mind was the possibility that she might turn out to be as useful as Thelma Todd had been and still was, but Jean was married to a wealthy businessman who considered her appear- ances in slapstick comedy undignified. Roach regretted her decision and forgot about it. Then, just before shooting on *Liberty* began, Roach saw Jean and her mother in a crowd of extras during the lunch-break on one of his sets and asked her what had happened. "Well," she told him, "I got a divorce." A modest deal was worked out on the spot.

Liberty opens with shots of some brave Americans in simulated news-reel footage fighting for freedom at various points in history as the sub-titles recall these events. The final one reads: "And even today – the fight for liberty continues", and we see Stan and Ollie in prison stripes trying to escape from a guard. McCarey's script has a wryer, more true to the real Leo, note creeping into it.

Credibility was a fundamental element in Stan and Ollie's screen characters. When spoken dialogue was added, the point of credibility was sometimes strained, since the words themselves had to be plausible while the situation in which they found themselves was pretty far out.

One of the unlikeliest of plot lines was given to them in their last silent film, *Big Business,* but it turned out to be as fine as anything they ever did. It spelled out its theme as usual in the opening title: "The story of a man who turned the other cheek – and got punched in the nose."

In the film, Stan and Ollie are Christmas tree salesmen in Los Angeles in the middle of summer. Eventually they reach the house of scowling Jimmy Finlayson, who slams the door on them, leaving their sample Christmas tree caught inside. They ring the bell and pull the tree free only to discover that Stan's coat is caught. This goes on for a minute or so until Finlayson tosses the tree as far as he can. Then Stan wonders if Fin would like to order a tree for next year. This inquiry sends Fin into his famous ticking bomb routine. We expect the explosion to be shattering, and it often is. He attacks the tree with a pair of shears, rendering it into several branches.

Ollie, boiling, cuts off a few of Fin's remaining hairs from his balding head. Fin destroys Ollie's watch. The boys are driven by this vandalism into an orgy of destruction – they tear off the doorbell, cut the telephone cord, and take an axe to windows and doors, while Fin rushes to the curb and begins demolishing their Model T.

An interesting sidelight to this production is the chronicle of the extensive damage done to the wrong house by Stan and Ollie, through no fault of theirs, which resulted in Roach having to pay for its reconstruction. Roach frequently recounted this "episode" but it smacks of the apocryphal. As Roach tells it, he had previously bought a house of an identical style a block away from the site of the one used in the picture. The crew was supposed to confirm its identity through a photograph. Unfortunately for the owners of the first house they came to, the Roach crew decided that the number of the house was slightly off but there was no mistaking the architecture – that fake miniature hacienda with its adobe and tiled roof. If true, it is the only known instance of a house being mugged by mistake.

It was Jimmy Finlayson's seventh appearance in a Laurel and Hardy comedy; he was becoming more of a staple ingredient than Charlie Hall. "Fin", as everyone called him, was one of the original Keystone Kops over at the Sennett Studio. He was a Scotsman who had come to America in 1911 with Graham Moffatt's "Bunty Pulls the Strings". His specialty was the double take, and comprehension was visible in the added thrust of his bristling moustache, eyes squeezed to disbelieving slits, and a cocking of his bald head that spelled trouble.

8 || The Boys Talk at Last - and Everybody Laughs

1   Without any publicity to herald the historic moment, Laurel and Hardy's *Unaccustomed As We Are* opened on 4 May 1929, and much of the dialogue was spoken. Stan's slightly liquid Lancashire accent seemed perfectly in character, and Ollie's careful enunciation was intended to make him a man of some consequence, but as that film and others were to prove, he was a well-spoken misfit. Audiences were delighted with the boys' voices even though it became evident that the gags were fewer in number, slowed down by dialogue, and some of the pathos in their repeated failures in life was drained off through the articulation of details of their plight.

But that was happening everywhere. Some of the mystery left Garbo; Jean Harlow, soon to be a major "discovery" at Metro, spoke with a mid-western nasality; and Buster Keaton's star began to slip over the far horizon since his frozen comic mask required him to speak in a monotone.

The premise of Laurel and Hardy's first talkie, again McCarey's story, is a primitive one, bottom-drawer material, and yet, in execution, it is among the funniest of the boys' conventional turns. *Unaccustomed As We Are* is that hoary bromide, a husband (Ollie) bringing an uninvited guest (Stan) home to dinner, which leads to Mrs Hardy (Mae Busch) walking out and forcing Ollie to cook dinner himself. Stan is asked to light the stove (and at this point in a typical Laurel and Hardy audience, everyone holds his breath), and Stan, after turning on the gas, comes into the dining area asking for a match. Ollie looks at his friend with disgust and rushes in to light it himself, getting blown into the living room for his trouble. Then their neighbour (Thelma Todd) hurries across to see what has happened only to have her dress set afire. The blazing garment is torn from her body by Ollie, and she is hastily bundled into a tablecloth. Edgar Kennedy, who made a career of constant suspicion and defensiveness, on the Roach lot, played Thelma's policeman husband.

It is obvious from this rough précis of the film's first five minutes that Stan and McCarey have outdone themselves to keep the audience unaware of the familiar ring of the story. They utilized the formula that they had devised over their two years of collaboration, the triple gag. First one gag – the explosion – which leads to another – Thelma rushing into the conflagration to see what has happened – followed by the topper: she sees her husband (Kennedy) enter the building, just as Mrs Hardy, having had a change of heart, returns. Thelma is stuffed into a wardrobe trunk by the boys.

Unaccustomed As We Are was immediately followed by the boys' last silent film, *Double Whoopee*. This had been made prior to the switchover and was memorable chiefly as the film in which Stan, as a hotel doorman, slams a taxi door on Jean Harlow's gown and as she walks inside, the entire back of her dress is ripped away.

Later that year (1929), Jean Harlow got a new agent, Arthur Landau, who had seen her on the Roach lot. Landau persuaded director James Whale and producer Howard Hughes to use her as a replacement for the heavy-accented Greta Nissen in *Hells Angels* (1930).

Roach was not too concerned. He still had Thelma Todd. What he could not have known was that Thelma would die mysteriously within five years and Jean herself would be dead less than a year after that.

The third blonde Roach would promote to stardom would be Carole Landis in his *One Million B.C.* (1940), but she was destined to kill herself over an unrequited love affair with Rex Harrison in 1948. It can be said without any equivocation at all that Hal Roach had no luck with blondes.

2   There has been considerable emphasis upon Stan and his recurring misalliances, but Babe Hardy was equally and even more delicately involved in an affair. The lady's name was Viola Morse: she was a dark-eyed, alluring young woman, a divorcée and the mother of a handsome small boy. Viola was from the deep south like Babe. They shared a love of good food, lively companions and the excitement of the casinos and the track at Tiajuana.

One's first impression of Viola was of her heavy-lidded gaze and half smile. Babe once likened her to the Mona Lisa, but it would be difficult to say who was more inscrutable, Viola or Babe.

Sometime in 1929, Viola Morse became Babe Hardy's mistress. He rented a comfortable house for her and the boy, who was away at military school much of the time. He left Myrtle and, for appearances' sake, moved into the Beverly-Wilshire Hotel. But all of Babe's friends, including everyone on the Roach lot, accepted him and Viola as a couple.

The sequence of events is somewhat murky today, and friends who were close to Babe disagree about it, but during that same year, his wife Myrtle became an alcoholic. No one disputes this fact, although there are various suggestions as to why she became one. In one version, Babe, and presumably Viola, went to Tiajuana on an autumn day and he lost $35,000 at the track, which would have been roughly eighteen weeks' salary before taxes. He came back broke and during the weeks that followed, while trying to maintain a home with the most limited of funds, a home that no longer held much meaning for her, Myrtle began drinking heavily. She knew that Babe was now taking Viola everywhere, but he couldn't bring himself to ask Myrtle for a divorce. It was in that limbo that the heavy drinking began.

During the spring of 1929 and throughout the summer, the boys were turning out one talking two-reeler after another – *Berth Marks, Men O'War, Perfect Day, They Go Boom, Bacon Grabbers* and *The Hoose-Gow*. Each one seemed a little funnier, a shade more expertly crafted than the last. William Randolph Hearst's Cosmopolitan production unit at Metro included a magic act for Laurel and Hardy to perform – the most inept and idiotic magic turn ever seen – in its *Hollywood Revue*.

The final touch that made their screen image familiar by ear as well as by eye came late in 1929 when their background music was taken over by a former band-leader from Nebraska, Marvin Hatley.

Hatley, who had played jazz piano for several radio stations and toured vaudeville as a one-man band before that, had a fluent inventiveness, but preferred being told what to do. "Give us a jazzy, up-beat number, Marvin," Roach might say, and Marvin would fiddle around at the keyboard. Within a couple of hours he would come up with *Honolulu Baby*, a swingy tune written for the team's *Sons of the Desert* (1933), which became one of the hit songs of the era.

One day in the studio music department, Hatley was fooling around with a "Coo-Koo" call that had been part of the offbeat melody when Stan walked in. "I like that thing," he said. "I think it's funny. We'll use it in my picture. The top part will be Babe Hardy and the cuckoo part will be me."

As worked out musically by Hatley, "The top part was a kind of bugle call – Hardy giving the orders to Stan, but Stan in counter-point was 'cuckoo, cuckoo'." It was written in six-eight time with a little lilt to it. Marvin was to become Laurel and Hardy's staff composer, and there would be lots of six-eight background music to come, matching Stan's gawky walk and the odd tilt of his head.

Marvin's memories of Stan are all warm ones: "Stan", he recalled, "had a wonderful personality. Everybody liked him. He was kindly, a very kindly man. . . . We took a trip to Portland, Oregon, for a première, and someone said, 'Let's go out and see the salmon.' So I had a camera, a cine-camera, with me, and there were some big falls where the salmon would jump up, and Stan said, 'Well, Hatley, there's a salmon, start shooting.' And I said, 'I don't see any salmon. Those fish are black.' So he got a big laugh out of that because that's actually black skin on the salmon, and when they can them, it's pink, you know."

Their short comedies were now advertised on *moviehouse marquees* along with the feature, and the next logical step was to put them into a feature of their own. But Stan especially was exhausted by the gruelling schedule of that year and asked for a few weeks off.

The truth was that Stan's work and his dedication to it had kept him from a normal home life for months. A permanent strain had developed between him and Lois, and the only way in which he knew he could maintain his delicate equilibrium was as a married man. Something had to be done quickly. The breach between them was far too wide to be resolved by a few gentle words and an ingratiating manner. So he told her that he was taking her to Hawaii on "a second honeymoon". In actual fact, they had never had a first, since Stan had been working for Roach without a break since the time of their wedding.

Before they sailed, Stan decided that the décor which Lois had chosen for their Bedford Drive home was partially to blame for his wretched moods there. According to Alice Cooke, it had the look of a medium-priced furnished flat, possibly the result of Lois's search for bargains. Stan called in Barker Brothers, a reputable department store in Los Angeles, and asked them to do the place over from his study to the nursery.

At Waikiki, Stan and Lois talked long and candidly about all that had come between them. Lois understood Stan better than anyone, but she said that she was weary of being "the understanding wife". She exacted promises from him that it would be better than that when they got back home. As proof of his good intentions, when he and Lois got back to Beverly Hills, she was pregnant again.

The Bedford Drive house had been redone in French Provincial and Stan complained to friends that Lois was a little too impressed with it. She encouraged him and his cronies to steer clear of the living-room except for those rare occasions when they had a formal gathering. Lois outdid "Craig's Wife" in her fastidiousness and Stan's hope that the new décor would elevate his spirits were dashed.

The only hope left for them was the birth of their second child. Stan was so convinced that it was going to be a boy, he began discussing plans for "Stan, Jr."

By all accounts, it was not an easy pregnancy. The toll of the past four years with Stan had undermined Lois's sweetness of temper to such an alarming degree that Stan sometimes confused her with his screen wives. Her nerves, too, were beginning to go; she was seldom amused. Lois must have realized before the child was born that the advent of another baby into the household could not possibly change Stan's character or habits. She felt a sense of hopelessness about it all. There were still those prolonged drinking bouts, sudden silences that might extend for a day or two, rumours and occasional physical evidence of other women, leading only to one dreary conclusion. Stan, again an expectant father, was hopelessly miscast in real life as a husband.

Stanley Robert Jefferson was born in Hollywood Hospital at 7.38 on the evening of 7 May 1930. Although he was "born alive", as his birth certificate reads, he was two months premature. Dr E. J. Krahnlik, who assisted at the delivery, did not encourage the parents to hope very strongly for survival. In the hospital incubator, Stan Jr. had to fight a host of problems that were allied to his prematurity. In that day, "preemies" did not stand the chance that they do today. Incidentally, it is significant that Stan told the registrar of births that he was a writer first and then an actor.

Dr Lou Earle, a specialist, was called in, but on the baby's sixth day of life, haemorrhaging began in the brain. That crushed whatever wisp of hope Stan held forever. Survival would now mean a mentally deficient child. He went home and drank himself into insensibility.

Nine-day old Stanley Robert Jefferson (Stan did not change his name to "Laurel" by court petition until 1934) died on 16 May. Stan, who could never bear even to attend a friend's funeral, wanted the entire episode erased from his mind and insisted upon cremation.

Meanwhile, Metro had begun production of a lavishly-mounted musical, *The Rogue Song*, a vehicle designed to carry Metropolitan opera star Lawrence Tibbett to the giddier heights of film stardom. Tibbett was to make six musicals in as many years, but he never won the kind of movie fame that was his in opera. Irving Thalberg felt that some of the onus or snob status of opera could be dissipated by the inclusion of some comic relief and proposed that Laurel and Hardy be added (this after the entire script was shot). There was no need for a contract of loan; Roach was already working for Metro.

The boys shot their scenes in the space of about ten days, and Tibbett was brought back for their single scene together.

It was now accepted around Metro that Stan and Ollie enjoyed an international popularity that was second to none among Metro's numerous superstars. Neither Garbo, Beery, Dressler, Shearer, Crawford nor any of the Barrymores was as widely known and admired. Gable was just beginning his career. But, unfortunately, in the final version of *The Rogue Song*, there was no place for Stan and Ollie. They were cast as comic actors, their identities changed if not totally concealed. In the revised film, they played Murza-Bek (Ollie) and Ali-Bek (Stan), two Russian sidekicks of a singing bandit (Tibbett). It was also a grave error having them directed by actor Lionel Barrymore, who had become a director with the very first talkies that were made by his studio (*Confession, Madame X,* 1929). After making several attempts to tell the team what to do in their first scene, Barrymore threw up his hands and told them that he didn't know the first thing about their kind of comedy. Hal Roach was called in to stage their scenes. Parenthetically, *The Rogue Song* utilized a primitive two-colour Technicolor process that was introduced commercially in a sequence of a Marion Davies film, *Lights of Old Broadway*, produced in 1924.

When *The Rogue Song* was released, there was some carping from the critics about the incongruity of Tibbett raising his considerable voice in defiant melody at the same time as being stripped to the waist, spread-eagled between two posts and whipped viciously. Nearly everyone was pleased that Stan and Ollie were in the cast, and the film did better than Tibbett's subsequent films. Since it is only during the past decade that intensive efforts have been made to secure and preserve prints of all films made during this rich period of early sound, *The Rogue Song* was destroyed by Metro during a house-cleaning some years back. No known print exists anywhere in the world.

Stan was unable to work for nearly three months following the death of Stan Jr and, Roach for a change, was all compassion. Although the obvious solution was to persuade him to go immediately into a film and lose himself in his work, Roach had problems enough without having to cope with Stan's drinking on the set, which, under the circumstances, he was certain to do. Charley Chase was having grave difficulties staying on the wagon at the same time. Roach must have wished mightly that he had not been unlucky enough to have two alcoholics as his major stars.

Disaster was also hounding Stan's old producer, Fred Karno. In January 1930, when Karno's numerous misjudgments, frivolities – including a huge pleasure-dome on the Thames called *Karsino*, into which the public could wander for a generous admission charge – and personal indulgences had driven him into bankruptcy, he caught the next boat to America. He had been told that the Marx Brothers could use his comedy ideas and if that didn't work out, he felt sure he could make a deal with a former colleague Jesse Lasky, who was then a major figure in motion picture production. But Karno's troubles, like his fame two decades earlier, had preceded him and, without a proper agent, there was no way he could get in touch with the Marx Brothers; Lasky was always "out".

Karno bought a second-hand car and drove to California where he looked up the supreme creation of his music-hall days Charlie Chaplin. Charlie was tactfully gracious and played an organ concert for him for two hours, then took his discoverer (Chaplin in a dinner jacket, Karno in a brown business suit) to a very late dinner at Marion Davies's beach palace in Santa Monica. But Charlie was evasive all evening about a place for Karno at his studio. In desperation, after exhausting every other possibility, Karno turned to Stan, who really owed him no favours. Stan persuaded Hal Roach to hire Karno for a few months "to see what he comes up with and learn the ropes".

Having failed to come up with a single idea that Roach could use, Fred Karno was released from his contract in June. Stan felt pity for the man whom he had once considered omnipotent. It gave him pause for thought. As they shook hands upon Karno's departure, Stan saw as distinctly as ever he would how fickle Dame Fame could be – but there was no time to brood.

The Laurel and Hardy Murder Case began shooting in late July. In a setting that seemed to have been drawn directly from a Richard Dix success of the previous December, *Seven Keys to Baldpate*, the boys are placed under house arrest by a city detective for the murder of a millionaire named Laurel when they arrive to claim Stan's "legacy". The victim may or may not have been Stan's uncle, the true relationship being of no real consequence since it turns out to be a nightmare of Stan's as he sleeps while fishing. Audiences were still easily frightened by screams in the night, squeaking doors and unknown footfalls in that second year of total sound, and the comedy remains one of the team's most successful.

Stan and Babe finally made their first feature, *Pardon Us*, in the late spring and early summer of 1931. It was directed by George Marshall, who was to guide W. C. Fields through his classic *You Can't Cheat an Honest Man* and revive Marlene Dietrich's career with *Destry Rides Again* in 1939.

Stan had previously resisted the full-length film, understandably afraid that audiences would not go along with an hour of their nonsense. The story was almost as slight as some of their two-reelers and far less detailed in its story construction and gag-work than a three-reeler such as *Another Fine Mess*. It cast Stan and Ollie as bootleggers who accidentally sell a bottle of beer to a policeman. They are imprisoned, but Stan's main problem while in stir seems to be dental, not penal. Whenever he tries to speak, a cavity in one of his back teeth buzzes, causing the warden, a tough cell-mate and others to think that he is giving them a Bronx cheer. One of the most amusing sequences occurs when Stan visits the prison dentist, who turns out to be criminally incompetent. The previous patient is wheeled out through the waiting room *in extremis*.

Everyone at Roach and all of Stan's friends knew by the end of 1931 that his marriage was in a state of crisis. Roach was alarmed because he sensed disaster for the team should Stan be shattered by a divorce. It seemed important to know just what Stan's true feelings for Lois were, but not even Stan could articulate that – and certainly not to Roach. One began to suspect that Stan required a wife who was stronger-willed than he was, who could manage his life for him or at least keep it on an even keel. Mae had had some of this quality and had managed to hang on for ten years. Lois was acquiescent or resentful except where money was concerned.

Stan's feelings for her began to seem less loving and more guilt-ridden.

Stan's work was affected; he was no longer a fount of gag ideas and comedy situations. The condition turned out to be contagious and creative doldrums set in at the gag-room sessions on the Roach lot. Finally, early in 1932, in desperation, one of the gag-writers proposed that they remake *Hats Off* (a silent, 1927), substituting a piano for the washing machine. In that early film, the boys are washing-machine salesmen who carry one of their demonstrating machines up a terrace of perhaps a hundred steps to a prospect's house high on a Hollywood hill.

The Music Box, chronicling a similar, needless climb (it turns out that a back road leads to the rear of the house), was an inspired piece of work. It is the purest example we have of the Laurel and Hardy formula – futility aggravated by a total lack of appreciation of their inept efforts. The hilltop home belongs to Billy Gilbert, the sneezing fat man with a temper as fearful as Jimmy Finlayson's or Edgar Kennedy's, who claims that he hates pianos and chops it up only to discover that his wife, arriving too late to prevent the assault, has bought it for him as a birthday present. The three-reeler won an Academy Award as the best *live action* short subject of 1932. The Disney Era had begun, and Walt was raking in an award or two every year from this time onwards. Stan considered the comedy the finest of their shorter works.

Roach was so gratified by the award that he decided to give the team a respite from their obligatory comedy-a-month schedule and permitted them to make a personal appearance tour of Europe, where their popularity was even greater than in America. In July 1932, they sailed for England, Babe taking his wife Myrtle along as she seemed close to a breakdown over his mistress Viola. The two men were having much the same problem at the same point in time, echoing a coda that appeared in Stan's life when he and Chaplin were associates; they were having little to do with each other socially (except for the fact that Chaplin was sharing lodgings with Stan to save money at one point), while their private difficulties were running parallel courses. Both Stan and Chaplin were heroically ambitious and personal attachments were secondary. Stan and Babe both sought domestic serenity, yet were equally trapped by its demands.

For Stan, the tour was a rescue from the morass; for Babe, it provided a chance to keep his marriage partner from further hurt and humiliation. Lois Laurel was apparently too upset by the impasse with Stan to go anywhere but to her home town of Santa Cruz.

9 || Surprised by World Fame

1   When Laurel and Hardy docked at Cobh in Ireland, there were thousands of fans struggling for a glimpse of them at the pier, and the church bells in the city beyond were playing the Coo-Koo Song! Sheltered in a very real sense by the Roach studio, they had no notion that their fame was so pervasive.

Moving on to London, they appeared at the Empire Theatre – one of that most important chain of variety houses controlled by Moss Empire where Stan had made his adult début in his father's *Home from the Honeymoon* sketch in Birmingham – and the queues in front of the house stretched for blocks. En route to that engagement, Stan and Babe had their first intimation that admirers can be terrifying. A mob of fans converged upon their limousine and tore off the door. They attended a performance of Noel Coward's *Cavalcade* and the tumult around them only subsided when the curtain went up and Coward's pageant of the British colonial empire was under way.

Home again in the Glasgow of Stan's youth, thirty people were rushed to the hospital from the crush at the station. The tour was no longer even remotely a vacation from the strain of all those films for Roach – it was becoming a struggle for survival against forces they never dreamed existed! Screaming fans bore in upon Babe and nearly suffocated him and bobbies were having to surround them continually. At one point, their limousine was picked up and carried by a dozen impulsive members of a massive, cheering mob. It seemed madness to both of them. It was as though their earlier dreams of great fame had become nightmares in which the world suddenly discovered they were the greatest living comedians. They couldn't know that Chaplin had gone through much the same thing every time he travelled away from Hollywood. Even the gentlemanly bobbies were overwhelmed at times by the size and hysteria of the crowds.

Stan's father and the last Mrs Jefferson, Stan's step-mother Venitia, met them at the boat in Southampton and travelled with them for several days. The reunion was not too successful. Stan had not seen his father for over twenty years, an impossible bridge of time. A. J. had the insight to realize that he had lost his son to the world, but he was enormously proud. That pride and A. J.'s deference to Stan, whatever he said or proposed, worked against any resumption of close ties.

Stan and Babe expressed a hope that people would be more civilized on the continent, but in France, the frenzy was repeated. They had looked forward to seeing the familiar landmarks: the Louvre, a glimpse of the Seine, Napoleon's tomb. But only the Eiffel Tower could defy the multitudes crushing against them. Evidence of the world's affection went beyond reassurance – it was out of control. Interestingly, the mobs seemed more drawn to Babe than to Stan in wanting to touch him, to know for themselves that he was flesh and blood. They ripped his jacket, tore off one of his shoes.

When the six weeks ended, the Hardys and Stan felt almost giddy with relief that they were aboard ship again. Shipboard decorum forbade mob scenes and they were largely left alone. While Stan later swore that he never so much as glanced at a woman during their wild, triumphant tour, and indeed women and men were mostly vast seas of joyous faces around them, by the time of their departure for New York, he had had quite enough of celibacy.

In the seclusion of his first-class state-room with its private deck, Stan once again "got involved". Her name was Renée, and, not surprisingly, she had a French accent, although her home was in

Houston. She had come to his door for an autograph and he had invited her in for a champagne cocktail.

Lois met the boat in New York, as they had agreed. It is conceivable that the long absence had changed his attitude and revived some spark of his old feeling for her, but Stan only seemed to see a woman who was a little bored, more than a little tired, a wife who was waiting because that was what was expected of her.

She immediately sensed his uneasiness, and on the train west she asked, "Is there another woman?"

"Yes," he told her. "I met a French girl and I think I'm in love with her."

Lois could not have been shocked. It was a repeat performance that only reinforced her conviction that Stan was still a little boy, that there was no hope that he would ever mature. She proposed that Stan get the young woman an apartment and live with her until he tired of her. She knew that it was inevitable that he would. Then, to minimize the cost of such an episode, she suggested that he put Renée to work as an extra in Roach's studio so she would be at least partially self-supporting. All of that was done.

Such a design for living was foredoomed. Stan was torn between Renée and Lois. His wife's practicality drove him to near distraction, but her undeniable sweetness was always there, like a conscience or virtue. The time he spent with Renée was something separate, impure and sinful. Stan never could shake off his Lancashire morality, no matter what he did. And there was baby Lois.

Roach, Ben Shipman and everyone else involved with Stan's career were afraid that he would leave Lois permanently and marry Renée, but Stan insisted that there wasn't a chance of that. "How could I marry a girl who'd sleep with me the first night I met her?" he would ask.

Within a few months, Stan eased himself out of Renée's life and attempted a firm reconciliation with Lois. Life had altered considerably for them during the past few months, changed as sharply by Stan's surprising world celebrity as by his fling with Renée. He bought a long, elegant Pierce Arrow car and hired an old vaudeville crony as chauffeur. He gave away his bicycle.

·   ·   ·   ·   ·

·

2 Stan was swept by alternating moods of doubt and relief. He had a family again, but he began to feel trapped. He fell into long silences and often, when tension became almost palpable, he picked up his gold-lettered overnight bag and disappeared. When he returned, there was a pretence of normality.

Then he began disappearing for days at a time without the overnight bag and Lois instinctively knew that he had gone back to Alyce's, where he kept a small wardrobe. This time around, Lois said "Enough".

Alyce was given up for the moment, but that only led to his becoming temporarily involved with yet another woman, perhaps in the belief that there was safety in strangers. He said some years later that he believed Lois had detectives following him. Under the circumstances, it is not unlikely.

The strain was harder on Lois than on Stan. At least he could get out of the house – all too frequently – to the studio or a hotel or a girlfriend's apartment. But Lois had a small child and a large home to run. She was looking after their finances and attempting to keep them solvent, and it wasn't easy. Close friends thought that she was beginning to go under.

When Stan was home, he and Lois were seldom alone. He was bringing a number of Roach writers to his study there in Beverly Hills and they would thrash out their problems on the film. Sometimes he would leave them suddenly to walk alone in the adjoining garden. Charlie Rogers and others had learned to read his moods expertly and these solitary strolls went unremarked.

At least once, after going off on one of his "sinful" week-ends and coming home exhausted, he began to weep and told Lois that he thought he must have something wrong with his mind. He had a curious belief that people who felt compelled to "sin" were out of their minds. A psychiatrist named Dr Parkins was called in to examine him, and Stan saw him several times over a period of three weeks. It was Dr Parkins' conclusion that he was over-tired, had no tolerance for alcohol and should abstain, but he was definitely not crazy.

Then Stan moved out of the North Bedford Drive house and into a suite at the Beverly-Wilshire. It was a kindness to both parties. He hadn't wanted the prolonged marital crisis to lead to this, certainly not consciously, but there was a strong element of self-destruction in Stan and, perhaps to prevent having to face up to this insight into himself, the serious drinking began again. His physical appearance on screen during this period (the spring of 1933) was affected. Even clown white could not entirely obscure the signs of anxiety and dissipation. His pranks on the lot were strained and were no longer simple hi-jinks. His stand-in Ham Kinsey had been leery about him ever since a recent episode when Stan had had him elevated on a wire high above the set in a rig used for "flying" actors and then ordered everyone to lunch. Ham had hung there alone for fifteen minutes. Stan was humoured in his unpredictable behaviour because he was a great star, but he was less gentle on himself. He later said that he knew that he had muffed his one chance at achieving some serenity at the top.

Ben Shipman met Lois's attorney and a settlement was hammered out. She was to receive the Beverly Hills home, two $100,000 trusts, and support for herself and their daughter. Through her astute management, this settlement would eventually grow to more than a million dollars, making Lois the wealthiest of all the Laurel wives, her fortune exceeding Stan's several times over by the time of his death.

Stan's only comment on the break-up was published in *Movie Classic* magazine:

When two people reach the place in life where they can no longer share a laugh together, then it is practically impossible to share the same bed and board. Laughter is not a trivial part of married life. To the contrary, it is very important. Neither my wife nor I considered the idea of divorce lightly. We have a little five-year-old daughter and for her sake, as well as our own, we both sincerely attempted to make a go of our marriage. . . . We reached the point where we were continually getting on each other's nerves. I'm sure that nothing I did was very amusing to my wife. When we were first married, little annoying things that we both might do were laughed off and forgotten. But in the past year we seem to have lost that saving grace of humour. When we realized that we had reached the point where we could no longer laugh together, then there was nothing else to do – difficult though it was for us both – but legally separate.

All of this sounded very logical and intelligent, and much of it was true, but if left out the most important element that would haunt Stan for years – he was convinced and he told others time and again that Lois was his true love and that he had lost the most precious thing in his life. Some of his friends and ex-wife Ruth believed that he never recovered from this loss.

3   During a film, Stan and Babe shared a camaraderie that was infectious. In the long breaks, they would pull a barber shop quartet together, with Charley Chase as baritone. Until his departure in 1930, Leo McCarey was on the piano; after that, it was sometimes Marvin Hatley. Stan was particularly fond of a Billy Rose ballad, "Little Old Lady (Passing By)":

> Little old lady passing by,
> Catching everyone's eye. . . .
> You are like that little old lady
> I hold dear to me.

It made little sense as a lyric, but it contained the kind of sentiment of which Stan was especially fond. The crew would gather around and listen with enormous enjoyment – both Chase and Babe had excellent voices. Stan had a trick voice, ranging from a phony deep bass to a high falsetto. Roach began thinking of ways in which this talent might be utilized on screen.

When the last shot was done, Babe would say goodbye and rush off to the golf course for a few holes before dark. Telephone conversations between Babe and Stan were rare. There was little socializing between them except at Roach affairs or by accident, unless something was set up by the publicity department. It was altogether a professional association, and yet there was such profound respect in each man for the other that the distancing off-camera seemed almost too deliberate, as though they feared closeness might spoil their act.

By this time, Roach was having every Laurel and Hardy film shot in four languages. They were not dubbed; they were completely redone in German, Italian, Spanish and French. Stan and Ollie read their few lines from phonetics on a blackboard that were held out of camera range like the idiot cards used by John Barrymore. These foreign versions were hugely successful and Metro, Roach's distributor, decided to do the same with all of their major productions. But despite their international celebrity, the films of Joan Crawford, Garbo, the Barrymores, Norma Shearer and Marie Dressler were not the guaranteed successes that every Laurel and Hardy comedy turned out to be. The cost of their failures – in four languages – fast became prohibitive and the practice was stopped.

The four-language system did prevail, however, through the production of *The Devil's Brother* (Fra Diavolo) in 1933, helping to make that operetta, with Dennis King in the title role, the most successful Laurel and Hardy film ever made in commercial terms. As late as the 1960s, there were long queues in Paris and Milan to see the French and Italian versions in re-release. As Stanlio and Ollie, they are robbed of their life savings in an Italian mountain pass. They immediately decide to become bandits themselves (cast so consistently outside the Establishment, they were frequently outside the law as well), their first victim being a woodcutter, who recounts such a catalogue of misfortune that the boys unhesitatingly turn over *to him* the few coins left in their pockets. Their charity quickly turns to shock and disgust when they see him in the distance adding their small change to a huge bag of gold. Emboldened by a flash of cynicism, they pretend to be the notorious Fra Diavolo and his henchman when the next stranger comes along, Ollie singing the refrain that is the much-feared bandit's trademark. But Ollie forgets part of the lyric and their intended victim finishes it for him. It is Fra Diavolo himself (Dennis King), who, happily, has a sense of humour and allows them to come into his ring of Italian merrymen.

Inexplicably, Stan was unhappy throughout the filming of this musical. He had numerous quarrels with Roach about the story, which was written by a woman, Jeanie MacPherson, hired by Roach to adapt the 1830 comic opera by Daniel Auber. Their leading lady, Thelma Todd, frequently attempted to cheer up Stan and sometimes succeeded. She had a bawdy sense of humour and was often in some difficulty over a boyfriend, which she would confide to Stan, punctuating her tale of amorous misadventure with laughter. When *Fra Diavolo* turned out to be one of the best comic operas ever translated into screen terms, Stan subsided permanently as critic of Roach's story sense, although they would continue to argue over details.

10 ‖ The Advent of Baby Ruth

1   In the spring of 1933, Virginia Ruth Rogers, a slender blond widow of twenty-nine, went over to Catalina Island for a week of fun with a girlfriend, Gladys. Ruth was a beauty; she was often taken for Marion Davies, but she had something of a lady clown's face along the lines of Giulietta Masina with a naturally broad mouth that smiled easily. Of mixed Scandinavian-German descent, she was a strange mixture of high principle and infectious gaiety. She projected an improbable sort of innocence and good breeding, and she had some doubts about the propriety of going with Gladys. Her girlfriend was frankly looking to be picked up by some available male.

The girlfriends made the short crossing from the mainland aboard a big white steamer. In those days, much was made of arrivals and leis were tossed at new arrivals; the Catalina Tourist Bureau made a large effort to persuade visitors that coming to Avalon was the next best thing to a trip to Honolulu. As the steamer approached its berth, they passed a small sloop with two men aboard. The men were wearing yachting caps, and the skinnier one, Stan, had a megaphone. Pulling his famous ear-to-ear grin, he waved to the young women at the rail and yelled into the megaphone: "Hi, there! How are you?"

Ruth told Gladys she thought they might be "official greeters". Gladys, thrilled by such luck so early, didn't encourage Ruth in her naïveté and said, "Those boys know how to get first dibs."

On the sloop, Stan's companion Bill Seiter, who was then also his director on *Sons of the Desert*, gave them a salute. Stan told him, "I'll take the redhead," meaning Gladys, and Seiter good-naturedly agreed. "The blonde's fine with me," he said. "She looks like my wife." Seiter was separated at the time from actress Laura LaPlante, who had just been nudged from her throne as reigning queen of Universal Studios by a husky-voiced young upstart from Broadway, Margaret Sullavan.

The men were waiting for the girls when the ship docked. Seiter introduced himself and then said, "This is Mr Laurel." Neither of the girls connected this "Mr Laurel" with Laurel and Hardy. For one thing, Seiter was not fat; he was rather handsome with dark, wavy hair. And Stan, too, had a certain breezy flash about him. "How about some lunch with us on the sloop?" they asked.

Ruth didn't want to go: her mother had told her often enough, "Never go off with a stranger." But Gladys already had one foot in the dinghy that would take them out to the sloop, so Ruth didn't want to be a spoil-sport. "We had a nice lunch," Ruth recalled, "and Stan took some pictures with a little Brownie he had. He also happened to mention that he was getting a divorce." Somehow while they were eating, the men had switched partners. Stan made no bones about his preference for Ruth and even leaned over once and kissed her on the cheek. She blushed, and he thought that was very funny.

Another boatload of tourists passed them slowly and several kids at the stern-rail recognized Stan. They grimaced and scratched their hair like monkeys. Stan echoed their gestures, enjoying it hugely and at that moment, it dawned on Ruth who Stan was. She had read something in the papers the previous week about his divorce case. She couldn't remember the details but she thought it was on the messy side. "I don't want to get mixed up in that," she decided.

Over the next several days, Stan and Seiter appeared several times at the St Catherine Hotel where they were staying and chatted with Ruth and Gladys. Ruth was polite but declined to go out with Stan. With reason, Gladys began to wish that she had come alone.

By Saturday night, it looked very much as though the girls were going to be alone for the evening when Stan and the director showed up again, accompanied by a third man. The men told Ruth and her friend that they were on their way to a cocktail party aboard a doctor's yacht and invited them to go along. Ruth again demurred, to Stan's obvious disappointment and Gladys' further annoyance. In fact, Gladys seemed about to wring Ruth's neck, but the men politely went off without them. Gladys asked Ruth why she didn't want to go, telling her, "I thought we came over here for a good time." But Ruth explained that she didn't drink and that even though Stan was a big celebrity, "we can't say we really know him. I don't like to go out at night on a yacht because they might not bring us back." So the ladies strolled casually along the promenade, and within a few minutes Gladys picked up a good-looking fellow wearing a navy yachting uniform with cap. He suggested that they all walk out on the pier attached to the hotel. Ruth noticed they were alone, no one was strolling about or fishing "and there was a gangplank going down. And the man who was with Gladys seemed to have two sailors in white uniforms and funny little caps waiting for him below on board a motor launch . . . I guess he gave them a signal because they grabbed me and rushed me down the gangplank and evidently Gladys had agreed to go with him because she said, 'Oh, Ruth!' when I told them I didn't want to go. Then she said, 'Oh, shut up! We'll just go out and have coffee and a sandwich. He'll bring us back.' But I wasn't convinced. I was sure that was the way they shanghaied girls. Then we passed the other yacht and Stan and Bill Seiter saw us, but we were headed out for a big ocean-going vessel, way out past the breakwater."

Ruth told her abductor that if he didn't take her back to the boat they just passed, she was going to jump overboard, even though she couldn't swim. The uniformed man then began to swear at her and said she was a bitch, but her words must have frightened him (Ruth said the man was Louis B. Mayer's son-in-law William Goetz, a founder of Twentieth Century-Fox Pictures). He ordered the sailor at the helm to turn the launch around and go back to the doctor's yacht. Stan, wearing a yachting cap, came running out from the salon, a drink in his hand. "Ruthie, what happened?" he asked. Ruth was semi-hysterical by this time and told him that she had been shanghaied. Although the scene might have been lifted from a Roach comedy and Stan was doubtless, in the back of his mind, considering what might be done with it, he took her by the hand and led her back to a deck-chair. He saw that she wasn't up to the party aboardship and gallantly offered to row the girls back to shore. Naturally, Gladys considered Ruth a very soggy blanket indeed by this time and, on the way back, told Stan, "She's so naïve." She couldn't know that this trait in a grown woman in Hollywood was greatly appealing to Stan.

That was the beginning of Stan's relationship with Ruth Rogers, doubtless the most significant of all his feminine alliances since in the immediate months ahead lay his greatest achievements as a performer. However misguided their marriage, it saw Stan's genius come to full flower. For nearly three years, he was able to relax around Ruth, keep most of his interior demons at bay and the creative juices flowing. She tried her best to remain on the sidelines, but an occasional suggestion of hers would find its way into Stan's comedy. She kept insisting that he and Babe do a comedy western and the story of *Way Out West* evolved while they were together, but she was out of his life by production time. The least of her achievements was that she made them a sought-after social couple, invited to the Thalbergs, hosting the liveliest table at the Mayfair Ball, their rose garden pictured in the photo section of the Sunday paper. It is only fair to give this delicate blonde from Watts her due since the great comedies and Stan Laurel as a man of consequence in Hollywood society developed during her years with Stan. There was probably an element of strain in Stan as a social animal. He was far more comfortable in his own home or in a bar. Still, he persuaded himself that all of this was fine at the time, "the happiest years of my life", he was to tell Ruth.

Sometimes he would rebel, and Ruth numbly acquiesced in the rebellion. He suggested one weekend that they should go to Catalina, and once there, insisted that they stay at a second-class hotel and not at the St Catherine. They were taken up to a room with faded wallpaper and a tattered rug on the floor. The bathroom was not spotless. It was the kind of hotel room in which he had lived with Mae for years on end, and he doubtless wanted to remind himself that such places existed both for those on the way up and those on the way down. It says something for Ruth's character that she silently shared this room, knowing that there was more comfortable accommodation aboard their fishing yacht anchored next to the Tuna Club.

Much of the time, Stan's pleasure at being married to a lady with a sense of humour was visible and infectious; it found its way into the camera and is still with us. *Them Thar Hills* (1933), *Babes in Toyland* (1934), films that were among Stan's own favourites were coming out one after the other.

Ruth was meanwhile running a successful women's dress shop called Rosemarie. She modelled the dresses herself, mostly for buyers from retail stores in the Los Angeles area, and sold them wholesale. Since Stan's marital and financial problems were both unsettled – and hopelessly intertwined, of course – there was no possibility that they could marry until he was legally free to do so. His vast earnings (he was then making $3500 a week) were going towards legal fees and the huge settlement into which he had been forced. When informed by lawyer Ben Shipman that his salary for the next five or six months might be tapped as well, Stan angrily declared "I'll go on strike."

According to Ruth, this is exactly what he did. There were no Laurel and Hardy comedies released between *Fra Diavolo* (May 1933) and *The Midnight Patrol* (August 1933). As might be expected, idleness was never a state that Stan could handle with any profit. His anger would subside and he would then fret over the finality of it all, saying that he really loved Ruth, but he still loved Lois too. This agonizing indecision rent him for days, reaching a climax one afternoon when Ruth received a phone call from Shipman, who asked her to rush over to the Roosevelt Hotel. It is the only known instance when Ben Shipman asked a favour of Ruth. Relations between the two were always strained. She was busy with her designers and told Ben that she would have to know just why it was so urgent. Ben then told her that Stan had just got his divorce papers and he was trying to jump out of the window.

"I've got a doctor here," Ben said anxiously, "and one of his buddies from vaudeville, and I wish you'd come out here and see if we can calm him down."

Ruth got into her Willys coupé and dashed across town to the

Roosevelt on Hollywood Boulevard. When she walked into the room, Stan was standing with his hands in his pockets and his shirt-tail hanging out. Baldy Cooke was there, Dr Parkins and Ben Shipman.

"Well, Baby Ruth," Stan said, "how did you know I was here?" Ruth was too upset to answer, but Stan seemed to bounce back to normal almost immediately, and he asked Ben, the doctor and Baldy to leave them alone. Ben, whose investment in Stan was considerable and who was now one of his closest friends, was reluctant to leave. Ruth felt that Ben didn't trust her with such a sensitive assignment. She was convinced that he was a misogynist even though he was married at the time. John McCabe, who got to know Ben well through Stan for a period of more than twenty years, agreed that Ben disliked Ruth, but not women generally and cited his long vigil beside his invalid wife, followed by a happy marriage to his secretary.

Baldy knew that there was no love lost between Ruth and Ben, saw what was happening and resolved the matter by telling Shipman and Dr Parkins that he would see them outside, that he had something to say to Ruth. After the two men had gone, he told her: "It's the most remarkable thing! We were grabbing him by the shirt-tail and pulling him away from the window . . ."

Ruth recalled that Stan had never been "sweeter" to her. "He ordered dinner," she said. "And then we played all kinds of silly games. He had just made *Fra Diavolo* and there were hand games in it – nosies, earsies, kneesies, and you'd pat your knees and touch your ears and pinch your nose."

Stan, having lost the Bedford Drive home to Lois in the divorce, had moved into a rented house on Palm Drive in Beverly Hills and had asked younger brother Everett, known as "Teddy", his wife Betty and her two sons to share it with him. Teddy, who had once toured in tent shows but was really more enthusiastic about cars than he was about the theatre or movies, was a chauffeur for the Ambassador Hotel manager. Pete Gordon and a black cook named Tomasina were the only members of Stan's household staff to accompany him.

Within a few weeks of the Roosevelt Hotel incident, Teddy went down with a bad toothache, and Stan sent him to a dentist who had a large clientele among the stars. An extraction was planned and Teddy was given a form of anaesthetic known as laughing gas. For reasons still unknown, he died in the dentist's chair of heart failure.

Ruth remained close to Stan throughout the next week – the funeral arrangements, his brother's burial. Stan himself avoided the services, but when they were over friends were invited back to the Palm Drive house for drinks. He said, "That's what we do in England." Ruth was hostess, although Stan's grief did not incapacitate him. He told Ruth that he believed in reincarnation. "How could children who come on stage and perform as though they had been performing for years," he asked, "how could they perform? They *have* to learn it in another life. After all, what's so different from the miracle of being born once and being born many times?"

Teddy was buried on a rainy day and it turned into a downpour as Ruth was driving home to Watts in her Willys Overland. Water was coming up above her running board, so she turned round and returned to Palm Drive. Stan was drinking heavily, which was no surprise. He seemed relieved to see her and said, "I'm having trouble. Betty (Teddy's widow) told me to forget about you and said she'd be my sweetheart and she's been trying to get in bed with me. Can you stay all night?"

Once again, Stan's life began to assume the outlines of a Roach comedy. Shocked by his sister-in-law's advances, he invited his fiancée to spend the night "to protect him".

Ruth, who seemed to have a patent on virginity, explained that "there were four bedrooms (occupied by a widow, her two sons and Stan) so it was all right." In the morning, Stan gave Betty Jefferson some money to get relocated.

Roach and his executive breathed a corporate sigh of relief when Stan made it clear that he was going to marry Ruth. He always cost them money when he was footloose, since that was when the binges began, no one ever quite knew where he was, and delays mounted on his pictures. Although Ruth was a far gayer spirit than Lois had been, she would not allow herself to be talked into "living in sin" with Stan before his divorce became final. She said "that would just kill mother".

Finally, Stan asked Alice and Baldy Cooke to move into the Palm Drive house to chaperone, so with that arrangement set up, Ruth moved in permanently. Stan told the Cookes that he wanted them to come overnight just to satisfy Ruth and that he was sure they could leave after that. But, no, Ruth insisted that they should remain until she was properly married and the Cookes could not return to their apartment until three months later. Alice thought it was a considerable imposition on their friendship:

I lost all my friends. And Baldy used to have to go home and feed the cat and bring me a dress every day. But oh the fun we had! My God! Stan had a coloured maid. I didn't have a thing to do but play "lady". But I wanted to go home and un-play lady. Every day we'd hope Stan would say, "Well, we're going to get married, Ruth and I." . . . But they didn't. They kept putting it off, and fighting and everything.

After the first few days of unconnubial bliss, Stan began drinking again. He was still making *Sons of the Desert* with Bill Seiter directing. Luckily, Seiter knew Stan well – they were old fishing buddies on Catalina – so he shot around him. Unhappily, Stan in middle age was a dreadful drunk when he was not in a party mood. Ruth, in her innocence, thought that she could "humour" him when he drank to excess, but on one occasion, when he began chasing her around the house with a carving knife, a more drastic remedy seemed required. Baldy overheard the commotion and came to her rescue, giving her the key to their apartment and telling her to drive there and remain until Stan sobered up.

The next day Stan was washed out, but sober and contrite. He asked Ruth to accompany him to the studio and "just be there". One of the assistant directors took her aside while a long scene was being shot and said to her, "If you can make Stan work like this and finish the picture, I'll bet Roach will put you on salary." This suggests that Roach's troubles with Stan were simmering throughout this period of his and Babe's best screen work. When asked about this, Roach said, "It was the wives", and it is possible that, despite the assistant director's vote of confidence, Ruth was a disappointment to him. He repeatedly said that Stan should never have left Lois and seemed to have forgotten that that marriage had deteriorated over a very long span of time.

The Roach-Stan Laurel relationship was a marriage of disparate

38. As gypsy thieves, Stan and Ollie are demoted to kitchen duty along with their dog, Laughing
Gravy, in *The Bohemian Girl*, 1936
39. Nothing certifies their childlike innocence more than the fact that they always shared the same
bed. Here they snooze in *The Fixer-Uppers*, 1935

Charlie Hall
sprays the boys
with cottage cheese
at the deli counter
in a series of *Tit
for Tat* assaults, 1935
Stan in a rare
guise as Hitler, 1937.
Actress June Collyer
(far left) and wife
Ruth are amused;
the James Hornes
seem occupied with
the menu. Chaplin
had not yet begun
work on *The Great
Dictator*.

41

42. The Fun Factory, a small studio theatre on Stan's estate in the San Fernando Valley, 1939. The bathing beauties are a gag to kid their wives.

43. That same Fun Factory more than twenty years later when it was about to be demolished by orchestra leader/ real estate promoter Horace Heidt. Also saying farewell to the landmark are (from left): Lucille Hardy Price, Eddie Baker, Jane Darwell (seated), Madge Kennedy, Joyce Compton, Francis X. Bushman, Vivian Duncan, Beatrice Kay, Babe London and Chester Conklin.

The boys join the Foreign Legion in *The Flying Deuces* (1939), but seem to have brought their nightgowns along. The sergeant straightens them out.

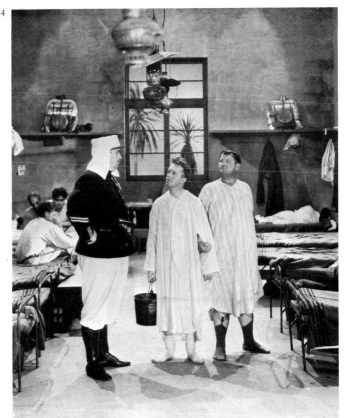

One of their lighter moments in the army in *Great Guns* (1941), their first film for Twentieth Century-Fox. The girl is Sheila Ryan.

46

47

46. Their plots become less amusing as Laurel and Hardy continue with the programmers for Fox. Here, in *A-Haunting We Will Go* (1942), they are threatened by gangsters.

47. Their last Metro film, *Nothing But Trouble* (1945), had them concealing a young king who is fleeing an assassination plot. Their employer, Mary Boland, wants to know who the intruder is.

48. Motorcycle cop Edgar Dearing detains the boys in this scene from *The Big Noise* (1944), their next to last Fox film as their career winds down.

49. The Hal Roach Studios at their busiest in the 1950s

50. In the middle of a skit in an English variety hall, 1952

spirits. Stan had begun to feel that Roach needed him far more than he needed Roach, but there was simply no way that Stan could leave the studio without Babe Hardy. He wanted to believe that he was big enough, important enough, to go it alone if forced to do so. When his contract expired, however, he was practical enough to decide to wait patiently for Babe's to do so some months later. He wanted to make a few personal appearances and thought that perhaps Roach might be generous enough to allow Babe to appear with him. But he was wrong in that expectancy. Hal Roach declared that there would be no joint personal appearances while Stan was challenging the studio. Roach's lawyers advised him that by conceding this, he would give Stan exactly what he wanted – continued public exposure while Hardy's contract ran out.

It is interesting that Roach blames Chaplin more than the earlier defector, Harold Lloyd, for his troubles with Stan. Roach's loyalty to Lloyd was as profound as his uneasiness about Stan. Roach knew that Chaplin and Stan had toured together, that they were rivals then (leading actor and understudy) and still rivals in Stan's mind. He may have known too that Stan was being apprized of Charlie's every professional move through Alf Reeves, Chaplin's studio manager who was remembered as Fred Karno's tour manager in America. Alf and his wife Amy were to remain close to Stan throughout his Hollywood career and get to know all of his wives. He was also Chaplin's source for news about Stan.

Stan often told his friends that there was no reason why Laurel and Hardy couldn't make their own pictures, but Roach was more perceptive than Stan on one point. He believed that Stan had almost no business sense, that he couldn't handle money. If Chaplin found it difficult to part with a dollar, Stan couldn't keep track of where it went. By foiling every attempt by Stan to achieve his freedom, Roach truly believed that he was acting in Stan's own best interests. Very possibly, in the end, Roach was to be proved right.

In his bid for freedom, Stan needed a lion for an agent or manager and he got a pussycat in Ben Shipman. Gentle Ben Shipman would approach actors and backers and say something like: "Would you be interested in . . . ?" He was incapable of the strong-arm tactics of a Myron Selznick or the flamboyant razzle-dazzle of a Leland Hayward even though with Laurel and Hardy he had the most marketable comedy team in the history of show business. His ineffectuality in this area was so great that one suspects collusion, but his friends insist that he was loyal to Stan to the end. It is true, however, that he was forever compromised by having been Roach's lawyer and financial adviser first. When Shipman asked Roach for what the studio head considered absurd and impossible salary increases *and* control over every production, it was a show-down and Stan was the principal loser. Shipman remained Roach's friend, and what he agreed to in private conversation with Roach can never be known. Babe Hardy was sympathetic to Stan but never felt very strongly that he was being underpaid.

While *Sons of the Desert* was in the final stages of shooting in the summer of 1933, Ruth Rogers was between dress seasons at the Rosemarie Shop with some time on her hands, and she accepted Stan's invitation to go out to the Roach Studio each day "and watch Stan make the picture. As a matter of fact," she recalled, "I was in one of the scenes at the steamship office. And Stan got the idea that if I was around he worked better."

None of the Roach staff recalls that this became a custom. Ruth's presence during the shooting of the rest of this movie was more than likely a turnabout – Stan was humouring *her*. He knew he had overstepped the bounds of courtship decorum with that carving knife and he was trying to atone. Still, we get a clear glimpse of the inside of that relationship during one of her visits to the set. Ruth recalled that it was a rain scene:

> It wasn't real rain, but it looked like it. And the boys were on the roof, hiding from their wives. They were hiding because they'd told their wives they were going to Honolulu for Babe's health, but they went to a convention instead, the Sons of the Desert Convention in Chicago. And there they were clowning around in the parade and jigging up to the newsreel camera and just acting silly. Then the wives happened to catch it in a moviehouse. . . . So the boys came home and they're standing outside the door and the wives are still at the picture show, but they don't know that, of course. They've got grass skirts and Hawaiian pineapples and ukeleles and they're singing "Honolulu Baby, Where'd You Get

Those Eyes?" And doing the hula and everything. So when the wives don't answer the door, Babe finds the key and they go inside. There is the daily newspaper with a glaring headline. The ship they were supposed to be on has sunk. Then they hear their wives coming home, so they climb up into the attic, and overhear their wives making all kinds of threats. Finally, they get out on the roof and the rain is blowing and they get soaked. . . . I was waiting off camera with his double, Ham Kinsey, and threw a blanket around him, then we rushed him into his dressing room and I grabbed a bottle of whiskey and put some lemon and sugar in it. You know, a hot toddy. And we had the shower running, and Stan took the hot toddy and started to cry. Then he said, "Baby Ruth, as long as I was married to Lois, she never took an interest in my work. She didn't care what I did. She never treated me this way."

Stan was forever trying to blind himself to Lois's virtues; she had deliberately stayed away from the studio because she didn't want to interfere with Stan's work. As a retired film actress, she knew how vital it was to keep intruders away from any shooting. On the other hand, Ruth had a strong compulsion to be in on everything. She was not aggressive about it, just gently nudging. It was to prove a fatal flaw in her coming marriage or at least give Stan an excuse to turn against her.

Until his retirement, Stan had only one loyalty beyond his friends and hireling buddies and that was to his work. The world is richer for that obsession, but it was hard on the women in his life. Stan once confided to Ruth that he was deeply affected by the disharmony within his parents' home and that of his grandparents. Until his late middle age, he would not have one relationship with a woman that was free of acrimony. His history with women was a long, complicated affair that was to be the most negative element in his private and professional lives. Three of them, Mae and Ruth included and one yet to come, created such havoc that his career was jeopardized. The ladies, of course, insisted that Stan was the impossible one. Until he was close to retirement and his last marriage, he was never with a woman he trusted implicitly. Women, to Stan, were not only mysterious creatures, they were conspiratorial. He countered with secrets great and small, hotel rooms (escape hatches) to which he vanished without a word, and brooding silences.

Sons of the Desert was released in Christmas week 1933, and Stan held open house on Palm Drive. Blond Ruth looked especially fetching in black velvet pyjamas and all of his friends turned up. Advance word on the picture was the most enthusiastic since the boys' classic two-reeler, *Towed in a Hole*, a year earlier. Theatre owner Frank Faust and his wife were much taken with Ruth. Leo McCarey dropped by, and the Cookes were there, wondering if Stan was going to let them have a holiday. It was a warm, affectionate group, and Stan charmed everyone except the studio publicity man. This fellow, after a number of drinks, began fluttering his tie in the manner of Babe Hardy, a gesture which Ollie always used to cover social gaffes or other indecorous situations. Since Babe was not there and not even invited, Stan took exception to this. When the man didn't stop, Stan cut off his tie. He later regretted this extreme measure even though it had won him a round of applause, and he sent his tasteless guest a box of ties.

By mid-January, Ruth had had enough of Stan's temperament. Later, she realized that there was always a tremendous let-down when a film was completed, followed by several days of non-stop boozing. But after taking verbal abuse for an hour or so, and fearing that it might turn physical again, she ran out of the house and refused to come back.

The Cookes were in a quandary. They felt their duties as chaperones were ended when the lady of virtue walked out, but they were afraid to leave Stan alone with just Pete Gordon. Pete was a drinking companion, and whatever Stan did was fine with him. Finally Stan said, "I'm going to call Ruthie." Alice was alone with him at the time, since Baldy had been called to work on a Charley Chase picture.

Stan reached Ruth at her dress business, and asked if she would like to get married. Ruth hesitated, but said many years later that she loved Stan far too much by then to refuse. "Well, it's all settled then," Stan told her. "I'll get hold of Baldy."

Although he was in the middle of a scene, Baldy was told to get over to Stan's house immediately. He drove back from Culver City in a panic, wondering what Stan had done this time. Alice said of that impulsive episode:

Baldy came in – thought something had happened to me, of course. I said, "Everything's all right. We're going to Mexico." So we took a car down to the depot and down we went by train to Tiajuana. Then Stan hired a taxi and we went to Caliente. He reserved two rooms with connecting bath at that gorgeous big hotel down there. And that night, Stan had the justice of the peace come over, a Mexican, and the man brought five others with him. They all had such long faces, so sober, that Baldy broke up. Then the Mexicans started to laugh, too. They laughed right through the ceremony. Afterwards, Stan ordered I don't know how many drinks. But when we finally went to our rooms, the Mexicans kept coming in with more drinks. About seven in the morning, Baldy and I were sound asleep, and Stan woke us up. He said, "Hey, I got a gin fizz for you. . . ." When we got back to Los Angeles, Baldy and I felt free. We said now we can go home, and I started taking our things out of the closet. Stan came in and asked, "What are you doing?" I said, "Why, you and Ruth are married. Now we're going home." "Oh, no, you're not," he told me, and he took everything and hung it back in the closet. He said, "You can't go home and leave us alone because we had such fun together, just the four of us, not until I find a house that I'm going to buy for Ruth." Well, it was two months more finding the house.

2 The house that Stan and Ruth liked best was a small Mediterranean-style villa on Glenbar Avenue in Cheviot Hills. Nearly everyone they knew was invited to inspect the new property before they actually bought it. One evening, Alice and Baldy Cooke, a close friend of Ruth's by the name of Thelma Black and her daughter Beverly, were all driven over after dinner at the Palm Drive house. Baldy regaled them with the balcony scene from *Romeo and Juliet*, utilizing the bedroom balcony and playing both parts. A few minutes later, he reappeared in the back garden with his head sticking out of the kennel, barking.

Cheviot Hills was a fairly new development of luxury homes just minutes west of Culver City, where the Roach Studio was located.

There was a handsome library on the first floor, where Stan could set up his bar and mementoes and work on comedy ideas. The night of the Cookes' inspection, he brought along his ukulele. He knew most of the latest tunes, like "Yes, sir, she's my baby", and he had a repertoire of hundreds of music-hall ballads. One verse from those early days which Ruth recalled was:

A little boy,
A pair of skates,
Broken ice,
Heaven's gates.

There was a sense of taste and even refinement in Ruth. She was a lady of the nineteenth century, always trying rather desperately to seem at home in the looser atmosphere of the twentieth. She succeeded only superficially. She thought of the man of the house as "the breadwinner". Dinners or parties in the Laurel home after Ruth's advent became very formal affairs, but she was a good hostess and often an amusing one. She would prompt Stan into doing turns which she knew he enjoyed performing. She drank moderately and held her alcohol better than most men. She was an expert driver, which Stan was not, and the newly-wed Laurels began collecting cars, having three by the time of their first divorce.

Some of the servants thought she put on airs, but that was just Ruth's manner; she was forever insecure around her social inferiors and sometimes uncertain when with her peers. Some of this stemmed from her origins. She came from a solid middle-class family north of Los Angeles, but her own parents were living with her in Watts, then a lower middle-class area of small bungalows and predominantly white, at the time when Stan was courting her.

Coming from a theatrical family who were, despite his father's success, outcasts socially, Stan saw *class* in everything that Ruth did. He turned over the decorating to her. Leaving nothing to chance, she called in two decorators to assist. She was as improvident as Stan, which did not endear her to the boys' lawyer-manager Ben Shipman, but throughout their marriage, there were few quarrels over finances. When funds ran low, they would do without; then when the money flowed in again, the spending resumed. It was only *after* their first divorce (they were to be married twice, or three times if we are to count the ceremonies) that money became the principal issue.

Stan made only one request when they were decorating the house, and it turned out to be not only expensive but an ingenious way of making the house unmarketable. He had the three bedrooms on the second floor made into one huge suite of a master bedroom, dressing-room and oversize bath. He said that he wanted no overnight guests.

When word of Stan's spending spree reached Lois, according to Ruth, Lois broke a vow to herself and phoned him. The main thrust of that alleged conversation was that she thought it would be wisest if *she* handled his money, an unusual proposal coming from an ex-wife unless it was accompanied by an offer to take him back. Stan and Lois talked for over an hour and Ruth overheard enough to be devastated. But she didn't let on to Stan that she was, and when he hung up, she said, "Stan, if you want to go back to Lois now, you understand you're perfectly free. I won't stop you."

Stan was considerably moved by her surprising generosity. "You're one of a kind," he told her, embracing her and adding, "I don't want her back, Ruth. I want to be with you. You've done everything that makes me happy and I feel better with you. I guess I love her some way, but I still don't want to go back to her."

They had a queen-sized bed, unusual in that day, and the first night they used it, Stan picked up a pair of binoculars, telling Ruth "I'm trying to find you." There were months of little jokes and horseplay. One morning, she woke up to find Stan wearing one of her blue hair ribbons and mugging as he had done in drag on stage with Mae. Ruth appreciated laughter as an essential ingredient of life every bit as much as Stan did. Of all of his wives, Ruth was the most convivial. They sought out friends who shared their high spirits and actress Alice Brady became close to them for a time. Alice was droll and delivered all of her one-liners with the utmost dryness and the straightest of faces.

Since Ruth had learned after several miscarriages that she could never carry a child full-term, they spoke of adoption. Baby Lois began visiting them regularly. The chauffeur would pick her up and she would spend part of a weekend with them. Ruth became very fond of the girl, remaining friends with her for the rest of her days and leaving most of her estate to Stan's daughter upon her death in 1976.

Through all of 1934, they were reasonably content. Ruth endured Stan's tantrums with only a little visible anger. And then it was always "cheer-up" time with flowers, candy and affection. There was a great reservoir of love in Stan, frequently dammed at home, and it flowed endlessly on the set.

If Ruth had realized that she was an episode, perhaps several episodes, and not the focus of Stan's life, the marriage might have been better. It was foredoomed, but it might have lasted longer than it did. Except for Pete Gordon, an ex-vaudevillian giant named Tunney who acted as chauffeur-bodyguard, and a host of down-on-their-luck performers who were maintained in various cheap hotels and boarding houses by Stan and came around regularly for their subsidy, the faces around Stan kept changing. Like a great many men, he was more loyal to his own sex than to women in a non-emotional way. This stemmed not so much from fickle-heartedness as from boredom. Any routine, especially the conventional demands of marriage, bored him to distraction. Children – even his own daughter – got on his nerves if they were around for long. Lois had grasped this, but Ruth never did while they were married.

Sometime in 1935, the Laurels' cook Tomasina left, and they hired Mrs Lillian Burnett, a black lady who had worked for the Hardys until their separation that year. Mrs Burnett is our chief witness to a series of incidents that undermined Stan's marriage to Ruth. She said that Stan was "cool" to Ruth much of the time. She further said that Claude Bostock, Stan's old vaudeville agent, and his wife seemed to be backing Stan up in this freeze-out of Ruth.

Another intriguing detail supplied by Mrs Burnett is that Ruth had a lady detective, a woman named Beulah Siep, staying with her. Ruth would call upon Mrs Siep again several years later for another long assignment. She and Stan were curiously alike in this one detail: they rarely confided in anyone who was not on their pay-roll – whether a detective, a lawyer or – in Stan's case – a crony.

Something serious and permanently harmful to their marriage

had occurred. If we are to pull the contradictory accounts together and make some sense of them, Ruth must have made herself "unavailable" to Stan as a bed-partner on numerous occasions. It went beyond the usual headache and sent Stan into a rage. His first thought was that she had been compatible only to become Mrs Laurel and he told Claude Bostock as much. It was Claude's advice to get rid of her with the least possible damage to his emotions and finances. When he became infatuated with a nineteen-year-old twin sister living in Downey, Bostock encouraged it.

In fairness to Ruth, it should be pointed out that, having been raised in a Victorian household, it was her intention from first to last to make their home a refuge for Stan. He was "the master", as she looked at it, and this coincided precisely with Stan's own concept of marriage. But where Ruth got into trouble was with her streak of independence. She had learned to say "no" to Stan. She had been a most successful businesswoman when she met Stan, and she could balk when she tired of something. She adored parties, and she was good at them. Stan, on the other hand, disliked them and was even irritated by them at times. Her husky laugh amused the fellows, and after a drink or two, she would dance with all the verve of early Joan Crawford. She wanted their life together to be less restricted than Stan's had been with Lois or even with Mae. Sitting at home all of the time was not for her and she thought it was unhealthy for Stan.

Stan's first rebellion was the affair with the twin from Downey. Detective Beulah must have tailed Stan or had one of her colleagues do it because Ruth learned of the girl's age, neighbourhood and even a considerable amount about her reputation, which was, according to Ruth, "that she had given the clap to every sailor in the Fifth Fleet."

A year before their wedding in Agua Caliente, Ruth had seen one of Clara Bow's last films, *Call Her Savage* (1933), an unintentional howler in which Clara had been angered by something that leading man Gilbert Roland had done. Wearing her riding habit, boots and carrying a crop, she came upon the manly Roland flailing her crop mercilessly and making bloody welts on his face. Ruth conceded that she was a great fan of Clara's and had remained loyal to the bitter end of her career. She confessed that the memory of that scene may have inspired her assault upon Downey.

In any event, Ruth put on her riding habit and boots and picked up a crop and set out in her new Ford coupé with lady detective Beulah and cook Lillian to confront Stan in the home of the twins. Upon their arrival in Downey, they had some trouble locating the correct house, and first came upon the twins' grandmother. That lady, wholly innocent of Ruth's mission, told them, upon being asked if Stan Laurel were on the premises, that Stan was *engaged* to one of her granddaughters and had just given the girl a diamond. Ruth was half-crazed by this piece of news and began roaring up and down the street calling for Stan to come out "like a man" and slapping her crop against her palm.

She failed to flush him out, and in a few weeks, Stan realized that the young lady was not quite the virginal creature he had thought she was. Since Ruth claimed that her first marriage to the tubercular Rogers was never consummated, she said that she was "as close to a virgin" as Stan would ever get. He pretended to believe her and came back to the Glenbar house.

Stan had given the Downey twin a diamond bracelet worth about $8000. After their "break up", through persuasion (possibly Ben Shipman's), the bracelet was returned and Stan gave it to Ruth. But Ruth angrily tossed it back at him. "I don't want such trash!" she said. The jeweller took back the bracelet at a considerable loss to Stan, and taking his cue from *Them Thar Hills*, the boys' latest and funniest sound comedy, in which they haul a primitive house trailer up into the Ozark mountains for Ollie's health (the doctor has told him that he is suffering from too much high living and Stan's first suggestion is that they move down to the basement), Stan went out and bought a huge, deluxe trailer, hoping that this might appease Ruth. It boasted hot and cold plumbing, electric refrigeration from its own generator and feather beds. They towed it to Arrowhead, Big Bear and Palm Springs.

It was not as luxurious as Buster Keaton's land cruiser, which was an early version of the motor home, sleeping six with two drawing rooms, bath, kitchen, and a separate driver's cabin. Buster, his friend Lew Cody, and occasional other guests spent weeks traversing the western half of the United States.

Those excursions in the Laurel trailer were happy times, as Ruth recalls them. Stan was relaxed. He laughed at nearly everything, and Ruth had to laugh, too. Quite often, she didn't know what they were laughing about, but that didn't matter.

Then Stan was called back to the studio for a new picture, *Babes in Toyland*. Roach had brought the musical comedy hit during a trip to New York and had subsequently realized that it had no story. People were flocking to see it because of the Victor Herbert score and its masterful use of gels and coloured spots. "Coming back on the train," Roach said, "I worked like hell, writing . . . Laurel was Simple Simon and Hardy was the Pieman."

The feature was to become the second most successful film of the boys' careers (trailing *Fra Diavolo* by only a little): It was much the most ambitious project of Roach's up to that time. It is unfortunate that it was filmed about six months before a refined Technicolor permitted an entire feature (*Becky Sharp*, 1935) to be made in colour successfully.

The story was made up from scratch, contrived by Nick Grinde and Frank Butler with considerable uncredited assistance from Roach. They combined elements of Mother Goose with the hoariest of screen villains, the heartless landlord, and bogeymen straight from the Brothers Grimm.

The boys, sans bowlers, wore Robin Hood-type hats with feathers for their roles as toymakers in Toyland. Bo-Peep, the ingénue, was played by Charlotte Henry, who had made her screen début as Alice in Paramount's rather incredible parade of their stars, which they had palmed off as *Alice in Wonderland* (1933). She fared much better in *Babes*. The movie won rave reviews from all the major critics and ran for weeks in such prestige houses as the Astor in New York. The *New York Times* critic, André Sennwald wrote:

> The film is an authentic children's entertainment and quite the merriest of its kind that Hollywood has turned loose on the nation's screens in a long time. Borrowing Victor Herbert's title and his music, as well as Walt Disney's dream-world secrets, the custodian of the royal custard has enriched the Christmas holidays with an original flesh-and-blood fantasy. Since the comic team of Laurel and Hardy has wandered into it, the elders, as well as their young charges, are advised to check their dignity at the door.

11 ‖ Stan Rebels

1   A number of simmering disagreements with Roach came to the boil in the immediate weeks following the release of *Babes* and in early March 1935, Stan walked out on the studio. Roach wanted to limit them to features, with only an occasional fling at two-reelers. He had prepared for them a parody of two enormously successful adventures set in colonial India, *Clive of India* (January 1935) and *Lives of a Bengal Lancer* (January 1935), which he was calling *McLaurel and McHardy*.

Stan's will towards self-destruction could always be counted upon to assert itself when things were going best. Hal Roach made an official announcement that Stan had left the studio and almost the next day released a statement that Oliver Hardy was going to co-star with comedienne Patsy Kelly as *The Hardy Family* with "Our Gang's" chief delinquent Spanky McFarland as their son.

Despite rumours flying from one column to another that Stan and Babe were feuding, the dispute was clearly between Roach and Stan. Stan brooded over stories in the presss of his "feud with Babe" and finally phoned Louella Parsons and said to her: "Please don't say my friend Babe and I have ever had a word. Babe is one of my best friends (*not quite true, but true enough for Louella Parsons' readers*) and the only arguments we have had have been an occasional difference of opinion on stories. There isn't an actor in the world who doesn't want to discuss a story idea and give his own personal viewpoint."

Patsy Kelly had emerged as a very funny screen comedienne after a long series of two-reelers with Thelma Todd. She was dowdy and acerbic, droll and credibly human. Stan respected her talent enough to believe that Roach was serious about replacing him with her.

After three weeks, he realized – and it was a frightening thought to him in many ways – that his screen destiny was ineluctably caught up with that of Oliver Babe Hardy. They were as inter-dependent as Siamese twins. But then a colder chill of reality blew through him and he knew that he as much as anyone had made Babe Hardy an extension of himself. Hardy, the actor, might do any number of other things. *The Hardy Family* (this was two years before Metro launched a fictional Hardy family with *A Family Affair* 1937) might well become a tremendous success. Babe did not pretend to be a writer, nor even a comedian in the ordinary sense. He was an actor who did comedy. But Stan had written and acted himself into a dead end as a possible single.

Throughout that year a quiet revolution was taking place in American films. The infidels seemed so innocent, no one suspected that they would rout slapstick so resoundingly that within six years only the Marx Brothers (in once-yearly productions), the Ritz Brothers (whose aesthetics were nowhere) and W. C. Fields would still be on the screen. (Abbott and Costello and Red Skelton came later, almost as an echo.) They were female for one thing, and they were nearly all beautiful for another.

In retrospect, what happened to American comedy with the success of *It Happened One Night* (1934) parallels rather closely the fate of director Frank Capra. He had come into films as a gag-writer on *Our Gang*, moved over to Mack Sennett, where he helped create Harry Langdon's screen image, moved with Langdon to First National to direct his features there, then seemed to go down with Langdon as success spoiled the trusting innocent, and was finally hired by Harry Cohn of Columbia because he was unemployed and came cheap.

In late 1933, Laurel and Hardy's seventh year as a team, Capra asked his boss Cohn to buy a magazine story by Samuel Hopkins Adams entitled *Night Bus*, which cost the studio $5000. Capra and his favourite screenwriter, Robert Riskin, withdrew to Palm Springs to work up a treatment, changing the title to *It Happened One Night* because there had been a number of "bus" pictures and Cohn saw failure stamped all over another screen trip by Greyhound. In Adams' story, there was a runaway heiress who falls in love with a penniless artist. Columbia's story editor Myles Connolly pointed out to Capra and Riskin that they had two unsympathetic characters – spoiled brat heiress and flowing-tie Greenwich Village painter. He told them to make the heiress bored with being an heiress and the man "a regular guy, someone we all know and like". Note Hollywood's opinion of artists and other creative types.

The evolution of this simple tale from the pages of conventional fiction to classic comedy almost didn't come off. Myrna Loy, Constance Bennett, Margaret Sullavan and Miriam Hopkins all turned it down. Claudette Colbert, who eventually played the heiress, wanted no part of it initially because she was tired and about to leave for a month-long vacation. If she made the sacrifice, she demanded double pay and a four-week shooting schedule. Harry Cohn, by now desperate, winced and gave in to her demands. Then Louis B. Mayer, annoyed with Clark Gable's rebellious insistence on better contractual terms, phoned Cohn and asked if he could use Gable in something, anything. Columbia was the Siberia of film studios just as the Pantages circuit was Parka country for vaudevillians. Gable needed "a lesson".

At the Sennett Studio, Capra had been schooled to satirize every institution known to man – motherhood, the law, schoolmasters and mistresses, wives, mothers-in-law, policemen, farmers, travelling salesmen, and, of course, every conceivable figure of power from school principal to tycoon. At the Roach Studio, he concentrated on the foibles of childhood, trapped as he was with Bob McGowan's "Our Gang" company. At First National with Langdon, there were cross-country walkers, Charles Atlas, the former ninety-pound weakling, and other targets. Now with *It Happened One Night*, he and Riskin decided to kid the pants, almost literally, off sex. It was heretical and trouble for Capra nearly all the way.

Initial critical reaction was lukewarm and it ran only a week at the Radio City Music Hall. Then word-of-mouth began to build, and critics went back for a second look. There were hold-overs at theatres all across America. It won eleven Academy Awards, including the best picture, best direction, best actor and actress. Coming on the heels of an earlier Capra comedy success, *Lady for a Day* (about the one-day transformation of a loveable old beggar lady, May Robson), Capra, schooled in ringing all the changes possible on a winning screen formula, found a new leading lady who was even more sympathetic than Colbert in Jean Arthur, whose voice he described as breaking "into a thousand tinkling bells". She would appear in three Capra comedies in the next five years.

Jean Arthur is important to this chronicle of the fortunes of Stan Laurel because she as much as anyone was a transitional figure. She was in some ways as innocent as Stan and Babe. She was daft in ways that were akin to those small madnesses that set Stan apart from Lloyd and even Chaplin. If she had ever appeared as Mrs Laurel in one of their comedies, she would have seemed almost too much at home. There would have been nothing for Stan to play against, since she was as much not-of-this-world as he. But Jean was attractive, warm and in every way enchanting. Beginning with her role opposite Gary Cooper in *Mr Deeds Goes to Town* (1936), she was the first – albeit quite innocently – to bring down the curtain on slapstick as a favourite movie mode. Shortly afterward, Irene Dunne joined her with *Theodora Goes Wild* (1936), and Carole Lombard, whose *My Man Godfrey* (1936) had come out at about the same time as *Theodora*.

Laurel and Hardy would survive this female revolution for another two years, but after 1938 it would be downhill for the rest of their careers. Some writers remarked that the movies had "grown up". Actually, as we survey the devastation and loss, the movies suffered a grievous wound that would never heal and audiences a deprivation of incalculable dimensions.

In April 1935, less than a month after his rebellion began, a chastened Stan returned to the Roach Studio and production began immediately on *Laurel and Hardy in India* (the new working title).

Roach, full of ideas for the film and eager to get it before the cameras, was more conciliatory than ever. Ben Shipman, representing Stan, had told Roach that Stan now wanted $100,000 per film, but Roach had laughed him out of the office and then beaten him down to a figure around $80,000. Still, that was far more than any other comedian on salary to a studio was getting at the time.

Roach assured Stan that the India film (soon to be called *Bonnie Scotland* paradoxically, since it opened and closed in the Highlands) would be more spectacular than *Babes in Toyland*. A retired Colonel from His Majesty's Forces in India was hired as technical adviser. It was also made clear to Stan – to his lasting sorrow – that there would be no more short comedies. Laurel and Hardy, Roach told him, had become too important for that.

The film was not the huge success that Roach had hoped for. It was a slight story idea superimposed upon a twice-told military adventure, and long on atmosphere (Scotland and India) but short on laughs. Oddly enough, it is a comedy that has improved with age. And it is obvious from the care Roach lavished upon it that he was manfully trying to sustain the world's enthusiasm for Laurel and Hardy during this critical period for film comedy.

Bonnie Scotland's partial failure was possibly to blame, but Roach, who took a justifiable pride in his ability to move with the times and often be ahead of the others, was ambivalent about his most famous clowns. Even though he assured Stan that they would do nothing but important features, he indicated to his staff that the movies had matured to a point where he had to consider doing "more serious things". This could mean the retirement or demise of such great long-running series as *Our Gang* and *Charley Chase*. Stan did not like the sound of any of it. Laurel and Hardy and "maturity" did not go together.

Roach was not alone. At that very moment Chaplin was editing and scoring the film that would be his last great excursion into low comedy (*Modern Times*, 1936).

Lois's final divorce decree had come through in the last week of September 1935, and Stan phoned Ruth from the studio to tell her the good news. Then, on an impulse, he proposed that they make their marriage absolutely legal by marrying again before a Justice of the Peace. The ceremony was planned hurriedly for 28 September and only a few friends were to be present – Kemper and Ethel Marley, Alla Counts and W. A. Thompson, all of Los Angeles. Stan was exuberant and most of the problems in his life seemed solvable as they drove home across the desert.

2 In mid-November 1935, and all through December, Stan and Babe were involved in the shooting of yet another antique operetta, Michael Balfe's *The Bohemian Girl*. The success of *Fra Diavolo* and *Babes in Toyland* seemed to have proved to Roach's satisfaction that his most valuable stars could survive in this way. He feared that Hollywood was about to scrap their former brand of comedy as something that the movies had progressed beyond – a relic from the early silents. The solution, obviously, was to allow them to romp in their typically loony fashion through a musical comedy that was more genteel than those the Warner Brothers were turning out. Roach had made a speciality of opera *bouffe*.

Thelma Todd, wearing a dark wig over her platinumed hair, was cast as the Gypsy Queen's daughter and opened the movie with a rousing Gypsy song. Tragically, Thelma was found dead in her garage on 15 December and when the film was edited in January by Bert Jordan, most of her footage was deleted from the picture on Stan's order. He said it would be morbid to leave Thelma in as one of the stars of the picture "because of what happened".

Thelma Todd's death shook Roach out of his complacent belief that his studio "family" were models of virtue to the Hollywood community, Stan excepted. With Stan and his "girls", Roach had anticipated the worst for years.

Thelma, in the decade of her screen work, had acquired a unique screen image, a wise-cracking blonde with every hair in place, a lady who kept her cool through the chaos around Laurel and Hardy, Edgar Kennedy, Zasu Pitts and even the Marx Brothers. She had come to Roach in 1929, and been teamed almost immediately with Miss Pitts in a series of comedies about the misadventures of an ill-assorted pair of ladies. Zasu Pitts had moved up from being typecast as a rather wan leading lady to comedienne, whose woebegoneness was only exceeded by her timidity.

When the Pitts' brand of fecklessness made her popular as comic interest in major features, Roach lost her. Without any hesitation,

Roach teamed Thelma with Patsy Kelly, who was much more her own type – wise-cracking, cynical, but with a fatal attraction to catastrophe. Also, she was as dowdy as Thelma was well-groomed.

Stan admired Thelma in her speciality and liked to have her in his films, but because of her brassy attractiveness, she could not be used often. *The Bohemian Girl* was only her fourth appearance in a Laurel and Hardy film.

Her death is a mystery still unsolved. She had gone to a party thrown by Ida Lupino at the Trocadero on Sunset Boulevard on the night of Saturday, 14 December. Her ex-husband, Pat DiCicco (who later married Gloria Vanderbilt) was invited, but he appeared at another table with actress Margaret Lindsay, and there was a sharp exchange between him and Thelma during the evening. Thelma drank more than usual, and after she'd left in her chauffeured car, theatre-owner Sid Grauman phoned Roland West, her business partner and fellow tenant in a small apartment that they had built over the restaurant they owned jointly. Grauman told West that Thelma was a bit "under the influence" and suggested that he see her safely to bed. Witnesses all agreed that her mood when she left the party was morose.

West once had been a moderately-successful director (*The Bat*, 1926, *Alibi*, 1929). He and Thelma had many friends in common and they became close in the months following her separation from DiCicco. They had opened "Thelma Todd's Cafe" with West putting up the money and Thelma giving her name and, often, her person to the establishment. Although West maintained a house on Pasetano Road, which was tucked behind Sunset Boulevard where it runs into the sea at Pacific Coast Highway, he usually stayed in his apartment above the restaurant, separated from Thelma's quarters by locked sliding doors.

Following Grauman's phone-call, rather than helping Thelma into her apartment, he bolted the front door to the two apartments. At the inquest, he had no satisfactory explanation for this. He said that he first heard his dog barking and shortly thereafter water running, at around 3.30 a.m. in Thelma's apartment, and assumed the lady was home. But, of course, there was no way that she could have gained entrance through the bolted door.

Thelma was found dead early on Sunday morning by her maid in a garage loaned to her by West behind his house on Pasetano Road, some 500 yards from the restaurant apartment. She was slumped forward over the steering wheel. What she called her "peg tooth", a porcelain replacement, had been knocked out as her face struck the wheel, cutting her lip. There was blood on her chin, her dress, her mink coat and on the car seat. The ignition switch was on, and there were carbon-monoxide fumes in the garage. No suicide note was ever found.

Stan and Ruth received a Christmas card from Thelma on the Monday following her death, a day before the funeral. A number of her friends, including Stan, also received gift parcels that week, her maid bringing them to the studio after her death.

Like the death of Starr Faithful, which was fictionalized by John O'Hara in *Butterfield Eight*, Thelma Todd's became a staple in the Sunday magazine sections. It was by far the most shocking scandal that year in Hollywood, and it rocked the Roach Studio, Roach himself in particular.

Today, Roach survivors speak of Thelma Todd's "killing". Some, Ruth Laurel among them, go further and say they think that she was murdered. "Why", Ruth asked, "would she come home in a limousine, climb all those steps up the cliffside to the garage to her convertible to kill herself? She was known to have had lots of pills and some other drugs that were not available at the pharmacy, and she could have taken an overdose.

The shock of Thelma's death was absorbed at Stan's home a little more easily than it might have been normally because of their holiday guests. Stan's father Jeff and his second wife, Venitia, had come over for Christmas. They stayed well into spring, and Stan and Jeff were barely speaking by the time of their departure.

Since there was no guest room in the Glenbar villa, the Jeffersons had to stay at a nearby hotel and come over each day to have dinner with Stan and Ruth. Their accommodation was paid for by Stan.

The reunion seemed to be fine for about ten days, then their daily visits began to set Stan's teeth on edge. Jeff had recovered from his pique at Stan for legally changing his name to "Laurel" in 1934 before his marriage to Ruth. He took such pride in the great old stage name Jefferson that he really saw no reason for it, and undoubtedly longed to garland the family escutcheon with yet another branch. In an interview upon his arrival in Hollywood, Jeff said that he had traced the family back to Wales, where the forebears of *Thomas* Jefferson were said to have lived. Then he capped this by stating that Stan, in young manhood, had borne a striking resemblance to the third American president, especially around the mouth and chin. The story was monumentally insignificant as by this time, his son's long-jawed face had become far better-known around the world than that of the author of the Declaration of Independence.

On one exquisitely tense afternoon during the Jeffersons' stay, Jeff said that he wanted to go over to the Fox Studio to see Shirley Temple at work, as Stan had promised him. Stan refused even to consider it for reasons best known to himself and denied ever having made such a promise. When the shouting reached embarrassing levels, Stan dashed out of the back door and Jeff out of the front. Ruth and Venitia sat mutely by, wondering how the relationship could be salvaged, yet that evening, they were laughing and drinking through dinner as though nothing had happened.

The next unfulfilled promise, according to Jeff, was a trip to Hawaii, which, he said, Stan himself had proposed. The Jeffersons settled for ten days on Catalina Island shuttling between Stan's fishing yacht and the St Catherine Hotel.

In early May 1936, Stan decided to show Roach that when his contract expired in November, he would not just be dealing with a recalcitrant actor. He filed articles of incorporation in Los Angeles with $100,000 capitalization for "Stan Laurel Productions". He then began mulling over story ideas that would be suitable for him as a single, but he did not approach realization of his essential dilemma as an artist. He was not a single and his wastebasket in the Glenbar study began filling up with misbegotten scenarios. Still, he was determined to go through with the corporation. During the summer, he put under contract at least one cowboy star, Fred Scott, and began shooting inexpensive westerns.

Roach thought that Stan was being most ungrateful. He really had convinced himself, and with some justification, that he created

Stan. Stan Laurel was a product of the Roach Studio just as much as "Our Gang" had been. The difference between them was that if the child actors in the Gang had marched into his office and demanded higher salaries and control over their productions, he would simply have fired them one and all.

If Laurel waited and snared Hardy, too, Roach foresaw a ruinous mass exodus from the studio, including composer Marvin Hatley (of the Coo-Koo Song) and certainly former comedy star Harry Langdon, who was now hanging around Stan much of the time.

Since Ben Shipman, Laurel and Hardy's lawyer-manager, was formerly Roach's lawyer and still his close friend, it seems reasonable to assume that Roach urged Shipman to keep Stan in line. When Stan insisted to Shipman that he was not going back unless on his own terms, a temporary compromise was worked out. Roach conceded control to Stan under certain conditions, and the next Laurel and Hardy feature. *Our Relations* (1936), was a "Stan Laurel Production". No percentage of profits was to go to Stan's production company, only his salary of $80,000. He would not own any rights to the negatives or prints, but he could have the control.

And so it was done. Based upon a short story by W. W. Jacobs, author of the classic "The Monkey's Paw", and with much twin confusion drawn from Shakespeare's "Comedy of Errors", *Our Relations* began shooting on a number of elaborate sets that summer, with a huge cast and a more adult slant than anything the boys had done in the past.

As two long-married bourgeois types, they encounter by the purest chance two long lost, black sheep twin brothers who are sailors, and have not been hanged for mutiny as their mother has written on an old family photograph. Two waterfront whores (Stan, on his own, apparently overlooked the fact that more than half of their audiences were children) mistake the bourgeois gentlemen for the sailors.

One day while shooting was under way, Stan and Ruth were in a restaurant in Hollywood and Stan noticed that the large ashtray on the table had a rounded, weighted bottom so that it could not be overturned – it would bob back up again. The next day, he had the writers insert a scene in which gangsters are brought into the plot when they see a valuable ring, belonging to the sailors' captain, going into Stan's pocket. The dénouement of this is that the boys are "taken for a ride" to the dockside, where their feet are encased in cylinders of cement – exactly like the bottoms of the restaurant ashtrays. They are left to teeter their way into the drink.

12 || Chaplin and Laurel Meet Again

1 Around the time of *Our Relations'* release in October 1936, two of the world's funniest and most beloved performers chanced to meet in the waters of the Pacific off Catalina. It was the rarest of occasions since Stan did not move in the same circles as Charlie Chaplin.

But it could not have been more timely, as Stan's ego had soared since he had become a producer for Roach. He did not hesitate to tell Ruth that "catching up with Charlie" was in his mind with his recent promotion. He had every intention of remaining his own producer to the end of his or *their* career.

Chaplin was at that time enjoying the world-wide success of *Modern Times*, his attack on the dehumanizing process that Henry Ford's assembly line had spawned. It had opened in February and the reviews and audiences were both wildly approving. Eight months after its release, it was still drawing huge crowds in the major cities around the world. It boasted as its theme song one of Chaplin's most haunting and successful original tunes – *Smile, Though Your Heart is Breaking*. And, as nearly everyone remembers, nine years after the début of *Vitaphone*, the Little Tramp was still silent. There were only sound effects and that magnificent song in the background.

Chaplin's constant companion at the time was the brunette actress Paulette Goddard, a former Goldwyn girl (a status in films not unlike that of the Ziegfeld Girl on the stage) whom Chaplin had selected to appear opposite him in *Modern Times* and whom he was about to marry.

Miss Goddard and Chaplin were aboard his newly-acquired fifty-five foot motor cruiser with three state rooms, and a small crew. By contrast, the *Ruth L.* looked functional and plebeian.

The craft clearly reflected their owners' life-styles. Chaplin's was elegant, large enough for entertaining the doctors, writers and philosophers he chose as his friends; Stan's was unembellished, ideal for a weekend of fishing – his greatest passion after the creation of humour – with pals from the studio. On this particular Saturday afternoon, in the company of Ruth, he had pulled in two bushel baskets full of bluefish. Ruth herself didn't much enjoy fishing since she panicked when they got on the line, but she "liked to see Stan happy".

Chaplin credited "the humiliation of being poor" for giving him the drive to become a wealthy actor. He later told a reporter, "My desire to make money came at an early age when I was growing up in poverty in Lambeth, on the south side of the Thames. I didn't starve, but I didn't know a regular bed. When I was small I had a terrific inferiority complex. Success helped me out of it and gave me confidence . . . the truth is that I went into the movie business for money. Art just sort of grew out of it."

As we are now aware, Stan's accumulation of riches was considerably less than Chaplin's. A handsome, small Spanish villa and the yacht were the sum total of his luxuries. It would have puzzled the millions of comedy fans around the world to have known of their differences. Stan had settled his disputes with Roach for a credit line and a fraction of what Chaplin took in from a single feature. Stan was paid in thousands of dollars, which seemed a great deal to Hal Roach, while Chaplin's income amounted to millions and was growing every day from world rentals of his huge backlog of comedies.

Chaplin was known to be tight with a penny, while Stan owed more than $50,000 in back taxes. As Chaplin suggests, their childhoods accounted for the contrast. Chaplin, as the son of a light baritone with a heavy dependence on alcohol, spent as much time in London's streets as in the dismal, overcrowded one- and two-room tenement flats shared with his mother and brother. It was the street urchin in Chaplin who gloried in the Beverly Hills spread, the Japanese servants, the yacht and, not least, the studio – his own.

In the Catalina waters, Chaplin recognized Stan and had one of his crew toss him a line. Stan chose to forget the times he had tried to talk to Chaplin by phone "just for a get-together" when Chaplin could not be reached. There followed a hearty reunion at sea, and as first one, then the other recalled incidents from their early days with Karno, the awkwardness of the years of separation fell away. The ladies lapsed into a chatty rapport; they both had husky, little girl voices, permanently sustained by being treated – when the mood struck their partners – like over-indulged children. Ruth and Paulette became a delighted audience for a couple of hours as the men competed with each other in dredging up the hoariest of music-hall ballads. Chaplin roared with laughter as Stan sang what he described as being a song for Mother's Day:

> Don't go in the poorhouse
> Until I come home
> And we'll all go in together.

Chaplin accepted a gift of freshly-caught blues and they parted, vowing to keep in better touch. But their lives were running on different tracks and years would go by before they would meet again.

2   The end of 1936 was a time of withdrawal for Stan. There did not seem to be any enthusiasm among the Roach executives for anything that he proposed. As his contract, which was really a brief extension of his old one with better terms, was expiring, he wanted to work out a long-term deal. He desperately needed a feeling of security. Roach's disinterest in such a deal was dumbfounding to Stan. If *Our Relations* had received mixed notices and lukewarm business, the trouble was with Roach, not with the team. Their curse was Roach's indifference and Stan thought that such an attitude was suicidal. Roach was far too preoccupied with

trends, yet the only lasting films he was making were those of the boys'. It wasn't that Stan had begun to believe his own press agents, but that he had become a film-maker with a vision. It was cock-eyed and lunatic but it was a vision that was clear to everyone. And it was an enduring vision – Stan was certain about that. If only time would prove him right – hindsight or one's final place in movie history often bore little relation to a star's standing at the box-office. As Louis B. Mayer pointed out, history did not sell any tickets to a movie.

There seemed no way that Ben Shipman could negotiate a new agreement except on a four-picture basis, woefully short on security. Shipman was no longer dealing from a position of strength (even though it must be stressed that he took no advantage of that asset when he had it). Roach had already bought the novel *Topper*, a very mild sex comedy in which the principal gag grew out of the fact that Topper, like H. G. Wells' "Invisible Man", had the ability to disappear at will. The studio head was committing himself to an extended schedule of big-budgeted sophisticated comedies and drama.

Roach thought that a renewal of the terms worked out on *Our Relations* covering a four-picture deal was more than generous: it would bring Stan a total of $320,000, not a modest commitment of money at the time. Roach knew that if there were to be any survivors from the great comedy period, they would be Laurel and Hardy, W. C. Fields and the Marx Brothers.

Stan did not agree to these conditions at once. While he was undecided, he was edgy and it was almost impossible for Ruth to be around. When things were difficult, they were the worst of partners. She had learned to be silent rather than vocally reassuring. All of her earlier attempts at lightening Stan's moods had been aborted by glares or sudden departures. This time, she was just as edgy as he was. She knew they had very little money to live on, and while she was very careful not to intrude on a man's province – that had been bred into her – she thought it only fair to know whether they had a future. More often than not, her answer was the sight of Stan's back as he hurried through the front door with his little black bag to be gone for a night or longer. Finally she told him not to come back.

Stan them embarked on a long vacation from Hollywood, winding up in New York. Ruth believed that he was with Alyce, and when he returned to Cheviot Hills, having sailed back from the East Coast on the President Taft, he found that Ruth had demolished their home. She had had Bekins Moving and Storage pick up every rug, drapery and piece of furniture. The only thing she didn't remove was a built-in radio. The house was an empty shell. Stan sat down on the front terrace and wept.

On Christmas Eve 1936, a divorce agreement was signed by both parties whereby Ruth was to receive five per cent of all of Stan's future gross earnings until her death or remarriage, even though "he is not now under contract for any services whatsoever" – an interesting comment to be included in a divorce paper, appearing to be more of a judgment than a vital piece of information.

Ruth also was given the Glenbar house (rendered unsaleable from Stan's redesigning of the interior), a 1935 Packard Sedan, a 1934 Ford Coupe, an annuity paying $172 a month for the rest of her life, a bank account totalling $17,000 and three real estate parcels. It was a tough agreement and Stan saw himself wiped out a second time by a wife within less than four years.

Ruth took a much smaller house on Hancock Place near the Wilshire District; she had furnished it with things from the Glenbar house and stored the rest. She was "seeing men" again, her phrase, and one of them, her attorney Roger Marchetti, kept inundating her with flowers. Later, she wasn't sure that this wasn't a trick of his to break her up permanently with Stan so that he would rake in the huge fees that such a divorce produced.

Stan visited the new house and saw the flowers and one of Marchetti's tender notes. Predictably, he was outraged. He insisted that she stop seeing the man whom he hated more than anyone on earth, and half a dozen other men of their acquaintance. "They're all no good," he told her. "You're too nice a girl."

Ruth could not understand why he should be free to live with Alyce Ardell or someone else and she could be so restricted. But she finally agreed that she would not go out with any of his friends or "people Babe knows or anyone at the studio". This somewhat limited her since she had been together with Stan for such a long time, and his friends were her friends. When she began saying "no" to all the men who called and found that there were long, lonely evenings stretching ahead for her, she got on a train and went to visit relatives in Kansas City. On an impulse, Stan went along with her.

A newspaper story in Los Angeles *Examiner* in January 1937, announced that Stan and Ruth were "Motoring to New York on Second Honeymoon". But that story also named Roger Marchetti, Ruth's attorney, as "Stan's lawyer". There was something very much awry. It was possibly then that Stan began to look at Ruth with some suspicion.

They were in Kansas City when Stan saw the item, which had been picked up by one of the wire services. He exploded and said it was a plot on the part of Ruth and her attorney. Kansas City was a "neutral corner" where they could discuss their differences; it was the home of Irene and Craig Norris, whom Stan liked very much. Irene was Ruth's first cousin.

After seeing the story, Stan said he was leaving, but Ruth insisted that she would go East for a while, saying that Stan should have a good stay with Irene and Craig now that he was there. He took her to the Union Depot and as they passed a book and magazine store, he asked if she wanted anything to read. She saw a bestseller in the window, *Live Alone and Like It*, and asked him to buy it for her. He gave her a look and said, "Don't be funny."

Stan's second production under his own name was progressing well as the new year began. *Way Out West* was no ordinary western – it had the lavish mounting of Cecil B. De Mille's *The Plainsman*, which had been released that January. There was no mere saloon; there was a dance hall where a dozen black-stockinged beauties did the can-can to the strains of *Won't You Be My Lovey Dovey*. Most importantly it was a parody western. It strove to take the most banal of western plots – the one about the gold-mine deed getting into the hands of the rightful and deserving heir – and turn it into an insane adventure. En route to deliver the deed to their late prospecting buddy's orphaned daughter, they give up their mulish mule in favour of a stage coach, which they hail in the middle of the desert. Another passenger is a middle-aged lady with whom Ollie attempts a casual conversation. "Only four more months to Christmas!" he remarks. She is silent *and* perturbed. "Do you believe in Santa

Claus?" Ollie asks. She now thinks she is at the mercy of a madman whose next move is likely to be anything. As soon as they disembark at Brushwood Gulch, their mutual destination, she informs her husband, the Sheriff, of the peculiar overtures. He tells them, "If you want to stay healthy, you better catch the next coach out of town." Ollie assures him that they will do so just as soon as their business is attended to, and the Sheriff strikes terror into their hearts by informing them that if they miss the next coach, they'll be riding in a hearse.

At the saloon, they spill the beans to the saloonkeeper (Jimmy Finlayson) about having the deed and needing to get in touch with local resident Mary Roberts. He rushes upstairs to the apartment he shares with wife Lola (the leading showgirl and his partner in crime) to tell her the news. *She* will impersonate Mary Roberts and shortly she appears in a pinafore, her blonde curls in pigtails, to confront the boys who have brought the sad news. "What did he (her alleged father) die of?" she asks them. "Of a Tuesday," says Stan.

Downstairs, the boys come upon the real Mary Roberts, who is a slavey in the saloon kitchen. When they discover their error, the film becomes a frantic pursuit, with the deed recovered, then filched again. In trying to recover it in the dead of night, they use their mule Dinah, who has reappeared, as a moving counterweight to hoist Ollie up to the apartment balcony. The first mule used in the film broke its neck during the hoist when Stan climbed out of the saddle and Ollie's great weight sent the animal flying. Stan was terribly upset as the death of any animal distressed him deeply.

There were several songs in the film, and in one of them, the team sings *In the Blue Ridge Mountains of Virginia, On the Trail of the Lonesome Pine* so effectively that there was applause at the preview. Nearly forty years later, in 1975, a record taken from the sound track of their duet became a surprising hit in England.

Way Out West was much the most successful Laurel and Hardy film since *Fra Diavolo*. It may even have made Roach reassess his priorities, although certainly only temporarily. The confirmation from his special effects man, Roy Seawright, that the technical problem of making Roland Young and Constance Bennett appear and disappear could be resolved meant that the first of three *Topper* features would be in production early in 1937.

Throughout 1937, there were numerous reconciliations and partings between Stan and Ruth; much of the instability of the relationship was directly due to its lack of focus. But the success of *Way Out West* and Roach's reaction to it convinced Stan of two things: that he and Babe were still as popular as ever, and that Hal Roach was too preoccupied with more sophisticated fare to help them sustain that popularity. When Ben Shipman was asked by Roach how Stan felt about the reviews and the good business generated by *Way Out West*, Ben was forced to admit that he was not happy.

Ruth had the wisdom to see that Stan's sole concern at this point was the future of Laurel and Hardy. She became a one-woman cheering section. Stan misinterpreted her enthusiasm, probably wondering why she was being so supportive all of a sudden. It might have seemed less obvious if there were some continuity in their partnership, but the Glenbar house was still shut down, Stan was living in a penthouse apartment, and Ruth was in a smaller home near downtown Los Angeles. They shuttled back and forth; they fought and made up. They went to Big Bear for a relaxing weekend and Stan was in a rage because the water was too low for fishing. Ruth told friends that she thought he was throwing a fit of some kind. By the end of February, Ruth realized that some vital spark was eluding them and threatened to stop seeing Stan. He had a legal agreement drawn up defining the terms of their "cohabitation", but that didn't work out and by spring, they were out of touch.

In early June, Ruth left California to spend the summer with cousin Irene and her husband in Kansas City. When she was in Los Angeles, Ruth believed that Stan kept a constant check on her to make sure that she wasn't seeing "the wrong men" whenever they weren't "cohabitating". In Kansas City, he was unable to do this and it apparently made him frantic. On 9 June, he sent her a telegram asking her to "Come on back", but she declined. Just before her departure, an incident had occurred that had made her deeply distrustful of Stan. She had met a fellow named Mike whom she had begun seeing quite often. The romance was derailed when

Mike left Ruth's house close to midnight one evening and sat down behind his steering wheel only to find a pool of black molasses on the car seat. Ruth was convinced that Tunney, the huge ex-vaudevillian Stan kept on salary as bodyguard and chauffeur, had committed this outrage on Stan's order – an assault that was compounded by the fact that Mike was wearing a new white linen suit.

Doubtless Stan was guilty. It was only a slight variation of the many affronts to dignity that passed on to film on the Roach lot for dozens of years.

In his divorce agreement with Ruth, she had been given sole possession of their lovely white elephant of a home in Cheviot Hills with its oversized single bedroom. Now, in desperation, Stan wrote to her saying, "You know how I can't stand to be in debt. Will you please put a loan on the big house? I'll pay you back."

Ruth agreed at once. She has been much maligned by ill-informed admirers of Stan as a grasping fortune-hunter and trouble-maker. While she knew how to stir up trouble, Ruth was never after money *per se*. She was after justice, which is something else. She had been legally promised five per cent of Stan's gross income and, since she had abandoned her successful career in dress retailing, she had no other income. In the divorce agreement, she had agreed never to use the name "Laurel" in any commercial way, so she lost out on a chance to create a line of "Ruth Laurel" dresses with a designer in Paris. There is some evidence to support a theory that "Stan Laurel Productions" was a shadow organization designed by Ben Shipman to do two things: to sustain Stan's artistic ego, which was sagging badly, and to swallow all of Stan's earnings so that Stan would get his *corporate* share, but Ruth would be denied her five per cent because it could be proved that Stan's personal income was zero.

Ruth knew nothing of any possible plot against her at this point and with her approval, Stan's secretary, Ernest Murphy, made a strenuous effort to get a bank loan so that his employer might pay his back income taxes. Several valuers inspected the unique one-bedroom property and came back with negative opinions. It was unrentable to anyone but a wealthy bachelor or a singularly harmonious couple and practically unsaleable.

Stan was grateful, but overriding his gratitude was his continuing irritation over her compulsive intrusiveness. On 30 June Stan wrote her:

Just received your last letter. I am sorry to know that you have written Bostocks. I wish you wouldn't do that. I don't want them interfering in my business any more. That is why I got rid of them. Now Ruth I want you to know once and for all that whatever has transpired, Marco (*Stanley Marco, an attorney retained by Stan in Los Angeles*) *has not* in any way shape or form had anything to do with it. My switching to new agents was entirely my own doing. Marco did not even know them till I introduced him. I don't know where you get all your strange ideas from. You get something in your mind and it becomes a reality. I am perfectly aware of all that's going on and am not a bit worried of the outcome. I will win out. It is tough sledding now but it won't be long. If Roach wants me, he will pay my price, if not, that's that. I have waited long enough and intend to go to work elsewhere, so you will soon be receiving your five per cent. Ernest is having the Bank appraise the house so will let you know as soon as we hear. I think you are foolish to buy a new car till you sell the other two. Why don't you trade the Ford in on one and try to sell the Packard alone. I will see what I can do for you. You can rest assured, Ruth, that you will never want for anything as long as I can help you. If you hadn't have raised so much hell and dragged me into a lot of mess we both would have been alright now. But it's no use digging up the past. It doesn't help matters now. It's all done and over with. . . . Guess you read about the three children that were kidnapped and found dead near Inglewood – terrible thing! Am seeing Feldman (*Charles Feldman, one of the best agents in Hollywood, had agreed to handle Stan although even he could not buck the trend, and their association was brief*) at 5 o'clock today. Will keep you advised as to what happens. Take care of yourself and have a good time.

Stan

Then in August, still without a salary in spite of his new agent, he wrote Ruth that he would like to see her when she got back "and have a long talk with you and try to explain to you the things you do that cause these mixups every time. Don't think for a minute I'm happy by any means and life's too short to go on with it.

"However I'll get away from it all one of these days even with all the obstacles I have trying to prevent me, and you could certainly help me if you would try to 'right' me instead of 'fight' me."

Stan's confusion over his relationship with Ruth was soon temporarily resolved when he met a Russian singer known as Illeana at a club for Russian expatriates, the Balaleika. She was as impressive as Mae, a statuesque blonde a good inch taller than Stan. She had tremendous gusto and was bursting with vitality. Her effervescence was as irresistible to Stan as her accent.

Babe had joined Stan in semi-bachelorhood in November 1937. Myrtle Hardy sued for divorce, asking for alimony of $2500 a month and accusing him of "extreme mental cruelty".

The facts behind the divorce were not clear-cut. Myrtle's drinking had driven Babe to take up permanent residence at the Beverly-Wilshire Hotel. Those who knew her and liked her, and there were many, were convinced that she only drank because of Babe's wanderlust. He was seeing Viola Morse often enough to give Myrtle grounds for divorce. From the gay, understanding helpmeet of the twenties and early thirties, Myrtle had become accusatory, often incapacitated by drink and, Babe learned to his horror, even unfaithful on one or more occasions. Both Babe and Stan betrayed an unbecoming time-lag regarding women and what was "proper". Babe, for example, would stop anyone telling an off-colour joke in Myrtle's presence, but yet he thought it was perfectly in order to deceive her with another woman. That was a man's prerogative, at least in the nineteenth-century world that enveloped him and Stan in a sepia mist, keeping them captive to fake and busy deceptions.

On 6 December 1937, Mae Laurel emerged from her decade of exile, went into a Los Angeles court-room, and sued Stan for separate maintenance, claiming that they had been legally "common law man and wife" for nearly ten years. At almost the same time, Ruth dragged Stan into court seeking alimony since he wasn't earning anything and her five per cent had stopped. She had evidently heard about assets that Stan had acquired – a Mexican cannery and his own movie company. Ben Shipman settled the Mae Laurel case out of court, but Ruth won $750 temporary alimony.

As Mae was leaving the court-room, reporters asked her if Stan had spoken the truth when he had admitted that she was always introduced as his wife, and she tearfully replied, "He is a gentleman. He told the truth." Mae took her modest settlement back East, where she remarried. She eventually died in a Long Island nursing home in 1969.

3   In October 1937, Hal Roach had obtained a firm commitment from the Italian government of Il Duce to finance four operas to be produced by Roach in Cinecittà, a sparkling new film centre at the edge of Rome. Mussolini had been much impressed by *Fra Diavolo, Babes in Toyland* and *The Bohemian Girl*. He informed Roach that he considered him an extraordinary talent and said that no other film producer in the world came near him in this special area. The dictator was, it must be said, a near fanatical Laurel and Hardy fan.

Roach saw absolutely nothing wrong with this arrangement. The seizure of Ethiopia by the Fascists in June 1936, and the *Axis* alliance of Hitler and Mussolini in October of that year, were political matters beyond his grasp. Roach threw a huge party for the twenty-first birthday of Vittorio Mussolini, Il Duce's eldest son, and on the frosting of the birthday cake (the young man had reached his majority on 28 September) stood a black-shirted Fascist soldier opposite a confectionery model of the ocean liner *Rex*.

Hal Roach was not alone in his naïveté. In 1936, producer Walter Wanger entered into an agreement with the Italians to collaborate with Mussolini's film aides in designing Cinecittà and producing two of his films there every year. He was disabused of this notion very quickly upon his return to America, his friends pointing out that he had been guilty of gross political innocence. The deal with Il Duce fell through. The difference between Wanger and Roach was that many of Wanger's friends were intellectuals and political sophisticates. Roach was to blunder deeply into this gaucherie before realizing his error.

Meanwhile, Roach and Stan were out of touch altogether. Stan still was holding out for production control and $100,000 a picture, but the studio head steadfastly refused to discuss such demands. Stan refused to concede that their comedy was passé. The audiences were out there, and if the film-makers continued to ignore them, they would soon enough make themselves heard. If Hitler hadn't distracted everyone so totally, perhaps they might have done so already.

Among these "serious and mature" film-makers, the most successful and influential of them all since the death of Thalberg were Darryl F. Zanuck and David O. Selznick. They were constructing film empires on the theory that the story was the thing.

Babe Hardy was extremely uncomfortable being squeezed this way and that. Privately, he wished Stan would "come off his high horse" so that they could continue making their comedies. He was still under contract to Roach, but he hated the idleness and even more he despised taking money for doing nothing. He was afraid that Stan might just succeed in ruining them both. Much of his time was spent at the track or at the Lakeside Country Club, where he was a golfing crony to director George Stevens (their former cameraman), Leo McCarey (who gave him and Stan their screen image) and a good half dozen other men at the top of the industry. Babe learned in this very direct fashion that he and Stan were more popular with the movie-going public than they were with studio heads, chiefly because of Stan's rebelliousness. The direction of American movies was changing, he was told, and if Laurel and Hardy were to survive, they had to have *continuity*, their continuing presence on the screen. A prolonged hiatus would mean the end of their legendary status. Flare-ups of temperament were certainly allowable in a genius, but Stan had to be his own employer. Prospective producers were at that moment feeling an occasional twinge of compassion for the great John Barrymore, who was in the process of coming apart through alcoholism, employing him and regretting it. There seemed to be no compassion at all for Stan, whose excesses seemed to be an exaggerated sense of his own worth and of his gifts as a film-maker.

4   Stan's wedding to Illeana Shuvalova in Yuma, Arizona, on New Year's Day 1938, could again have been a scenario for a Roach two-reeler. Ex-wife Ruth was in Phoenix when she heard in a radio newscast that Stan planned to marry "a Russian countess". She phoned Roger Marchetti, her attorney, who was then in New

York, and he allegedly told her that the divorce was illegal. It is difficult to see any merit in this contention when the seven-page divorce agreement of 24 December 1936 is just about the most detailed decree ever drawn up, spelling out specific rights and obligations, and granting property to Ruth right down to the furniture.

Ruth sent Stan a telegram to his apartment, the La Belle Tour Apartments on Franklin Avenue in Hollywood, telling him that she was rushing to Yuma to save him "from this mistake. Sober up. I am tired of threats. Intend to fight for my rights. I am your wife. Mrs Stan Laurel."

By the time Stan received the wire, he and Illeana were back in Los Angeles and Ruth was registered at Yuma's Del Sol Hotel, where the honeymoon suite had been vacated only hours earlier. Stan wired her there: "My divorce papers legal. Defy you or Marchetti to prove otherwise. . . . Why don't you sober up. Go ahead and fight for your rights. You are not my wife or ever will be. I am very happy now so please leave me alone."

When reporters interviewed her in Yuma, they asked Ruth if she was going to press bigamy charges. She said she wasn't sure, although some reporters wrote that she was. She told them that she had been shocked to learn from the hotel clerk that there had been "another Mrs Stan Laurel" in the honeymoon suite.

Roach finally signed up Stan for another four-picture contract. By that time, late January 1938, his marriage to Illeana was becoming a project that required as much energy as his career. It was also expensive and he needed the money.

At 48, Stan had embarked upon new and certainly uncharted waters. Illeana's background was as dubious and murky as her "title", but to Stan's friends, she was a "firecracker". He was always demanding action around him and became morose when there was none. Now he had an unpredictable, fiery Russian by his side whenever he was not at the studio. He seemed delighted by the way in which his life had picked up steam.

Many of his friends could not take the turbulence. In nightclubs, Illeana would suddenly burst into song at her table and do a Russian number *a capella* in a mezzo that lifted the roof off the place. Stan would smile indulgently and pretend that she was so gifted, the other patrons should be grateful for the contribution. At the home of one of Roach's executives, Illeana noticed some ants crawling out of the cut flowers in the table centre-piece. She shrieked and declared that she could not sit down at the table "until those animals are removed".

Since all of this required some insulation, Stan's alcoholic intake increased to the same alarming peak that it had done when he was with Mae. Very soon, a great deal of time and energy in the Laurel household was directed towards getting Stan sufficiently dried out to get to the studio. Former drinking partner Pete Gordon was now involved in getting Stan to take showers and drink plenty of black coffee.

As for Illeana, she was arrested so frequently for public drunkenness that she would eventually be ordered by the court to leave Beverly Hills. But she was flamboyant to the end and would burst into song in her prison cell. The jail guards became rather fond of her. She was wild and, to all eyes but Stan's and those of her coterie of other Russian émigrés with dubious credentials, irreparably lost. There were rumours of previous arrests for prostitution and deportations from such ends of the earth as Singapore and Hong Kong. Stan dismissed them as libellous.

Stan's judgment was not altogether impaired. A number of his friends remember only Illeana's liveliness, her "drink and be merry" attitude towards a life she was convinced was brief enough. And there was a domestic side to Illeana, which Stan felt augured well for their future. She was the mother of an eight-year-old boy, who was kept at military school most of the time. She insisted upon that, indicating that her sense of values had not gone along with her inhibitions. She had a great fondness for her little Russian mother, who lived with them part of the time and spent many hours in the Laurel kitchen instructing their black cook, Lillian Burnett, in the making of bortsch, blintzes and the proper way to serve lamb.

In their first and only summer together, Stan, Illeana, and his retinue of cronies, servants and her mother moved to Canoga Park near the home of Charlie Rogers, who had co-directed *Fra Diavolo* and *Babes in Toyland* and co-authored *Way Out West*. Charlie had accepted Illeana, as he had all of the women in Stan's life, with no reservations. He understood Stan far better than most of the other Roach people. He knew that he was fiercely proud and enormously gifted, and that one trait had served the other while he was on the rise. Stan leaned on Rogers for support at that time. In some ways, he was isolated in the midst of all the parties. Many of the guests were Russian émigrés, fake counts and phony countesses.

The country place that Stan purchased was run-down. There was only a small stone cottage there, barely large enough for the servants, but it was part of his plan to make this marriage work and to help ensure his future as a screen comedian. Although there were some miles between them and the frenetic night-life of Los Angeles, Illeana's wild friends turned up all too often at the weekend. Stan hoped that once she was settled down to the routine of running a home, she might drink less and be less exposed to arrest and newspaper reporters, who found her exploits such good copy that she was often on the front page. The press seemed intent upon making Illeana into the most notorious Hollywood wife in town. Stan was becoming aware that it was within these newsmen's power to tear his reputation to tatters.

Stan had a high brick wall built around the property and a gate installed. A house was built from his own design consisting of a massive living-room with corner fireplace and a large master suite. He called the place "Fort Laurel" and announced that it was his refuge from "blondes" and "ex-wives", the terms being, in his case, synonomous. He intended also to escape from all the newspaper reporters.

Illeana, who had impressed no one as being delicate, now claimed that ex-wife Ruth's frequent phone-calls, inquiring after Stan, were driving her to the verge of a breakdown. In April, a restraining order was placed on Ruth by the court, barring her from further communication with Stan or his household. Not surprisingly, it was Ruth's contention that she and Stan were still married, that they had been reconciled just before this foolishness with Illeana. She expected, she said, that when Stan returned to his senses, they would be back together again. Many years later, Stan would tell John McCabe that Ruth was forever writing the scenario of something she wanted very much in her mind, realizing some part of it in fact (her announcement that she was the only legal Mrs Stan Laurel), and then believing all the rest of her fantasy. This seems to have been a perceptive observation for she persisted in this sort of thing almost to the end of her life. Stan was a remarkably keen analyst of the weaknesses of others, which was part of his genius, of course, unless he was emotionally involved with them.

Alice Brady, who had befriended both Stan and Ruth a few years earlier, had recently completed her most celebrated role as Mrs O'Leary in Zanuck's *In Old Chicago*. She tried to remain in touch with Stan despite Illeana. She sent him a pair of duelling pistols and told him to run an ad in the Los Angeles *Times* stating that in the event that Ruth Laurel was kidnapped, he had no intention of paying any ransom. Miss Brady was kidding, but Ruth was terrified by reports coming back to her about Illeana and never went anywhere for the next six months without her armed female private eye, Beulah.

Swiss Miss (1938) was completed during the time of this uproar off-screen. It contained one of the most charming and devastatingly funny scenes of any Laurel and Hardy comedy, Stan trying to take a bottle of rum away from a St Bernard rescue dog. Its big scene has Stan and Ollie being pursued by a gorilla as they try to move a piano across a wooden footbridge – over a gorge in the Alps – to a composer's château. The piano was supposed to have contained a bomb, placed there by one of the composer's several enemies (he was not a lovable man). The gorilla begins to swing the bridge so violently that it snaps, and he and the piano fall several thousand feet into the gorge, exploding upon impact. But someone decided that that was one complication too many, so the bomb was removed from the script.

Even better than *Swiss Miss* was their second feature that year, *Block-Heads*, released in August, and now considered vintage Laurel and Hardy. It is filled with echoes of earlier films by the team, but they are reprised with such finesse that the laughs are bigger than ever.

Then in September, while *Block-Heads* was being praised by knowledgeable reviewers, any semblance of peace in the lives of Stan and his fiery Russian collapsed within a day. In one version, while Illeana was out with friends "to cool off" after an all-day domestic battle, Stan, in an effort to atone, was cooking dinner (it was a Thursday and the cook was off for the day). A dark-haired thug broke into the house, ripped out the telephone wires, roughed up Stan, ordered him to open his safe, and made off with $10,000 in cash. The rumour was that the intruder was Mr Shuvalova, Illeana's "ex", although Stan later feared that she had never bothered to divorce him. Presumably, if not Shuvalova, it was someone in his hire since it was so obviously an inside job. The man knew where the safe was and that it contained a large amount of cash. When Stan came to his senses, he raced outside, jumped into his car in pursuit, and nearly crashed into a police car as he careered down the wrong side of the street. Arrested on a variety of charges, including drunken driving, Stan spent the night in jail, his only such experience.

Whatever really happened on that September evening, Stan chose to protect Illeana. In fact, he was as gallant towards her as he had been towards Mae – there was this fundamental decency in Stan that was the cornerstone of his screen character. Once committed to anyone, particularly where his emotions were involved, he could be dragged through the mire but he wouldn't abandon that person. Stan later confided to Ruth that Shuvalova did shake him down for large sums of money, either forcibly or through blackmail. Ruth believed that the threat was that Shuvalova would expose his own wife as a bigamist on the world's front pages. But to the press, Stan said on this occasion that Illeana was terribly late for the dinner he was preparing, and that he finally got in his car to search for her when he was arrested.

Days passed following the incident and there was nothing but idleness for Stan. Production was in the planning stages of a new film at the Roach Studio, tentatively entitled *It's Spring Again*, which sounded like a Deanna Durbin confection, but was about two bumbling friends and a pet elephant named Zenobia.

Stan told the press that his new film would not be for Roach at all, but for Mack Sennett, who was planning a comeback. Sennett had a script about the normal-sized son (Stan) of midget parents, which he called *The Problem Child*. Stan was enthusiastic and there were a number of conferences at Fort Laurel about it, but there were major financial problems that could not be resolved. Stan needed money and Sennett was talking about percentages of potential profits.

Beyond this, Stan, who had a keen sense for such matters, knew that Sennett had not kept pace with comedy development. His last movie, *Hypnotized* (1932) was not terribly different from a score of others he had made ten years earlier. *The Problem Child* was shelved and Sennett never did manage to pull another film project together.

Meanwhile, *Zenobia* was made with Oliver Hardy alone and Harry Langdon in support and it was released in May 1939. As completed, the Langdon part was not comparable to any Laurel role. Thus Roach was able to tell the author, as did its director Gordon Douglas, that the part was not really written with Stan in mind.

While technically Stan might have felt free to make an occasional outside picture on his four-film deal with Roach, his employer was not pleased with his indifference. Roach justifiably believed that he had contributed more than anyone to Stan's success, that he had been more than generous, and silent in the face of the most shameless – to him – public behaviour. When Stan declined to come in to discuss another possible film, Roach abruptly fired him.

For several weeks, Stan retreated into near-total seclusion. He would discuss the Roach débâcle with no one but lawyer Ben Shipman, who presented Stan's reply in the courts. He sued the Hal Roach Studios for $700,000 ($200,000 due to him under the last contract and $500,000 additional damages).

Fort Laurel finally became a true refuge during that ordeal. The gate was kept locked at all times and reporters were turned away. Stan concentrated on his "farming", which consisted of a large vegetable garden and hot-house, where he was attempting to wed a potato with an onion (and succeeded, although he never could persuade anyone to eat them); his quackless ducks which were being fattened for the table; and his plans to build a little vaudeville house on the property where new gags and routines could be tried out.

The suit against Roach dragged on. No trial date was set and Stan could not stand the endless uncertaintly any longer. He booked reservations for Illeana, his cook and himself on the Twentieth Century Limited and left on a cross-country vacation. In New York, they settled into the Waldorf for a week in a four-room suite. Mrs Burnett's presence in one of the front elevators was challenged by a foreign guest, who told her, "You can't ride on this elevator. You have to go on the freight elevator." Mrs Burnett was not a lady to suffer such indignities in silence and Stan was furious, phoning the manager and telling him, "Mrs Burnett is registered here just as we are. And we are paying for her. She doesn't have to go down the back elevator. She's my personal maid. Don't bother her any more."

The vacation was costly. Illeana was prodigally throwing money around that was no longer coming in: perfumes, furs, caviar. Stan bundled her on to the train again to hurry back west before she spent him into insolvency.

Harry Langdon, who had preceded Stan on a rather similar course, attempting to control his own work and only succeeding in destroying his career, had become especially close to Stan during those months. He hadn't wanted to be used as a bludgeon by Roach against Stan in the "Zenobia" business, but he was broke and there were ex-wives after him for back alimony. When Stan got back from New York, Harry came over with some sketches he had done during Stan's absence of how the little vaudeville showcase should look. They were turned over to an architect and blueprints were made.

Langdon and Pete Gordon were Stan's audience as he spoke of his future plans. He would expand his own producing company with lawyer Ben Shipman and Babe Hardy as partners – Laurel and Hardy Feature Productions. He would retain ownership of the films, as Chaplin had done so successfully. He spoke of these matters with some excitement; there was no hint that he might be entering the twilight of his starring career.

Harry Langdon had been through this entire cycle – discovery, stardom and decline – and he said nothing to disillusion Stan. Perhaps Stan could beat the odds. Stan's own view of Langdon's failure was that he had not caught on as a screen clown because his comic image had not jelled, whereas his and Ollie's screen images were fixed in the public mind as solidly as any since Mickey Mouse. Stan did not seem aware that the medium, the industry itself, was about to abandon him and Babe, despite vast audiences for their comedy throughout the world. The anomaly would be lost on Stan to the very end. It was inconceivable that Hollywood would close the door on an entire school of beloved entertainers.

Stan seemed determined to narrow the gap between himself and

Chaplin, both in status and in wealth. He knew that he could never catch up and he had no illusions about Chaplin's place in film history. In Stan's view, he was the greatest of them all. But Stan had followed his own celebrity closely – he was far more ego-driven than Babe could ever be. He knew what the Laurel and Hardy films had grossed abroad. He read the trade papers – *Variety* and *The Hollywood Reporter* – the way Babe read *The Racing Form* – and at home he had his secretary, Ernest Murphy, to help him answer the many fan letters that came in. Stan was certain that he knew better than Hal Roach where he and Babe Hardy stood in American films.

In February 1939, Roach answered Stan's suit with "an explanation". A Roach spokesman told the press that Stan had been uncooperative and had "violated the morals clause of his contract".

Stan reeled under this last charge. If he was anything at all as a human being, he was moral. He believed in marriage – too firmly, many of his friends felt. If he didn't enjoy the presence of children for longer than half an hour, still they were his greatest fans, especially in America. He wanted and felt he deserved their respect. But now, incredulously, the studio's lawyers were saying that he had "brought himself into ridicule and contempt and failed to have regard for public conventions and morals and has shocked and offended public morals and decency". It was incredible! Stan's first thought was that Roach was simply trying to weasle his way out of his last contract with him.

Once the initial shock wore off, Stan began to realize that the women in his life had done this to him: Mae and Ruth and Illeana. Even Lois, discreet and reclusive as she had been ever since their separation, had hit the headlines when she divorced him. The parade never seemed to stop. Now Illeana and her skirmishes with the Beverly Hills police led Stan to believe that he was jinxed.

Stan would never forgive Roach for pinning the label of immorality on him, but he was not vindictive. Just as he had once told everyone that Mae was "Mrs Laurel" out of gentlemanly consideration, so now he declined to mention any lapses in Roach's rectitude. But all partying with Illeana stopped. His cook often saw him walking over the grounds for hours on end. Sometimes, he would hum an old English music-hall song as he walked, his hands clasped behind his back. When he lectured Illeana on her behaviour, bitter quarrels would erupt, and she would enumerate Stan's own flaws at the top of her lungs.

By the spring of 1939, word had got around that Stan Laurel was difficult. He had not made a picture for a year; he had failed to show up for a production planned for him and Hardy; personal appearances were booked and he had not appeared. Two talent agents were suing him over this last default. The gossip columnists had him quarrelling with Babe. He was nearly broke.

Stan was dividing his time between Fort Laurel and his small fishing yacht, the *Ruth L* (he had written to Ruth, reassuringly saying that he had no plans to change the name to the *Illeana*, as had been reported in the press, that he never would humiliate her in that fashion). He had to abandon his plans for the little theatre on the grounds of Fort Laurel because there was no money to pay for its construction. He had earned something over a million and a half dollars in his thirteen years with Roach, but it was nearly all gone – much of it to ex-wives. Now he was spending some of the little that was left on making inquiries into the background of Illeana. He still loved her and hated the thought of giving her up, but his suspicions had been aroused. He felt that he had to know what she had been doing in Hong Kong prior to coming to California. It was confirmed through a detective agency that she had been arrested there, too.

In May 1939, Stan divorced Illeana. He said that he simply could not get her to "behave" and that she kept the household in a perpetual turmoil. "It all interfered with my work," he told the court, "and in fact nearly completed my career, because it put me in such a state of mind I was not able to work. . . . Her conduct caused unfavourable publicity and she mixed with people I didn't care for her to associate with." Stan, forever the gentleman, grossly understated Illeana's fatal attraction to hoods and phoneys. Stan's greatest distress at the time was caused by his failure to obtain custody of Bobby Shuvalova, whom he had come to love and want to protect.

Illeana drifted into a dreary life of alcoholism and drug addiction. Her attractive slavic features were soon blurred by puffiness as body water bloated her when her liver began to fail. She died in her early forties.

It was a sad chapter in Stan's life, but more than that, she had caused his standing in the film community more damage than half a dozen bad pictures could have done.

Still, Stan's sense of humour was sharp, and when the mood struck him, he would act out a gag idea for Charlie Rogers or Langdon. Buster Keaton was dropping by more and more frequently. But Stan made no move to return to the Roach fold – he was waiting for Roach to apologize.

Babe Hardy, abandoning the off-screen limits that had become traditional with them, came out to Fort Laurel on several occasions just to reassure Stan. Babe's contract with Roach would expire soon, and Ben Shipman was putting out feelers within the industry to find a studio interested in a Laurel and Hardy series. He was not having much luck. There was no thaw in the freeze-out of the great screen comics. *Gone with the Wind* would be premièred in Atlanta that autumn, and slapstick's Ice Age would deepen.

Since the success of *Topper* and its sequel, Roach had re-equipped the studio for the production of nothing but major features. He pretended not to be aware that he was the last real hope for the slapstick comedian in America. No doubt, he saw himself at that moment as Sam Goldwyn's peer. "Our Gang" and Charley Chase were closed chapters in his career. It may have saddened him a little to realize that Laurel and Hardy seemed ignorant of that fact.

5   Nothing was quite the same after Stan's enforced sabbatical. His private life was a shambles. There was no contact with Roach, and there were many in the industry who felt that the studio head had gone too far in condemning Stan. He had done to Roach exactly what Bette Davis and Humphrey Bogart had done to Jack Warner. And is a man to be fired for having no luck with wives?

Stan, in one of his now frequent spells of near paranoia, voiced a fear that "women's clubs will ban me". Shades of Fatty Arbuckle! Much of Stan's difficulty stemmed from his basic innocence and, though some of his scrapes might suggest otherwise, his fundamental puritanism. He had been sheltered by his mother as a child and by the theatre as an adolescent and adult. Backstage life often seems lurid and shameless to pious civilians, but it is frequently childlike in its lack of sophistication. For every Noel Coward, there are a dozen

Stan Laurels. It is a con artist's paradise every bit as ripe as a boarding house for old ladies.

The rise of the Metro studio (Roach's distributor until 1939) in the late twenties and its pre-eminence throughout the thirties and forties paralleled almost exactly the decline of low comedy in American movies. The forces against it were not very visible at first. Buster Keaton was urged upon Metro by Joe Schenck after several years of having his films made by Joe. By some miracle, Buster wrested control from the studio chiefs on the first comedy feature he made for them (*The Cameraman*, 1928), and it remains among his funniest. It was never allowed to happen again.

Since Metro was the industry leader, few dared to go against the trend. Chaplin did not. He called it satire in his last four films. He was happy to oblige those who insisted that pure and unadulterated comedy was out-of-date and began to take himself very seriously indeed. By the time of his last screen appearance, he even endeavoured to show the world how hypocritical and harmful McCarthyism was in America in *A King in New York* (1957), but the political satire was embarrassingly humourless, its dialogue arch and sermonizing, and its characters two-dimensional.

Stan began to believe that, like his soldier in *With Love and Hisses*, he was the only one out of step. He and Buster and Langdon and Lloyd and the Marx Brothers.

When the war began in Europe and there was intense pressure upon Metro to give the public some "relief", they signed Red Skelton, and some years into the war, Abbott and Costello were brought over from Universal.

Lou Costello, the stubby, calamity-prone dimwit, with his tall, bland foil Bud Abbott, had emerged from burlesque just as it was dying. Costello had studied both Laurel and Hardy carefully. He borrowed Stan's cry and his blink and Ollie's tie-twiddle; only Costello twiddled his fingers instead of his tie. Stan resented the borrowings intensely, and it was salt in the wound when Universal first began promoting Bud and Lou in *Buck Privates* (1941) with all the intense publicity which Stan had hoped would be his and Babe's when they went independent.

Abbott and Costello were more energetic than Laurel and Hardy. They had borrowed equally from Olsen and Johnson, whose speciality was turning theatres into bedlam. Quite unwittingly, the team had come along at the very moment when Stan was seeking greater status for Laurel and Hardy and they seized the single niche in films that might possibly have been Stan and Babe's throughout the war years, holding it until the boys felt compelled to give up and retire.

Laurel and Hardy could have co-existed with Red Skelton, but not with Abbott and Costello. Skelton, too, was a veteran of burlesque with a trunkful of characters – a rube, a drunk, etc. – and echoed the taste of the English music-hall more closely than anyone else in films, although he was an American. They might even have survived the domination of film comedy by the ladies. Lombard, Dunne, Jean Arthur and Colbert had been joined by Kate Hepburn, Ginger Rogers and Rosalind Russell. Laurel and Hardy were unique, but when placed in competition with Abbott and Costello, it appeared (quite erroneously, as it turned out) that they had created but not survived a genre.

And yet when the Second World War began, what a vacuum existed! There were several million soldiers and sailors, as well as civilians, seeking relief from the tensions of battle and battle reports, air raids and bad news from the front. Beyond the last films of the Marx Brothers and W. C. Fields, these audiences had to settle for Frank Capra's populist fantasies, the films of the ladies mentioned above, second-rate Laurel and Hardy soon to be consigned to the rubbish heap at Fox, frantic Abbott and Costello, Skelton and Danny Kaye. The latter befriended Stan in his retirement and is a nearly perfect example of Hollywood's diminution of a first-class talent.

In isolation at Fort Laurel during the weeks that followed the show-down with Roach, Stan made an effort to pull together the fractured parts of his life. He even phoned ex-wife Ruth and asked her to "come home". Much to Ben Shipman's dismay, Ruth complied, although Fort Laurel was entirely new to her. "How's my baby Ruth?" Stan asked, as she got out of the car.

Stan told Ruth that he had lost his friends. This was not absolutely true, but Stan's mood was very blue. "Today you're everyone's host," he told Ruth, "but tomorrow you're nobody's guest." It was a shrewd analysis of the cycle of success in Hollywood. "I'm all washed up, Ruthie." Producer Boris Morros might have been mulling over the possibility of bringing the boys back to the screen at that very moment, but Stan had yet to be approached.

Ruth said she didn't mind if he was friendless or even jobless except that it made him unhappy. "Maybe we'll have a chance now, you and I, Stan," she said. "Without all those hangers-on and phoneys. It was outsiders who wrecked our marriage." But Ben Shipman was still very much in the picture and he was unmoved by her return, even though she had come back without any hope that Stan's future could brighten perceptibly.

Stan suggested that Ruth and he "start going together again". She was not keen on any relationship outside marriage, an attitude that was harmful to them both, but she tolerated the situation for a few months. Lillian Burnett believed that Ruth must have loved Stan very much to put up with what she had to endure during that period. There were many dinners when Stan was absolutely silent and looked at Ruth balefully while she tried to make conversation. The walk-outs with the little black bag resumed.

Stan was apparently nicer to his old vaudeville cronies and studio friends than he was to Ruth. Although he had taken the initiative and called her back, that was a mood of the moment and until another such impulse struck him and they remarried in 1941, life around Stan was an uneven, chancy thing for Ruth Laurel. Wives, to Stan, were still episodes that invariably had unhappy endings.

Two months after Ruth's return, an independent producer at RKO, Boris Morros, would reunite the team in *The Flying Deuces*, and persuade many of those who had worked with Stan at the Roach Studio to participate: cameraman Art Lloyd, writers Charlie Rogers and Harry Langdon, and actor Jimmy Finlayson. *The Flying Deuces* was a gamble for nearly everyone concerned. Morros, a Russian ex-patriate, who would become a double agent for Russia and the United States during the forthcoming war, had appeared literally from nowhere as a producer with financial backing. This was not extraordinary in Hollywood. Although it cannot be documented, it is probable that Morros met Stan during the wild, but often very social period he spent with Illeana. Many of their friends had been from the White Russian colony in Hollywood.

51. Babe and his chow with Stan, 1949

52. Babe's birthday party on the set of *Atoll K* in Paris, 18 January 1951

53. At an exhibition of Scottish merchandise in Edinburgh during their 1947 tour, Lucille Hardy at left and Ida Laurel at right

54. The boys pause during a tour of British music-halls to visit Stan's sister, Olga Beatrice Healey, and her husband. Flanking Mrs Healey are Babe and Ida Laurel.

55. Stan and B.
judge a beauty c
test at Butlin's
Skegness, 1952

56. Stan's sister and two secretaries help the boys to answer fan mail in England, 1952
57. A radio interview in the dressing-room at an English music-hall, 1952
58. Some of the mob surrounding Laurel and Hardy during their 1952 tour of England. It was Babe Hardy's last public appearance.

58

59

59. A Paris movi[
house during t[
revival of *Fra Diav[
(1951), their bigg[
grossing film
60. Stan and I[
Laurel, Lucille a[
Babe Hardy po[
beside ''Lake Laur[
and Hardy'' on t[
old Roach lot, rea[
the studio tank us[
in so many of the[
comedies. 1954

60

A city setting on the back lot at the Hal Roach Studios after demolition crews began to tear down the place, 1967

Stan Laurel's grave California

61

STAN LAUREL
1890 – 1965
A MASTER OF COMEDY
HIS GENIUS IN THE ART OF
HUMOR BROUGHT GLADNESS
TO THE WORLD HE LOVED.

62

63

63. Oliver Hardy and Stan Laurel caught in a reflective moment on the Metro lot after completing their final Hollywood film, 1945

RKO, which seemed to be changing hands every day, was the only major studio willing to take a chance on the boys. The firm was to take an even more capricious fling into the unknown with *Citizen Kane* eighteen months later. Director Eddie Sutherland had not done a film for nearly two years. His private life was no less chaotic than Stan's, but he came on to the picture, trailing an only slightly faded banner. At one time, he was Bing Crosby's favourite director; he had guided or followed Mae West through the production of *Every Day's a Holiday* (1938); he had staged Clara Bow's only success-ful talkie, *The Saturday Night Kid* (1929), in which he had cast two Jeans in supporting roles before great fame overtook them – Harlow and Arthur. During his most productive phase, the early thirties, he was married to the beautiful Louise Brooks. Then, like Stan, he had a prolonged bout with the bottle.

Sutherland was agreeable to letting the boys do what they did best. There would be no innovations. Story conferences often became a search for something that had worked well before. If this suggests that Stan was about to spoil his only chance of doing something new, embarking on a more original path than he and Babe had trodden before, it should be remembered that Stan Laurel was never known for his daring. We enjoy Laurel and Hardy as much because they are familiar as we do because they envelop us in their loony, eccentric world of failed suicides, heartless females, rampaging gorillas in the Alps, and hard times in the Foreign Leg-ion. *The Flying Deuces* has parts of several of their earlier successes (*Beau Hunks*, 1931, *Bonnie Scotland*, 1935) and is not one of the better films. But it was released when much of Europe had fallen to the Nazis and did well enough to recoup its investment.

The fact that it had been made, released and reassured their fans was important. It brought about a reconciliation of sorts with Hal Roach. Through Ben Shipman, he told Stan that he still owed the studio two pictures. Deeply in debt, Stan needed that $200,000. Babe went back on salary as before, and the generous loan-out to RKO ended.

Babe took away from that production something that was far more valuable than renewed popularity. He fell precipitously in love with the script-girl on the film, Virginia Lucille Jones. It was sudden and unexpected, even to Babe, since Viola Morse had told all her friends that she and Babe were finally going to the altar. What agonies of remorse Babe must have felt when he broke the news to Viola!

And how envious Stan must have been to see Babe so blissfully happy with the right woman. To Stan, Lucille seemed almost too perfect. She was a woman of innumerable graces. She was at ease with everyone. She was not only beautiful, but she had a deep, infectious laugh. She was so quick on the uptake, she usually laughed before you could finish a story. Lucille, born in Texas and raised in Arizona and California, had been a dancer and a secretary, then because of her quick, retentive mind, a freelance script-girl. Nearly everyone on *The Flying Deuces* was either freelance or borrowed from another studio.

The romance itself had not begun until they were mid-picture. Lucille had tripped over a rolled-up carpet, struck her head on an arc light and was carried off to the hospital. It was while Lucille was unconscious that Babe got his first real look at her. He was dismayed by the accident and considerably moved by her immobile beauty. A goddess on a stretcher! He wondered how he could have missed noticing her before. Flowers followed and endearing little notes about how much she was needed on the set. Lucille resisted Babe's overtures for several weeks, but then something in the roguish twinkle of his eyes suddenly became attractive to her. And there was, of course, his never-ending courtliness. In March 1940, they were married.

Babe and Lucille bought a two-and-a-half-acre ranch in the San Fernando Valley. They raised chickens, ducks, turkeys and even pigs, and made pets of all of them. When the pigs, who were the most affectionate, reached the size where they could knock down the Hardys whenever they jumped up on them, they were given away. They couldn't bear to kill anything. They had fruit trees and a vegetable garden. Until the government sent him into an internment camp in 1942, they had a Japanese caretaker. Babe began spending more time at home and much less time at the country club.

13 || Roach Brings Back the Boys - to Oxford

1   In the autumn of 1939, while Babe was courting Lucille, Hal
       Roach invited the boys to return to film *A Chump at Oxford*.
Some primal comic urge had stirred in Roach amid all his many
plans for such films as *The Housekeeper's Daughter*, a comedy-drama
then in production. He even turned over the reins of that film to his
son, Hal Jr., and plunged into story conferences on *Chump* with all
the enthusiasm of the Hal Roach of the mid-twenties. He and Stan
behaved together as though there had been no unspeakable breach
between them.

The title of the new Laurel and Hardy was a play on Metro's *A
Yank at Oxford* (1938), which had been publicized as the first Anglo-
American production made in England at their British studios. But
the similarity stopped there. What the comedy was saying was that
it was better to be stupid and loved – by at least one friend (Ollie) –
than brilliant and feared.

Running less than an hour, it was sublimely assembled. As
street-cleaners, the boys' fondest wish is to be educated sufficiently
to help them rise – at least as far as the sidewalk. While they are
having lunch on the pavement, Stan tosses his banana peel away, a
robber running from a bank slips on it and is apprehended, and the

bank president wonders how he can repay them for their heroic deed. Ollie doesn't hesitate a moment in telling the man that they are in desperate need of an education, and we next see them on a street in Oxford, in caps and gowns, with Eton collars.

Undergrads are amused to see such old chaps around the university, and quite obviously obtuse ones at that. They begin ragging them at once, as malicious as Third Avenue hooligans – sending them through a privet maze, pretending to be professors and assigning them rooms in the Dean's own residence. When the Dean arrives to find them in his own bed, they refuse to accept his identity, but when the Dean's valet enters, knocking down a privacy screen, the five undergrads are revealed, crouched there to watch the amusing confrontation that they have engineered. The Dean roars in outrage that they shall all be expelled and, as they are leaving in disgrace, one of the students turns to call the boys "Snitchers!"

The valet, Meredith, is amazed to see Stan, who is, he insists, Lord Paddington, the greatest athlete and most brilliant scholar in the history of the university. Outside the building, a rabble of undergrads are shouting "Fee, fie, fo, fum; We want the blood of an American." Stan, alarmed, is watching the scene from a window when it slams down on his head, restoring his memory and changing him back into Lord Paddington.

The students burst into the room to find Lord Paddington staring down at them in a superior manner. "We're going to take off your breeches," they tell him. "What?" he says in tones of offence, "Take off my breeches in the presence of Meredith?"

When the students again call him a snitcher, he calmly asks Meredith to hold his handkerchief, his ears begin wiggling ominously – a portent of dreadful deeds to be done – and as the students throw themselves upon him, they are tossed one after the other through the window as a terrified Ollie watches from a ledge outside. When the Dean runs into the room to see what is going on, he, too, is tossed unceremoniously out of the same window. Ollie dashes in at that moment, but realizes too late that this Lord Paddington does not remotely recognize him and out he is pitched, too.

Ollie is hired as Lord Paddington's manservant and for more than a third of its length, the film is all Stan's. When the Dean wonders

how his Lordship can tolerate such a stupid servant, Lord Paddington says, "He's got a jolly old face, you know. Breaks the monotony
and helps fill up the room." Then, at the Dean's suggestion, he
agrees to help straighten out Albert Einstein and his theory when he
arrives shortly from Princeton.

Now the student body gathers beneath Lord Paddington's windows to salute him with a few choruses of "For He's A Jolly Good
Fellow" and Lord Paddington walks to the window to glance out
coolly at this demonstration. The window slams down on his head
once again – and he is Stan restored, with all the old wistful dumbness. Ollie is overjoyed.

The film remains to this day one of the most popular the team ever
made. It is Hal Roach's own personal favourite and he ranks it with
Fra Diavolo. Because of its brevity, it was double-billed everywhere,
but it was in every way a triumph, for the boys, for Roach, for
director Alfred Goulding (whose last film it was), for editor Bert
Jordan, and for scenarists Charlie Rogers, Felix Adler and Harry
Langdon.

In early 1940, Stan and Babe filmed their last feature for Hal Roach.
Saps at Sea was not an especially distinguished farewell to a professional association that had so enriched the world for a decade and a
half. Its director, Gordon Douglas, who began working for Roach as
a very young man, acting, cutting and assisting on *Our Gang*,
eventually taking charge of that series, recalled that the day *Saps at
Sea* was scheduled to go into production, they had only twelve
pages of script. From this and other evidence, it seems clear that
Roach's excitement over *A Chump at Oxford* was impulsive and that
his real interest and loyalties resided in such matters as *One Million,
B. C.* For this epic about prehistoric man, he had hired D. W. Griffith
as co-director.

Stan looked at the few sheets of paper they were calling the script
and ordered Douglas into his dressing-room. The writers were on
the floor above, working on the thirteenth page. "What do you
think of it, Gordie?" Stan asked.

"Frankly, Stan, I don't think too much of it. In fact, I think very
little of it."

"Well, do you want me to tell you how I feel about it?" And with that, Stan began tearing the script into little pieces, so they were reduced to having no pages at all. After that, Stan, the writers and Douglas would sit down each day and go over what they might be doing the next one. They were winging it all the way. They would check the Roach sound stages to see what was standing in the way of construction. Stan and Douglas would walk around and say, "Hey, we'll use that saloon." Or, "We'll make that into a boarding-house . . . a lobby of a hotel." They would order the crew to "dress that end of sound stage two. Just put tables in it and a lot of horns for the interior of the factory."

The film was finished and went out, and their fans were delighted. But both Stan and Babe knew that there would be no more films with Roach. He was far too busy checking out miniature dinosaurs and other details of his excursion into the days of the big reptiles. He was also locked in a crisis of temperament with D. W. Griffith, who was soon to lose all control of his part in the production.

Laurel and Hardy, when their world audiences most needed their peculiar brand of lunacy, slid into a temporary limbo. Paris was occupied by the Nazis, England began getting a rain of buzz-bombs, rockets were launched from France against her cities. With mounting horror and anger Stan read the record of wiped-out communities – Bristol, Coventry – places he knew intimately as a touring variety comic, and he grieved.

2 Stan and Ruth were remarried (their third ceremony) on 17 January 1941, at the Hitching Post in Las Vegas. According to a newspaper report, he had been eating tripe and onions, a combination that, for Stan was as steeped in nostalgia as it was in potential heartburn. Asked years later if Stan didn't have an incurable affection for her, Ruth laughed and repeated a story that Stan often told interviewers. When asked about his hobbies, Stan said, "I married all of mine."

Ben Shipman, as agent for Laurel and Hardy Feature Productions, Inc, canvassed the major studios to see if anyone was willing to take over the financing and distribution of their films. Stan wanted control over all production. Once again Ben had no luck, but when Louella Parsons learned of the boys' difficulties, she phoned Darryl Zanuck and told him that he simply had to hire Laurel and Hardy or he would be making a huge mistake. It was for Zanuck to ponder on whether that was a threat or a sound commercial suggestion. Louella was not normally the dreadful lady she has been painted, despite her enormous power and abuses of the same. She gave critical assistance to Marilyn Monroe, Marlon Brando and dozens of other stars in trouble before they regained their footing on slippery Olympus. Now Laurel and Hardy were rescued from seeming oblivion through Louella's intervention. The Fox Studio, however, refused to concede any control over the films to Stan. Thoroughly frustrated but deeply in debt, Stan signed along with Babe. The boys were back where they had been in their early years at Roach before they had been teamed, contract actors who had to do whatever they were told.

The favour to Louella Parsons cost Darryl Zanuck very little. The boys were to be turned over to the production chief in charge of programmers or "B" films, Sol Wurtzel. Stan's fee per picture was substantially reduced since he was now merely a comedian on hire and had nothing to do with the writing, direction or editing.

Stan's ordeal was most visible in the dressing-room when he and Babe first began work on *Great Guns* in the summer of 1941. A studio make-up man came in to work on his face and it did Stan no good to protest. The clown white was no longer to be used. Throughout his days at Fox, Stan would appear to have a suntan, just one small detail in the stifling of his creativity that went on there.

Great Guns opened to surprisingly good notices. It wasn't the script or the production that were praised, but nearly everyone hailed the return of the screen's greatest comedy team. Here was Stan playing tic-tac-toe on thin air and erasing it with his shirt-sleeve, and here, too, was Stan shaving by the light of a bulb screwed into his mouth.

More typical is *A-Haunting We Will Go* (1942), their second Fox film. This programmer, running to slightly more than an hour, lacked a single redeeming feature. Only their utter confidence that a money-making machine, portable variety and sold to them by con artists, can pay their $6.80 Pullman dining bill reminds us of the Laurel and Hardy of old. But it also serves to throw into sharp relief the awful tripe in which they are trapped. This tale of gangsters and a misplaced coffin that is to be used as transport by a *live* hood so that even the movie's title is a cheat is most shameful when we watch Ollie attempting to perform with the delicacy of their vintage films, the material defeating him at every turn. The movie makes Dante, the magician, who had no previous acting experience, just about the only convincing character on the screen.

There was no escaping the status of these formula comedies. They were "companion" features, the bottom half of a double bill. The boys' absence from the screen those many months allowed Abbott and Costello to capture the loyalty of children that had once been theirs. On the surface it seemed the strangest of ironies that *Great Guns* had been inspired by *Buck Privates*, made a year earlier by Abbott and Costello. But Fox was routinely humbling Stan and Babe in this fashion. *A-Haunting We Will Go* had followed Abbott and Costello's *Hold That Ghost* by exactly a year.

Now that the team was working again, Ben Shipman found other studios that were interested. Under the terms of their Fox contract, they were allowed to do outside pictures. The boys signed with Metro on the same terms as at Fox, the contracts running concurrently, as prison terms often do. It was a hard time all the way for Stan.

Metro, who had considered Laurel and Hardy as part of their galaxy throughout most of their years on the Roach lot, did try a little harder than Fox with their first comedy there, *Air Raid Wardens* (1943). Stan thought the story had real possibilities. He had served as an airplane spotter for a number of months earlier in the war, wearing a helmet and scanning the skies with binoculars.

Edward Sedgwick, who had directed Buster Keaton's first two features for the studio, including his classic *The Cameraman*, was assigned to the film. Jack Jevne and Charlie Rogers, both great gag-men and comedy constructionists with Stan for years, were hired to collaborate on the screenplay. Their old cameraman from Roach, Walter Lundin (*Bonnie Scotland*, etc.) was brought in to photograph it. But despite all this, Stan and Babe were defeated by the studio system. Stan was not allowed to touch his make-up. The script his friends had turned out was gone over by a permanent member of the Metro writing staff to make it all smooth and devoid of any hint of spontaneity. Stan was not encouraged to suggest any changes during production that might make the picture funnier. The result was another let-down for their fans, who had now to accept the reality that it seemed to be the end of the line for the loveable boobs.

In the weeks following their return to the screen in the autumn of 1941, the boys toured Army and Navy bases as far away as the Caribbean. Sponsored by Camp Shows, they did their Drivers' Licence Sketch, which Stan had created for a Red Cross benefit performance at the 1939 San Francisco World Fair. In this routine, the boys wander into a police station to get Ollie's licence – which turns out to have been handed down to him by his grandfather – renewed. The cop on duty is so confused by their buffoonery that they manage to consume his packed lunch while he is questioning Ollie. The cop poses a hypothetical driving crisis: "You're on top of a hill and you're coming down that hill at sixty miles an hour."

STAN: "What? In his grandfather's car?"

COP: "Yes, in his grandfather's car."

STAN: "But we've got no brakes."

COP: "Nevertheless, you're coming down the hill at sixty miles an hour. (STAN, *getting very interested, sits down in the cop's chair at the desk.*) Now you throw it into second gear – and it won't work. Finally, you throw it into *third* gear, and *still* it won't work. (*Cop takes off hat in the excitement.*)

STAN: "Why don't you throw in his grandfather? He won't work either!"

The boys manage to give *all* the wrong answers and the licence is refused. The cop chases them out and Ollie hands him an apple core from his lunch, provoking the cop to take pot shots at them as they run out.

Stan and Babe were invited to join a "Victory Caravan" of stars on a cross-country tour selling war bonds. Frank McHugh, who had brightened many a Warner Brothers musical or farce, recalled that Laurel and Hardy got much the biggest hand from the crowds everywhere they went.

Stan's last marriage to Ruth was deteriorating rapidly. They had both wanted it to succeed, and it might have done if they had been left alone and Ruth's health had not failed. Ben Shipman was vastly annoyed with her; he resented the fact that she had come back into Stan's life. Then Ruth had a wisdom tooth extracted that led to a prolonged, massive infection. In a matter of weeks, her gaiety and good humour left her and she became a semi-invalid. She was never to recover fully from this minor dental surgery and she chronically coughed up a green mucus which no antibiotic could eradicate. Ruth, who never kidded herself, believed that Stan lost all romantic interest in her at that point.

Before they returned to Fox, a long personal appearance tour was planned by the Music Corporation of America for the boys. Stan and Babe (with Lucille accompanying him) did four shows a day in Omaha, St Louis, Chicago, Milwaukee, Minneapolis, Cleveland, Columbus, Cincinnati, Newark (New Jersey), Boston, Buffalo and Hartford. Their two studios read the trade paper accounts with astonishment. Without exception, each city was going wild over Laurel and Hardy. They were drawing huge crowds at every theatre the lines stretching for a block in some places. It was far beyond anything that could be expected from a typical film star personal appearance.

The difference between a live appearance of the boys and someone like Robert Taylor, for example, was essentially that they were more than film stars. They were living legends on the same plateau with Charles Lindbergh and Babe Ruth. Their Roach films had brought them up to the level of Chaplin himself, and it is doubtful that at this point in time little Charlie, promoting *The Great Dictator*, could have drawn the frantic, delighted mobs and the cheers that Laurel and Hardy were drawing everywhere.

For Stan, it was a return to the medium he loved best – live audiences. In St Louis, it was even nostalgic as they were booked into the Grand Theatre, where he and Mae had appeared nearly twenty years earlier. For Babe, it took him back to that moment eight years ago when he and Stan first stepped on to the stage of a British music-hall.

Radio interviewers were after them to put in brief appearances on their shows, and whenever they could squeeze it in, they obliged them. Ruth recalled that they worked constantly during the time of those appearances, from breakfast until bedtime. She joined them for part of the tour and was impressed with the effortless way in which they made the transition from films to live shows. The only panic occurred one day when Babe's suit did not come back from the cleaners as showtime was approaching. He was pacing back and forth in his room in his shorts while someone was dispatched to locate the vital suit.

The success of the tours (there were two of them over a period of twenty months) caused Fox to reappraise their handling of Laurel and Hardy and Malcolm St Clair was brought in as their director. He had learned comedy at the old Sennett studio, and had collaborated with Buster Keaton on one of his early two-reelers, *The Goat* (1921), which remains one of his best. He had handled such diverse talents as Rin Tin Tin, Clara Bow, Pola Negri and Louise Brooks and in 1928, he directed the first screen version of *Gentlemen Prefer Blondes*. In the late thirties, Mal had been signed up by Zanuck to direct his comedy programmers, especially a long-running series known as "The Jones Family" with Jed Prouty and Spring Byington. Like Stan and Babe, he had known better days and even a taste of glory. There is little doubt that he saw in Laurel and Hardy one last opportunity to revive his sagging career.

Mal St Clair had the respect of both Stan and Babe. Sadly for all of them, there was no rising above the quality of the script of *Jitterbugs* (1943), their first film together, though it did introduce an attractive new ingénue, Vivian Blaine, who would become a major Broadway singing star in *Guys and Dolls* five years later. The film allowed Stan to dress in drag, always one of his more engaging turns, as Vivian's aunt, while Babe played a gallant southern gentleman, a type he knew intimately. His scene with Lee Patrick as a phoney southern lady was a felicitous high point.

But it was all downhill after that. Stan thought that the studio writers had their characters confused and were giving Ollie lines and actions that Stan should have had. They were placing them in situations that were supposedly comic exaggerations of the real world, forgetting that Laurel and Hardy's world was unique. Their present studios had screened their old movies searching for gags that could be re-used and overlooking the eccentric nature of the boys' characters.

Their farewell to American films (*Nothing But Trouble*, Metro, 1945) appeared to be in the tradition of their great Roach opera *bouffe*, except that there was no music and the story was a mechanical contrivance about treachery surrounding the temporarily deposed Crown Prince of a mythical kingdom. There were four writers involved in this frantic pancake and no one at any level of authority had the wisdom to ask Stan for a suggestion. By now, there was a beaten cur attitude in Stan that made him a production pariah. Both Stan and Babe seemed unable to communicate their anguish to anyone, even to each other. But upon seeing the rough cut of *Nothing But Trouble*, their indignation gave them the voice to object and they begged Shipman to get them out of their contracts. Both Fox and Metro obliged them.

Laurel and Hardy left the Hollywood studios with no films in prospect. Even Louella Parsons, who had reminded Zanuck of their availability, avoided mentioning their names because she had asked them to appear *gratis* (as she did everyone) on her successful radio show, *Hollywood Hotel*, and Stan had informed her that they wouldn't do the show for less than $5000. Since Louella booked appearances on her show through an obvious kind of blackmail (those who dared refuse such an invitation to perform for free could be ignored in her Hearst column or, if she felt they had let her down badly, vilified), in the case of Laurel and Hardy, she clearly felt that they *owed* her an appearance.

At fifty-five, Stan thought that their vogue was over. Perhaps it was time to turn over the screen to younger, more energetic comedians. He particularly admired the films of Danny Kaye – Kaye's success took some of the hurt out of the success of Abbott and Costello. They had slowed down Kaye's pace, and the scripts were becoming as wholesome as those of Laurel and Hardy had been. Except for the obligatory romantic interest and his character's obviously higher I.Q., Danny Kaye was purveying the same lunatic comedy that the boys had done through two decades.

At about this time, there appeared the first ominous sign of something that was graver than weak scripts. Stan complained of fatigue and it was found that he was suffering from the initial symptoms of diabetes. From then on until his death, he was under a doctor's care much of the time. Some of Stan's flaws might well be attributed to this discovery – the short temper, the depressions.

But he and Babe were free of all Hollywood commitments after twenty years of stardom, and they no longer had to worry about their reputations. That was a nagging concern of Stan's – another year of such films and their names might have been sullied beyond redemption. Surely at that moment Stan saw clearly how ineffectual Ben Shipman had been in handling their careers. But he felt such a strong sense of loyalty, such a deep attachment for the man, that he didn't dwell on it. For one thing, Ben would be the first to point out his own shortcomings. When something backfired or Stan blew the whistle and cried "enough!" then Ben would slip into an old act he did on such occasions and swear that he was going to join the Foreign Legion. Stan would try to talk him out of it, his role being to take the threat with the utmost seriousness. Ben Shipman was stooped, white-haired, small, with a gentle voice and far too delicate a spirit for the Legion even to consider him. Finally, one afternoon Ben phoned with some good news. MCA wanted the boys to go out on the road again, a hugely profitable enterprise for all concerned, but Stan's health would not permit that until 1946.

Ruth had moved to Palm Springs, and when she learned of Stan's illness, she decided to return to Ben Shipman the alimony cheques that Stan had been ordered to pay her by the court. This gesture earned her no gratitude. Ben was not convinced of her concern. He remembered all those days of litigation, of battling the wives and mistresses out in court. Ruth hadn't withdrawn her suit then because Mae had appeared from out of nowhere at the same time.

Ruth was to learn some months later, or so she insisted, that Shipman had not informed Stan of the return of the cheques. Perhaps he had not. He may have simply returned the money to the corporate account, which was routinely divided in this fashion: two-fifths to Stan as President; two-fifths to Babe as Vice-President; and one fifth to Shipman as Secretary-Treasurer. If Ben was ever dishonest, it was by omission. Naturally, Stan sided with his lawyer and loyal old friend. Ruth was embittered by the episode and Shipman, quite understandably, intensified his actions against her. From that time on, Ruth's five per cent became a random affair, having little to do with Stan's actual earnings. Everything he earned went into the corporate account, as did Babe's. Only Shipman and his accountant could trace Stan's income and he rarely bothered to do so on Ruth's behalf. When Stan was reminded (by Ruth) of the obligation, a quarterly cheque would go out. Much of the corres-pondence between Ruth and Shipman became exhibits in a later suit filed against him by her, following Stan's death. Those documents make it clear that Ruth's charges were directed against Ben Shipman and never against Stan.

On 30 April 1946, Ruth won an uncontested divorce from Stan in Las Vegas. She stayed on for a while after her decree came through and she thought of settling there permanently. It was an ambience that suited her – an entirely urban hodge-podge set down in a last wasteland. Ruth had always preferred the town to the country, and in Vegas there was little evidence of nature – even the palm trees looked thirsty. People were more open there, she thought, less devious. If someone liked you, they would come right up and tell you so. In fact, a rather handsome man in his forties came up to Ruth and invited her to his hotel suite one afternoon. She was miffed that anyone might think she was "fast", until she learned that he had heard that she was Mrs Stan Laurel and had thought she was Illeana.

Traumatic though their relationship had been, Stan must have been thinking of Illeana a great deal of the time and wondering what had happened to her. He had drifted back into a life of eating out and spending evenings in bars where the food was appetizing, some of them Russian ones he had frequented with Illeana. In 1945, Stan took a party of ten for dinner at the Moskwa in the San Fernando Valley. Seated across the room was a compelling-looking blonde, imperious, blue eyes flashing, a diva, he learned. "Please send her over," he asked, and Ida Kitaeva (Keaton) Raphael entered Stan's life.

Ida's Russian accent intrigued Stan at once. She was recently a widow; he was in the process of getting a divorce. It seemed a repetition of his meeting with Virginia Ruth Rogers except for one small detail. Ida Kitaeva Raphael was in show business herself. She had a small career going with a few impressive movie credits, mostly from her work with director-writer Preston Sturges, who had used her in *Hail the Conquering Hero* (1944) as a prima donna primed to burst forth with some hallowed anthem at the welcome home reception for the "marine war hero" and in *The Sin of Harold Diddlebock*, which remained on the shelf for five years and was then released twice to sparse audiences, the second time as *Mad Wednesday* (1951), Harold Lloyd's last movie. She was working on the Lloyd picture when she met Stan at the Moskwa, and within days, he was chauffeuring her to the studio. She said it was heartbreaking to see his expression as she left him each morning since he was the one who should have been going before the cameras.

At first, Ida had no idea who he was. She was not a movie fan, her passions being opera and the classical theatre. Then she was shocked to learn how important he had been as a star. He seemed quite lonely and that won her heart more than anything. One night, as she later told John McCabe, "He said to me, 'I want to propose to you but I'm not divorced yet. Here we go – that word *again*!'" The lines did echo those he had spoken to Ruth Rogers eleven years earlier, but Stan had changed a great deal. He was no longer flirtatious. The world in which he moved had soured for him.

"So we met", Ida said, "and agreed the very next day, and he sent me a big box of roses – twenty-four. It was so exciting! He explained to me he was between pictures and I could tell he had been unhappy with the studio. . . . He lived then in his beautiful home, Fort Laurel, in Canoga Park."

Following the divorce in April, they drove to Yuma in early May to get married, but Stan got lost along the way and darkness fell long before they got their bearings again. They were deep in grazing land for miles and there were cattle all around them. They had to get the justice of the peace out of bed to marry them.

Newspapers asked "WHERE IS STAN LAUREL?" but reporters found him with his bride in San Diego's Grand Hotel. Ida told the press: "Please! Please, you boys quote me. Be sure it's accurate: *No more divorces for Stan Laurel!*" Everybody laughed at such an improbability, but Ida was right.

14 ‖ Goodbye Time

1   With the pressures of film-making behind him, Stan slowly eased himself into the role that most suited him – the mellow, charitable show business veteran, who could sit back now and enjoy whatever was left of his fame. Often at the Roach Studio, he had been abrupt and prankish; now he was a gentleman down to his toes. His illness had forced him into some of this reform. Whisky was not allowed, although once in a great while he would take a jigger or two. He was compelled to slow down his pace, so his old craving for action was now suppressed.

When the drinking stopped, the open bar at Fort Laurel was shut down. Pete Gordon drifted off, chiefly because Ida had very firm ideas about how life around Stan should be managed. Besides, Stan laughed a great deal with her around and their closeness tended to exclude Pete. Chauffeur and bodyguard Tunney left, too. As the place emptied, Stan realized that Fort Laurel was as much a relic of the past as the high life had become. He and Ida decided to sell it.

They moved to a more conventional two-storey house in Sherman Oaks, which lies just beyond Beverly Hills off Mulholland Drive. Before they were well settled in, Bernard Delfont, Lord Grade's brother, invited the team to play the Palladium in London.

Laurel and Hardy were the first Americans to be booked on the two-a-day policy at the huge music-hall, several years before Judy Garland's triumph there. Stan, Ida and Babe (Lucille was ill) went over on the *Queen Mary* in 1947. When they reached London, even though there was a heavy downpour, thousands of fans were at Waterloo Station waiting for a glimpse of the boys. The contrast between their low esteem in the eyes of American film-makers of the 1940s and this exuberant and affectionate mob was startling.

Delfont had booked them throughout the British Isles in the major music-halls. When they reached Newcastle, there was no heat either in the theatre or in their hotel, and they sat together bundled in heavy coats and phoned Lucille in California to tell her of their huge success and cheer her up. Lucille said it was ninety degrees there, which news made Stan and Ida especially miserable. Babe seldom minded the cold because of his weight and perspired even in temperate weather. Stan put the last piece of coal in the grate and said, "There'll always be an England!"

Stan's little joke lifted their dampened spirits considerably with Babe roaring, his great stomach heaving up and down. And so it went through fair weather and freezing rain, with crowds everywhere. Delfont told them that they could come back any time at all and make the same tour with sell-outs just as before.

In Paris, they played the Lido, a big cabaret where noisy drunks drowned out the boys' dialogue, and, backstage, the ladies of the chorus ran around nude. Stan was indignant and informed the manager that many parents brought their small children to visit them. The naked women didn't receive any coverings as a consequence, however, and Stan subsided. Then they moved on to the Low Countries, where Stan had once nearly starved during the tour of *Fun on the Tyrol*. After that, they toured much of Scandinavia.

When they got back home, Stan and Ida lived quietly in their undistinguished suburban house, so much like its neighbours. Ida cooked only a few exotic Russian and Chinese dishes (she and her family had come to America by way of Manchuria), and there was a small mountain of tin cans in their rear driveway, which a handyman would clear out periodically.

Ida gave up her small film career entirely. Hers was a quiet unselfishness, never visible. From a diva with a distinct continental bravura, she became known to her friends for her lack of any pretensions whatsoever to do anything beyond keeping Stan comfortable. But she remained an individual and projected great inner strength, and in guarding Stan's privacy, she could be abrupt at times. She knew that he was always eager to greet his fans, but there were a few occasions when his health would not permit it. Stan accepted her taking over the management of his affairs – everything but business deals, which were left in Shipman's hands. Ida became a buffer between Stan and the world, and he was given the chance to become the dean of American film comedy. At almost the same time, a drunken Marion Davies was eased out of Chaplin's presence despite their having been the closest of friends a decade earlier, apparently a sight too painful for him to bear. Stan and Charlie were getting old.

But Chaplin had reserves within him that Stan did not, which he would prove in a very short time. He was then involved in a paternity suit. The scandal was far worse than anything Stan had suffered, and for the first time, his feelings about Charlie changed. He still believed that there was no greater clown ever, but he saw him as human now and he felt considerable compassion for him. He was afraid that they (the mindless mob and the Establishment) were out to get him. There was a tinge of irony in that. Stan was edging ever more closely to becoming a part of the Establishment himself, quite unconsciously. He said that Charlie had never grown up. He was still a child, but no one seemed to realize that. Charlie never had known a real childhood so he spent the rest of his life living out his childish fantasy.

Television had developed to a point where there were competing networks late in 1947. Stan and Ida bought a set and many of Stan's hours were spent watching the new or reclaimed comedians – Sid Caesar and Imogene Coca, Milton Berle, whose career reached a dizzying height that he could not have imagined possible a year or two earlier, and a little later, Jackie Gleason and the biggest of them all, Lucille Ball.

While Stan had very little to say publicly about *Lucy*, he did watch it, and there is little doubt that he was astonished to see the many details of characterization and attitude which Miss Ball had borrowed from Laurel and Hardy, especially from himself. This was the first hint Stan had that, among other performers, he had become an idol and someone to be emulated in tribute, the way he had copied Dan Leno. In *I Love Lucy*, there were pratfalls, dunkings in water and wine, loony to the end. But Lucille Ball, like her obvious idols, knew the borderlines of taste and stayed within them always.

More than any other producer in Hollywood, Hal Roach had anticipated the quick dominance of television. He began turning out "quickie" half-hour dramas in late 1948, directing them himself. One of them, entitled *Sadie and Sally*, took only one day to shoot. He leased sound stages to other television producers, and he sold nearly all of the hundreds of comedies in his backlog in huge blocks, netting a fortune. *Our Gang* was syndicated as *The Little Rascals* and rapidly became one of the most popular children's shows on the air. Charley Chase was a late night favourite on many channels, and Laurel and Hardy began to appear almost round the clock.

In that age of the birth of television, the word "residual" had not taken on any pertinence, but within three years, Gene Autry would sue the distributors of his old westerns for "residual" income, based upon the contention that they were starring vehicles, could not have been made without him, and as their *raison d'être*, he was entitled to a share. Stan followed the story with hope and excitement, but Autry lost the case.

In some areas, Stan and Ollie were morning favourites. In New York City, they usually appeared just before the evening news or very late at night. Their audiences in cinemas had amounted to hundreds of millions around the world, but Laurel and Hardy fans suddenly reached astronomical figures. Not since the peak of their popularity in the mid-thirties had so much fan mail been sent them. Their ubiquitousness in classic old films must have ruled against anyone wanting to bring them into the medium live at that time, although a few offers did come in eventually. The other comics going into television were veterans of the stage or radio with only a few film appearances behind them – Ed Wynn, who survived for a few seasons, Fred Allen, who should have made a big success but did not, Eddie Cantor, Jimmy Durante and Bobby Clark.

Stan always felt a real obligation to his fans. If his feelings for his employers were mixed and often negative, his audiences were the recipients of Stan's total regard and respect. Within weeks following the mass exposure of those old movies, Stan fell hopelessly behind in answering fan letters even though he spent part of every day at a small desk with an old portable typewriter, composing appreciative notes. He watched the movies himself with a running commentary to Ida or anyone else present on what worked and what could have been better. Sometimes the films were butchered when they were edited for television, and Stan offered to do the job free but no one took him up on it.

Roach's success in the new medium prompted him to take the plunge with a more ambitious project, a half-hour series of situation comedy produced with the same finesse that had gone into his movie series. It was called *My Little Margie*, it starred Gale Storm, and it was vastly popular. The studio had every sound stage working. Hal Roach, Jr., took over the production of the few film features still being made before coming into television. Many of the same crew that had been on the great Roach comedies of the thirties were still there – Bert Jordan in the cutting room, Bob Davis checking out equipment and locations, and Bones Vreeland as chief grip and manager of the back lot. Television had brought a booming prosperity to all the Roach veterans except his old actors, who were either dead or in enforced retirement like Stan and Babe.

2   During the late winter of 1949–50, a film offer came in from an unexpected corner. A production firm based in Paris calling itself Les Films Sirius wanted to bring Laurel and Hardy back to the screen. They had a story of sorts: Stan and Ollie inherit a Pacific Island and on their way to establish residence, a storm comes up very quickly and they are forced on to a deserted atoll, where a Robinson Crusoe lifestyle is pursued (it was to be called *Robinson Crusoe-Land* in its United States release). Together with a girl in flight from a jealous fiancé who happens by and a young man who was part of their crew, they set up their own little Republic, a utopia (the film was reissued in the United States in 1954 as *Utopia*). All runs smoothly until uranium is discovered and the little island is overrun with various governments' representatives and other assorted crooks and pirates.

It was an ambitious film project and an Italian company (Fortezza in Rome) was ready to co-produce. An actress of modest fame and talents, Suzy Delair, was signed as the ingénue. The boys agreed to come out of retirement, and on April Fool's Day, 1950, the Laurels and the Hardys sailed for Europe.

Seldom had a film production been so accursed. Stan had never fully regained his strength from his struggles with diabetes, which had taken a turn for the worse in 1948. But he wanted to work even though illness had etched deep lines in his face, which no make-up could possibly conceal. And Babe was grossly overweight, up to 300 pounds. They were barely recognizable caricatures of themselves; producer Raymond Eger and director Leo Joannon must have been shocked by the sight of them. Joannon was in charge and seemed not to hear anything that Stan had to say, or perhaps there was a basic linguistic problem. Communication between the stars and the executive staff, all French-speaking only, broke down early.

The language difficulties could have been surmounted if there were genuine artists involved. One can easily imagine Lina Wertmuller, whose own *Swept Away by an Unusual Destiny* contains identical story elements, handling Laurel and Hardy with exuberance, delicacy, and an appreciation of mime that would have pushed aside the language barrier.

They were supposed to be filming for twelve weeks; the schedule stretched to a year. When they reached Paris, they learned that the script was not ready. Stan was used to that back on the Roach lot, but then he was ten or twenty years younger and half the time the comedy would pour right out of Stan between takes. The creative juices were no longer flowing unimpeded. Stan was sixty years old and in failing health. The entire project was becoming a melancholy charade.

Stan finally got the point across to Joannon that *he* would write the story with the help of two Americans, who were sent for. Gradually a story took shape, and production began in a Paris studio. Then they moved to a location on an island near Cannes. Ida recalled that the director, Joannon, "dressed himself like Cecil B. De Mille – puttees, pith-hat and carried a megaphone – everything. Honest to God. Stan used to say, 'Joannon is funnier than the picture – although *that's* not saying a hell of a lot.' . . . Joannon liked to take films of the water. Just of the water, that's all. Stan used to say, 'I guess he just *likes* water. Maybe because this is the story of an island Joannon thinks it's important to take a lot of water shots. Only he ought to get the island in there, too.'"

Finally, more than two months after their arrival and with only the beginnings of a movie, Stan found that his urinary tract was blocked. A local doctor treated him, but he did not improve. A specialist was needed but Stan continued working, looking like death. He phoned Ben Shipman in California and Ben came over, saw the chaos around Stan and, at Stan's suggestion, sent for Alf Goulding, who was living in England following his last – and extremely capable – directorial assignment, *A Chump at Oxford.* No one could wrest control from Joannon, but the latter did allow Goulding to direct most of the boys' comedy routines, with Stan making suggestions along the way as in the vintage Roach years.

Mid-film, Stan collapsed and was rushed by ambulance to the American Hospital at the edge of Paris. A surgeon discovered a growth on his prostate. Ida later said it was a boil, but that sounds quite unlikely. It was removed, but recovery was slow, with nurses round the clock and Ida never leaving the hospital, hanging around, the French press said, *comme une chienne*.

Meanwhile, Babe was suffering from the strain of the extreme heat in the south of France where they had been working. He had at least fifty pounds excess weight, and was anxious over Stan, the production, and the feeling that he was trapped and might never get home again. For the very first time, his heart began to act peculiarly. It began beating irregularly and Lucille insisted that *he* see a doctor; she learned that he was suffering from fibrillation. The doctor suggested that he reduce, although he was not told why. Babe's size was no longer a marketable commodity on the amusement scene.

Stan had lost weight during his illness, dropping from his usual 165 to 114 pounds. They erected an infirmary on the location, and Stan returned to work, unable to stand before the cameras for longer than twenty minutes at a time. On 1 April 1951, the Laurels and the Hardys finally left France.

Stan spent most of that year recovering. He gradually got his weight back, and his diabetes under control. *Atoll K* was released in 1952, the longest film they ever made in every conceivable way (nine reels) and a painful experience for all of their fans. Fortunately it never had a wide release, although it was eventually sold to television and appears on rare occasions, puzzling those who chance to see it and who are familiar with the *real* Laurel and Hardy.

In 1952, the boys were well enough to take on a tour of England again. Bernie Delfont had a long itinerary planned, and Stan was ready with a new act. He had written a sketch loosely based on an early two-reeler, *Night Owls* (1930).

The sketch contained one of their funnier confrontations with the law. As vagrants sleeping on a park bench, they are persuaded by a cop on his beat to rob the police chief's house so that he can take the credit for their capture and then "fix it up" to get them off. Since the corrupt cop insists that he will have to run them in as derelicts anyway, they agree. They make a dreadful mess of the attempt and when the cop picks up the silverware they have dropped to show to the chief, *he* is accused of the burglary. The boys run off, banging into garbage cans.

Lucille had put Babe on a sort of diet, but he had not been sufficiently frightened by his heart condition and still weighed nearly 300 pounds. Stan looked almost well again. The tour was another great success for them and nearly erased the painful memory of their ordeal in France. It had become a pattern for a number of washed-up film stars to tour for a little while – usually pitiful affairs in which the aging actress or actor was cast in a dreadful comedy that would never reach New York. But Stan and Babe had beaten the odds against survival on those terms. Bernie Delfont urged them to make their British tour a tradition and, before leaving England in 1952, they agreed to return in 1953.

An American actor, John McCabe, was in the midst of a three-year graduate course at the Shakespeare Insitute in Stratford when he learned that Laurel and Hardy were appearing at the Empire in Birmingham, twenty-five miles away. McCabe had been a dedicated fan since boyhood back in Michigan, and he was thrilled to be seeing his favourite comedians, so long off the screen, in person. Stan had written a new sketch, *Birds of a Feather*. Set in a mental ward where Ollie has been taken after trying to fly out of the window of a distillery where he and Stan are whisky tasters, it derives most of its humour from the revelation that the psychiatrist, Dr Berserk, is nuttier than they are. While it did not respect the later taboos against mental illness as a subject for comedy, it was relatively innocent in their hands, and certainly without malice.

On an impulse, McCabe decided to try to get backstage to meet Stan. This proved easy and Stan seemed eager to chat between shows; Ida was in France visiting relatives and he was lonely. He liked McCabe immediately and he didn't mind his many questions, since there was nothing personal about any of them. As a performer himself, McCabe was interested only in Stan's methods of work as a film actor, how those grand old comedies were put together. They spoke for over two hours that first day and Stan invited him back the next. By the third day, McCabe realized he was learning a great many valuable things about the business of being Stan Laurel and Oliver Hardy. He proposed that he begin setting down what Stan was telling him in the form of a book, and John McCabe's *Mr Laurel and Mr Hardy*, a highly readable introduction to their films and an affectionate review of their lives, took shape. It was published in 1961 and is still in print, its popularity prompting an additional flow of fan mail to Stan and Babe. Babe, who never felt the obligation that Stan did to their audiences and admirers, found it a nuisance, but Stan plodded ahead with his correspondence, eventually answering everyone who wrote to him at least once.

3   In early 1954, Babe was made painfully aware of his illness. He was felled by a heart attack which was complicated by an ailing gall bladder. He was hospitalized for weeks, but he warned Lucille not to let anyone know it was anything more than a gall bladder flare-up. He and Stan were in the midst of negotiations with Hal Roach, Jr., who was taking on more and more authority at his father's studio, to do a series of hour long children's films in colour to be called *The Fables of Laurel and Hardy*. They were to be familiar tales, including *Babes in the Woods*, *Aladdin* and *Puss in Boots*, and Stan would control them completely. Any chronic illness as serious as a heart condition would make Babe uninsurable and the deal would be off.

Stan actually wrote an outline of *Babes in the Woods*, and presumably it met with Roach, Jr.'s approval. Stan planned to remove the emphasis from the physical humiliations and feature more of their

"White Magic", such as that seen in *Way Out West* in which Stan uses his thumb as a match.

In the winter of 1954, television producer and personality Ralph Edwards contacted Ida and Lucille about the possibility of Laurel and Hardy appearing on his weekly half-hour reprise of a celebrity's past entitled *This Is Your Life*. The show, with considerable fanfare, presented old school chums who recalled offences that the celebrity had committed in childhood and ex-sweethearts now happily married to someone else, and was held together principally by Edwards' enthusiasm. The appearance of Laurel and Hardy would serve to remind the public that the boys were still around and even recognizable, despite Babe's larger size. Hal Roach, Jr. was pleased that the team was getting this exposure in advance of their *Fables* show. He even agreed to appear, representing their old studio, although his father declined.

With Stan and Babe left entirely in the dark about the project, the production machinery went into operation. Cherished family photos were whisked from their places in their living-rooms during brief absences, copied and rushed back.

Edwards opened the show in typical fashion: "Now tonight we have a startling surprise in store for you. Now listen to this; we are going to recreate not one, but *two* lives. Wait till you see who they are. Right now our two subjects are in Room 205 of the Hollywood Knickerbocker Hotel . . . they are talking to a friend of theirs, one of England's most prominent producers, Bernard Delfont of London, whom we've brought here to Hollywood just to make our surprise work . . . we have a television camera hidden behind French doors in the kitchenette, you see, of the hotel suite over there. Now on my signal the door will fly open, the lights will go on, the speaker will go on so they can hear, and you'll see what will happen. . . . This is Ralph Edwards speaking to you from the El Capitan theatre on Vine Street here in Hollywood. Your very good friends there, Mr Bernard Delfont and Mr Ben Shipman, have joined with us in this surprise tribute to one of the greatest comedy teams of our time. Two heads, two bodies, but one big laugh for over thirty years. Tonight *This Is Your Life*, I should say These Are Your Lives: Stan Laurel and Oliver Hardy. (*Music*) Now Stan and Oliver, Laurel and Hardy, we have a lovely evening planned for you. Please hurry downstairs. Come over to our theatre stage. How ya doing, boys? Fifty million of your fans are eager to see your lives unfold – lives that have brought the blessing of laughter to a troubled world for some thirty-five years . . . They took a taxi, did they, boys? . . . They are here? . . . Oh, my; this is more than a two-reeler. Here they come. (*Applause*) Hello, Oliver Hardy. Hello, Stan. This is great, wonderful. Let them get a look at you coast-to-coast. You don't mind this trick we pulled on you?"

Then a gentleman with a Lancashire accent by the name of Parks spoke into the microphone and recalled Stan's début as a boy comedian in "your Dad's coat, a long-tailed coat that was far too big for you. It was trailing along the ground and there was Stan walking around, pulled the coat right in two. Later on Stan, with the tails under one arm and the rest under the other, had to march home and what happened when he got home heaven knows."

The forgotten Mr Parks was followed by a Mrs Horne, who remembered that "Norvell and I always walked to school together. Instead of carrying my books, I carried his so that he could sing and dance all the way there." Babe failed to identify the woman and looked puzzled until Edwards revealed that she was Alcia Miller. "You haven't seen each other for forty-five years," said Edwards, giving us a clue to the sort of show it was.

Neither Stan's sister, Olga Beatrice in England nor Babe's half-sister Elizabeth, could get to California, but the programme came off smoothly. Hal, Jr. accepted a plaque designating the old back-lot tank – the setting for any number of water scenes in the boys' comedies – as "Lake Laurel and Hardy".

Stan and Babe were given kinescopes (film copies) of the show. Stan ran the film through his projector over and over, pointing out flaws in their "performances". He really was annoyed because they had had not time to prepare, but he seemed deeply moved by the tribute, and both he and Babe were inundated by messages from friends and fans who had seen them.

Then abruptly, the boys' career was terminated beyond recall. That winter, Babe was struck down by a second heart attack. The *Fables* programme was shelved when it became obvious that Babe Hardy had to change his diet *and image* drastically; he had to become a thin man or die. His doctors put him on a low cholesterol diet.

Gourmet that he was, he hated it, but the weight dropped. Within a few months, he lost 150 pounds. The wizened old man with the folds of flesh hanging from his jowls no longer resembled Ollie. There was no chance for a come-back after that.

Stan fretted in idleness. He had counted heavily on the deal with Roach, Jr., and there was no way he could see of ever performing again. He felt that he was nothing without Babe.

During the period of anxiety, Stan suffered a stroke, which temporarily paralyzed his left side. His leg, arm and hand were affected. His memory was clouded. The illness angered him and he fought back. Within a few months, he was walking again, although with a slight limp. His memory cleared and he regained much of the use of his hand and arm.

Lois, Jr., Stan's daughter, had married an actor, Randy Brooks, and they had settled in Tarzana, where they were raising their children, a boy and a girl, and running an ambulance service. Little Lois was not in close touch with her father, perhaps because of the divorce so many years ago and the fact that she had remained a friend of her stepmother Ruth. But when Babe was allowed to move around a little, Lois Brooks invited Stan and Ida and Babe and Lucille for Sunday dinner in their home. Stan brought along a young man named Andy Wade who had been his most devoted fan since childhood. Young Wade, then in his early twenties, had gone to California every year from his home in Florida, often accompanied by his father, just to stay in a motel near Stan and visit him each day. Wade would come up Stan's walk whistling the "Coo-Koo Song" as a signal that he was on his way. His devotion and obsession made him something of a nuisance and Stan often sighed when he heard that whistle; if he had been less kind, he would have ducked out of the back door.

Andy Wade brought a movie camera with him and began shooting home movies of Stan and Babe together. There was a strong feeling on everyone's part that this was their last social get-together – Babe was far from recovered and seemed to be there more through an effort of will than anything else, and Stan's limp was evident on camera. Stan warned the youth: "Andy, you can take this as long as you don't let it be seen by anybody but your family."

Another comedy buff named Bob Chatterton heard about the

home movie and begged Andy to let him borrow it before he returned to Florida. On Andy's way back to his Florida home, he was killed in an accident. When his father wrote to Chatterton inquiring about the film, which Andy had written him about, Chatterton said that he had loaned it to a third party, who had committed suicide soon after getting the film in his hands. Stan was acutely distressed by all of this. Either that film was jinxed in some terrible way or someone was not telling the whole truth. Within months after the suicide, the Tarzana finale of Laurel and Hardy began appearing in stores across the nation. Apparently, it is still being sold.

Just before Christmas 1955, Babe suffered a third heart attack with accompanying complications. He was determined to spend Christmas at home, so Lucille had them bring him from the hospital on Christmas Eve. She had a hospital bed set up in the dining-room and she decorated a tree. She learned how to administer the shots of demerol that he needed every few hours.

As the months dragged on, expenses mounted alarmingly. Lucille decided to sell the house and Babe was moved again – to the home of her mother in North Hollywood. He couldn't speak; he had little comprehension of anything around him. The television set in front of the bed was on for most of the day and Babe would watch the images blankly, but through some old instinct, magnetized by the small black and white screen. Although the stroke had rendered him mute, he would sometimes try to speak when Lucille bent to kiss him. Once she saw him form the words "I love you" with his lips.

Get well messages poured in from everywhere, and Lucille couldn't make a dent in them, so she asked the syndicated writer Bob Thomas to thank everyone for her. He wrote a tribute to Babe some weeks before he died, telling the fans how grateful Lucille Hardy was.

After eleven months of semi-consciousness, Babe Hardy died on 7 August 1957. Lucille told reporters, "It was a blessing for Oliver. He is finally out of his suffering, and he did not suffer at the end. Oliver suffered another stroke Sunday; and a third, Tuesday, sent him into a coma from which he did not emerge. His heart just stopped beating."

When Stan heard the news, he asked "What's there to say? It's shocking, of course. Babe was like a brother. This is the end of Laurel and Hardy." He meant, of course, the end of any hope that they might revive their career. The faint hope that through some miracle, Babe might rally and recover as much of his old mobility as Stan had, had kept Stan busy part of each day working on a new routine.

Living on Stan's trust fund and Ida's sizeable inheritance, the Laurels decided to rent their two-storey house and move to a small apartment in a building catering for overnight guests (indeed, listed in numerous directories as a motel) known as the Oceana in Santa Monica. There was one bedroom and a modest sitting and dining area. Fronting it was a balcony overlooking the Pacific directly across the boulevard. For Stan, it was an ideal blend of environments – the convenience and on-tour feeling of transient accommodation and, since he had no intention of ever moving again, the permanence of a home.

When Babe died, Stan knew that he was not up to attending the services. Not only was his own health poor, but he never could bring himself to attend a funeral, not since his mother's when he was sixteen. Ida went alone, and Lucille understood perfectly. Ruth Laurel made the atmosphere just a little tense by attending with Joe Rock and Alice Cooke. The upshot of that indiscretion was that Alice got into hot water with Ida and felt compelled to cut herself off from Ruth entirely in the future in order to atone and remain within Stan's circle of friends. There was a great deal of egg-walking among Stan's old friends around Ida. When anyone or anything threatened to disturb Stan's tranquillity, she was fanatically on guard. So distant was she with a few old Roach staffers who attempted to visit Stan that they thought she was a nurse.

Ruth, her innocent air with her to the end, approached Stan's widow at the services for Babe, even though her ears had been salted on numerous occasions when she had called inquiring about his health. Ida would answer impatiently, "It's all right. It's all right. I'll tell him you called," and often adding, "Why do you pester this man this way?" Ida listened in silence as Ruth thanked her for taking such good care of Stan, then without even nodding, turned on her heel and walked to another corner of the chapel where family and close friends were waiting to accompany the body to Valhalla, in North Hollywood, for burial.

Ruth said that Ida's gesture stung her as sharply as a slap in the face. In her will, Ruth had left a substantial part of her holdings, mostly real estate, to Stan, despite the two divorces and the wall that Ida had erected around him. But the humiliation at the chapel was more than Ruth could bear, so she had a new will drawn up that week, eliminating Stan.

In Ida, Stan had finally found the right woman at the right time in his life. For her, he was precious and vulnerable, and it amused him to see her fly at someone to protect him or his interests during those last two decades of his life. When Hal Roach was interviewed a year or so before Stan died and was asked about Stan, he had said that there was no better gag-writer anywhere except perhaps Chaplin, but that Stan was "terrible on stories". The remark was unfortunate and untimely. The Laurels had been invited by someone on Roach's staff to a preview of a compilation feature, made up of sequences from old Roach comedies. Ida sent off a letter cancelling their plans to attend and telling the Roach people why.

When Stan's daily routine became settled and there was always an hour or two set aside for fans and visitors, unless they were mutual friends, Ida would retire to the bedroom when the doorbell rang and never show herself. In his last years, however, Stan persuaded her to join the party.

Ida's most amusing side was her attempt to hang on to her own health and maintain a regimen around Stan that seemed sensible. Stan could not drink, but she would quaff down a double shot of vodka, Russian style, undiluted, each night before dinner. Stan smoked occasionally, and Ida dampened her cigarette's filter tip with a little water, saying, "Stan, this you should do. This is good for you."

4   Stan never fully recovered from Babe's death. Even though it had been expected for months, his final departure was a body blow. They had become so close over the years as performers, much like those breathtakingly skilful trapeze artists who do triple somersaults and catch each other's wrists; they had blended, or as Stan said later, "We seemed to sense each other.

Funny, we never really got to know each other personally until we took the tours together . . . I loved editing and cutting the pictures, something he wasn't interested in. But whatever I did was tops with him. There was never any argument between us, ever. . . .''

Stan was in the phone book, and many fans, startled and delighted to see his name there, took the opportunity to call on him. Stan liked that. Altogether, over a few weeks, they added up to a fair-sized audience. That was the way the television comedian Dick Van Dyke met Stan; he was among the first of a long line of show business callers.

Stan gave a quiet impression of being in on the arcane spirit behind comedy – he didn't mean to, but it was clearly part of what drew other comedians there to the Oceana. Few could get to Chaplin in exile in Switzerland; Harold Lloyd did not encourage strangers to drop by Green Acres; there was a desperation yet in Keaton for whom a cult was just then in the making. But Stan was there, in the phone book and with the front door open. With these people off the street, comedians or otherwise, he was not noticeably witty. He listened carefully to them and told them what they wanted to hear. An oracle. And he laughed from his belly, often. He was warm and human. Perhaps this was the Stan he had always wanted to be, but the demands of performing had got in the way.

Dick Van Dyke often told interviewers that Stan was his idol, that it was seeing Stan and Ollie in their two-reelers at Saturday matinées that had inspired him to become an actor and eventually a comic. After his initial visit, a friendship developed.

Stan liked Van Dyke's comedy shows on television. On at least two occasions, Van Dyke had impersonated Stan, one of the shows being an hour-long tribute. Van Dyke was a fair Stan Laurel, more skilled than most, marred slightly by his employing a grimace in place of Stan's vacant stare. One would have to possess Stan's mind to know how he managed to empty it in order to look out at the world in quite that fashion.

Jerry Lewis contacted Stan and liked to drop by to run through routines with him and get his opinion on them. Stan liked Lewis as a friend and was indulgent, but he had serious reservations about him as a comic. He thought he was far too undisciplined, "going off in all directions", though he liked the "little boy" thing which Lewis did and saw promise in that. Lewis offered Stan a high salary just to act as a consultant on his comedy hour. It was something which Stan knew he could do, but after considering it for several days, he decided against it. He said that he didn't think it would be fair to accept so much money when he would be powerless to help reshape Lewis's comic image.

Soon, the visits to Stan took on an aspect of pilgrimages among comics. Dick Cavett, before he was a star in his own right, wrote him an admiring note, and Stan replied, "Dear Dick Cavett, Thank you for your letter, containing such kind sentiments, so graciously expressed . . ." This was Stan, the retired gentleman clown, who meant every word of his courteous but grateful reply. When Cavett finally met Stan at the Oceana, an effortless manoeuvre, they fell into an easy rapport, and Stan confessed that his high regard for Babe was not always returned.

Danny Kaye came several times. He owed Stan a great deal and there may have been an acknowledgement given, although Stan never discussed it. Marcel Marceau, then the most esteemed mime in the world, came for a long afternoon visit. He did the Laurel cry and the funny, flat-footed walk across Stan's living-room. It was a delightful, jovial afternoon. Afterwards, Marceau told reporters, "I have met the master", and said that he had been a member of a Laurel and Hardy fan club in Europe that had numbered two million members and that, like Dick Van Dyke, he had been inspired to go into show business by Stan's performances.

When the Oscars were awarded in 1961, Stan was informed by the Board of Governors of the Academy that he was being honoured with a special Oscar "for creative pioneering in the field of cinema comedy". The Board wanted Stan to be present to receive it and, up to the last minute, Stan planned on going. But on the day of the big event, his eyes began giving him trouble – an affliction that had developed as a side effect of poor circulation – and he was afraid the strong television lights would blind him. He sent his regrets and Danny Kaye accepted it for him.

Stan was thrilled by the ceremony, watching it at home with Ida. He did become a little impatient when Kaye was not able to deliver the statuette until a day and a half later, but he was considerably moved when it was finally in his hands. All through his life, he had one reason for existing and that was to provoke laughter. He had seen that pursuit so often thrown off course and unrecognized that he had often felt he was clowning to an empty house, but this was proof positive that his peers knew what he had been doing all along.

There was even the possibility that his financial situation might improve (he was not living in poverty as numerous journalists, especially in Europe, reported) when a man named Larry Harmon, given the rights to use their characterizations by Stan and Hardy's widow, Lucille, found the backing to do a series of animated Laurel and Hardy comedies in colour for television. A pilot had been made, but nothing came of it, possibly because there was some threat of litigation. Hal Roach claimed that *he* owned the names and screen images of Laurel and Hardy. Eventually, Roach lost in the New York Supreme Court – after all, the team was born with those names but Stan was long dead and the series derailed years before that.

The years rolled by like the waves visible below, washing over the same sands again and again. Stan never ceased enjoying the narcotic appeal of the ocean. He rarely went out, but every day there was a stream of callers. On one occasion, forgetting the Andy Wade home movie incident, he agreed to walk and caper just a bit before the movie camera of Robert Board because he liked the young actor and trusted him. He spent four or five years saying goodbye to his fans. And there was always the same little speech about how he and Babe had got together on the screen; how the church bells played the Coo Koo Song on their tour of the British Isles, ad nauseam; a thousand, two thousand times or more, and always with the same animation, as though he were telling this perfect stranger the story for the first time. But that was Stan's "act" with the Babe gone.

On 20 December 1962, the Hal Roach Studios were sold at auction to a real estate developer, and in 1963 everything was levelled: sound stages, dressing-rooms, screening-rooms, the old administration building and writers' quarters where Roach's parents had lived. Dust billowed above the macadam paving the town street where Our Gang had run from the local constabulary; Lake Laurel and Hardy was drained and torn apart. Hal Roach, now a legend himself, must have grieved. There would be a long line of film scholars with tape recorders coming to see him in the years ahead, and most of them would note the sadness in him when he talked of the old studio.

Perhaps it was the manner in which it was all lost that distressed him most. In the late nineteen-fifties, Roach had turned over most of the studio operations to his son, Hal, Jr. In 1960, Junior lost six and a half million dollars in four months and looked desperately for a large loan to save the company. Reaching out with a helping hand was an industrialist with ties to organized crime, Alexander Guterma. Guterma made the Roach operation a part of a huge holding company known as The Scranton Corporation. It was promptly swallowed whole and spat out in bankruptcy court with Guterma convicted of stock fraud.

Stan followed the reports of the Roach Studio's struggles and then the trial in the daily papers, feeling very remote from it. But he must have seen the irony – all those years ago, Roach pointing an admonishing finger at him for bringing scandal to the studio (with his marital woes) and now the studio itself destroyed by an arm of the Mafia.

In mid-February 1965, Stan suffered a heart attack. Ida, who had been nursing him and giving him his insulin for years, sat by his bedside as nurses attended him. Theirs had been a nearly perfect marriage in a life overburdened with marital catastrophe.

On 23 February, Stan began sinking rapidly. He knew that he was going and he beckoned the nurse on duty to his bedside. "I'd rather be skiing than doing this," he told her. "Do you ski, Mr Laurel?" "No," he said, "but I'd rather be doing that than this."

It could have been a line from one of the old comedies – the delivery was nearly the same. And his timing was as fine as ever for in the next moment, he was dead.

All of the surviving film clowns gathered at the Church of the Hills in Forest Lawn for Stan's services: Harold Lloyd, Buster Keaton, Andy Clyde, Clyde Cook and Patsy Kelly. From television there were Tim Conway and Dick Van Dyke, the latter delivering the eulogy: ". . . the halls of Heaven must be ringing with divine laughter." The easy democracy of the old Roach days was briefly revived as Hal Roach picked up his former chief grip Bones Vreeland along with director Leo McCarey to ride out to Glendale together in the Roach limousine.

Film legends tend to be remembered more sharply than past sports heroes, arch criminals and patriots, chiefly because we continue to see them at their best. Laurel and Hardy's fame soared higher than ever as the chaotic nineteen-sixties moved to a close. Life had become more complex; values were changing; it was difficult to cope. But in Stan and Ollie, we saw two hopelessly inept souls surviving amid chaos, often of their own contrivance. If they could muddle through somehow, so could we.

Catalogue of Films

Compiled by Richard W. Bann and Fred Lawrence Guiles

(Listed by order of release dates)

STAN'S FILMS

1917
Nuts in May (2 reels; Nestor)
The Evolution of Fashion (producer unknown)
Lucky Dog (2 reels; Sunkist, previewed 1917) also featuring Oliver Hardy

1918
Hickory Hiram (one reel; Nestor-Universal)
Phoney Photos (2 reels; LKO)
Who's Zoo? (2 reels; LKO)
No Place Like Jail (1 reel; Rolin-Pathé)
Huns and Hyphens (2 reels; Vitagraph)
Just Rambling Along (1 reel; Rolin-Pathé)
Bears and Bad Men (2 reels; Vitagraph)
Frauds and Frenzies (2 reels; Vitagraph)
It's Great to be Crazy (1 reel; Nestor-Universal)

1919
Do You Love Your Wife? (1 reel; Rolin-Pathé)
Hustling for Health (1 reel; Rolin-Pathé)
Hoot Mon! (1 reel; Rolin-Pathé)

1921
The Rent Collector (2 reels; Vitagraph)

1922
The Egg (2 reels; Amalgamated-Metro)
The Weak-End Party (2 reels; Amalgamated-Metro)
Mud and Sand (3 reels; Quality-Metro)
The Pest (2 reels; Quality-Metro)

1923
When Knights Were Cold (2 reels; Quality-Metro)
The Handy Man (2 reels; Quality-Metro)
The Roach Films, released by Pathé, all 1 reel in length:

The Noon Whistle   *Save the Ship*
White Wings   *The Soilers*
Under Two Jags   *Scorching Sand*
Pick and Shovel   *Mother's Joy*
Collars and Cuffs   *Smithy*
Kill or Cure   *Postage Due*
Gas and Air   *Zeb vs. Paprika*
Oranges and Lemons   *Brothers under the Chin*
Short Orders   *Near Dublin*
A Man about Town   *Rupert of Hee Haw*
Roughest Africa   *Wide Open Spaces*
Frozen Hearts   *Short Kilts*
The Whole Truth

1924
Mixed Nuts (2 reels; a Samuel Bischoff release)
The Joe Rock Films, released by Standard Cinema-Selznick:
Mandarin Mix-up (2 reels)
Detained (2 reels)
Monsieur Don't Care (2 reels)
West of Hot Dog (2 reels)

1925
The Joe Rock Films (*cont'd*):
Somewhere in Wrong (2 reels)
Twins (2 reels)
Pie Eyed (2 reels)
The Snow Hawk (2 reels)
Navy Blues Days (2 reels)
The Sleuth (2 reels)

Dr Pyckle and Mr Pryde (2 reels)
Half a Man (2 reels)
Direction only:
Yes, Yes, Nanette (1 reel; Roach-Pathé)
Unfriendly Enemies (1 reel; Roach-Pathé)
Moonlight and Noses (2 reels; Roach-Pathé)
Wandering Papas (2 reels; Roach-Pathé) featuring Oliver Hardy

1926
Atta Boy! (6 reels, produced by Edward H. Griffith for Pathé)
Get 'Em Young (2 reels; Roach-Pathé, also directed by Stan)
On the Front Page (2 reels; Roach-Pathé)
Seeing the World (2 reels, "Our Gang" series, Roach-Pathé)
Eve's Love Letters (2 reels; Roach-Pathé)*
Now I'll Tell One (2 reels; "Charley Chase" series, Roach-Pathé)
Should Tall Men Marry? (2 reels; Roach-Pathé)
Direction only:
Madame Mystery (2 reels, co-directed by Richard Wallace for Roach-Pathé)
Never Too Old (2 reels, co-directed by Richard Wallace for Roach-Pathé)
The Merry Widower (2 reels, directed by Richard Wallace assisted by Stan Laurel for Roach-Pathé)
Wise Guys Prefer Brunettes (2 reels; Roach-Pathé)
Raggedy Rose (2 reels, co-directed by Richard Wallace for Roach-Pathé) starring Mabel Normand

THE LAUREL AND HARDY FILMS

(See 1917 listing for *Lucky Dog*)

1926
45 Minutes from Hollywood (2 reels, silent, Roach-Pathé)

1927
Duck Soup (2 reels, silent, Roach-Pathé)
Slipping Wives (2 reels, silent, Roach-Pathé)
Love 'Em and Weep (2 reels, silent, Roach-Pathé)
Why Girls Love Sailors (2 reels, silent, Roach-Pathé)
With Love and Hisses (2 reels, silent, Roach-Pathé)

*Includes scene in which a calling card is shown reading "Sir Oliver Hardy", although Hardy himself does not appear.

Sugar Daddies (2 reels, silent, Roach for Metro-Goldwyn-Mayer)
Sailors, Beware! (2 reels, silent, Roach-Pathé)
The Second Hundred Years (2 reels, silent, Roach for
Metro-Goldwyn-Mayer)
Call of the Cuckoos (2 reels, Max Davidson series, silent, Roach for
Metro-Goldwyn-Mayer)
Hats Off (2 reels, silent, Roach for Metro-Goldwyn-Mayer)
Do Detectives Think? (2 reels, silent, Roach-Pathé)
Putting Pants on Philip (2 reels, silent, Roach for
Metro-Goldwyn-Mayer)*
The Battle of the Century (2 reels, silent, Roach for
Metro-Goldwyn-Mayer)

1928
All produced by Hal Roach for Metro-Goldwyn-Mayer release:
Leave 'Em Laughing (2 reels, silent)
Flying Elephants (2 reels, silent)
The Finishing Touch (2 reels, silent)
From Soup to Nuts (2 reels, silent)
You're Darn Tootin' (2 reels, silent)
Their Purple Moment (2 reels, silent)
Should Married Men Go Home? (2 reels, silent)
Early to Bed (2 reels, silent)
Two Tars (2 reels, silent)
Habeas Corpus 2 reels, silent)
We Faw Down (2 reels, silent)

1929
Liberty (2 reels, silent)**
Wrong Again (2 reels, silent)
That's My Wife (2 reels, silent with sound effects)
Big Business (2 reels, silent)
Unaccustomed As We Are (2 reels, sound)
Double Whoopee (2 reels, silent)**
Berth Marks (2 reels, sound)
Men O'War (2 reels, sound)
Perfect Day (2 reels, sound)
They Go Boom (2 reels, sound)
Bacon Grabbers (2 reels, silent with sound effects)
The Hoose-Gow (2 reels, sound)

*The first Laurel and Hardy comedy in which Leo McCarey and Hal Roach put
on film those character traits and reactions that their fans best remember.
**featuring Jean Harlow, who was discovered by Hal Roach.

The Hollywood Revue of 1929 (120 minutes, sound, skit by Laurel and Hardy)
Angora Love (2 reels, silent with sound effects)

1930
All of their films were sound and all were produced by Hal Roach for release by Metro-Goldwyn-Mayer. Since sound films were now established as *the only* film form, no mention will be made of it again in this filmography.
Night Owls (2 reels)
Blotto (2 reels)
Brats (2 reels)
Below Zero (2 reels)
The Rogue Song (115 minutes, Technicolor, starring Lawrence Tibbett)*
Hog Wild (2 reels)
The Laurel & Hardy Murder Case (3 reels)
Another Fine Mess (3 reels)

1931
Unless otherwise indicated, all of their films were produced by Hal Roach for release by Metro-Goldwyn-Mayer.
Be Big (3 reels)
Chickens Come Home (3 reels)
The Stolen Jools (2 reels, produced by Pat Casey for National Variety Artists to raise funds for the Saranac Lake Sanitarium, cameo appearance)
Laughing Gravy (2 reels)
Our Wife (2 reels)
Pardon Us (56 minutes)**
Come Clean (2 reels)
One Good Turn (2 reels)
Beau Hunks (4 reels)
On the Loose (2 reels, Thelma Todd-Zasu Pitts series)

1932
Helpmates (2 reels)
Any Old Port (2 reels)
The Music Box (3 reels – Academy Award Winner for Best Live Action Comedy Short Subject)

*The Rogue Song is considered a lost film since no known print exists anywhere in the world.
**Considered the first Laurel and Hardy feature.

The Chimp (3 reels)
County Hospital (2 reels)
'Scram!' (2 reels)
Pack Up Your Troubles (68 minutes)
Their First Mistake (2 reels)
Towed in a Hole (2 reels)

1933
Twice Two (2 reels)
Me and My Pal (2 reels)
The Devil's Brother (*Fra Diavolo*, 90 minutes)
The Midnight Patrol (2 reels)
Busy Bodies (2 reels)
Wild Poses (2 reels, Our Gang series)
Dirty Work (2 reels)
Sons of the Desert (68 minutes)

1934
Oliver the Eighth (2 reels)
Hollywood Party (68 minutes)
Going Bye-Bye! (2 reels)
Them Thar Hills (2 reels)
Babes in Toyland (79 minutes)
The Live Ghost (2 reels)

1935
Tit for Tat (2 reels)
The Fixer Uppers (2 reels)
Thicker Than Water (2 reels)
Bonnie Scotland (80 minutes)

1936
The Bohemian Girl (70 minutes)
On the Wrong Trek (2 reels, Charley Chase series)
Our Relations (74 minutes)

1937
Way out West (65 minutes)
Pick a Star (70 minutes)

1938
Swiss Miss (72 minutes)
Block-Heads (58 minutes)

1939

The Flying Deuces (69 minutes, produced by Boris Morros for RKO)

1940

A Chump at Oxford (63 minutes, released by United Artists)
Saps at Sea (57 minutes, released by United Artists)

1941

(The year that marked the end of their long association with Hal Roach)
Great Guns (74 minutes, produced by Sol M. Wurtzel for Twentieth Century-Fox)

1942

A-Haunting We Will Go (67 minutes, produced by Sol. M. Wurtzel for Twentieth Century-Fox)

1943

Air Raid Wardens (67 minutes, produced by B. F. Zeidman for Metro-Goldwyn-Mayer)
Jitterbugs (74 minutes, produced by Sol M. Wurtzel for Twentieth Century-Fox)
The Dancing Masters (63 minutes, produced by Lee Marcus for Twentieth Century-Fox)

1944

The Big Noise (74 minutes, produced by Sol M. Wurtzel for Twentieth Century-Fox)

1945

The Bullfighters (69 minutes, produced by William Girard for Twentieth Century-Fox)
Nothing But Trouble (70 minutes, produced by B. F. Zeidman for Metro-Goldwyn-Mayer)

1950

Atoll K (98 minutes, production managed by Paul Joly for Les Films Sirius, Franco-London Films and Fortezza Film)

Bibliography

Allen, Frederick Lewis, *Only Yesterday*   New York, Harper, 1931
Barr, Charles, *Laurel & Hardy*   London, Studio Vista, 1967
Blesh, Rudi, *Keaton*   New York, Macmillan, 1966
Cahn, William, *Harold Lloyd's World of Comedy*   New York, Duell, Sloan and Pearce, 1964
Capra, Frank, *The Name Above the Title: An Autobiography*   New York, Macmillan, 1971
Chaplin, Charles, *My Autobiography*   London, Bodley Head, 1964; New York, Simon and Schuster, 1964
Cooke, Alistair, *Garbo and the Night Watchmen*   New York, McGraw-Hill, 1971
Disher, M. Willson, *Winkles and Champagne*   London, Batsford, 1938
Everson, William K., *The Films of Hal Roach*   New York, Museum of Modern Art, 1971
Everson, William K., *The Films of Laurel and Hardy*   Secaucus, Citadel, 1967
Fowler, Gene, *Father Goose: The Biography of Mack Sennett*   New York, Crown, 1934
Gallagher, J. P., *Fred Karno: Master of Mirth and Tears*   London, Robert Hale, 1971
Gifford, Denis, *Chaplin* (The Movie-Makers Series)   Secaucus, Citadel, 1972

Honri, Peter, *Working the Halls* London, Futura, 1973

Kerr, Walter, *The Silent Clowns* New York, Knopf, 1974

Maltin, Leonard and Bann, Richard W. *Our Gang: The Life and Times of the Little Rascals* New York, Crown, 1977

Maltin, Leonard, *Movie Comedy Teams* New York, Signet, 1970

Maltin, Leonard, *The Laurel & Hardy Book* New York, Curtis, 1973

Marx, Samuel, *Mayer and Thalberg: The Make-Believe Saints* New York, Random House, 1975

McCabe, John, *Charlie Chaplin* Garden City, Doubleday, 1978

McCabe, John, *The Comedy World of Stan Laurel* Garden City, Doubleday, 1974

McCabe, John, *Laurel & Hardy*; Text compiled by Al Kilgore, Filmography by Richard W. Bann New York, Dutton, 1975

McCabe, John, *Mr Laurel and Mr Hardy* New York, Grosset & Dunlap, 1961

Nizer, Alvin, *Laurel and Hardy* *Liberty* Magazine, Summer 1975

Pearsall, W. H. and Pennington, Winifred, *The Lake District: A Landscape History* London, Collins, 1973

Pratfall Magazine: Complete folio Los Angeles, California

Robinson, David, *Hollywood in the Twenties* London and New York, The Tatnivy Press in association with A. Zwemmer Ltd. & A. S. Barnes & Co., Inc., 1968

Scagnetti, Jack, *The Laurel and Hardy Scrapbook* Middle Village, New York, Jonathan David, 1976

Sennet, Mack with Cameron Shipp, *King of Clowns* Garden City, Doubleday, 1954

Shulman, Irving, *Harlow: An Intimate Biography* New York, Bernard Geis Associates, 1964

Thomas, Bob, *Bud & Lou: The Abbott and Costello Story* Philadelphia, Lippincott, 1977

Index